A Term To Remember

A Term To Remember

Edward Mezvinsky

with Kevin McCormally & John Greenya

COWARD, McCANN & GEOGHEGAN, INC.   NEW YORK

Photographs by Dev O'Neil, except where otherwise identified.

SBN: 698-10751-9

Library of Congress Cataloging in Publication Data

Mezvinsky, Edward
  A term to remember.

  Autobiographical.
  Includes index.
  1. Mezvinsky, Edward. 2. Legislators—United
States—Biography. I. McCormally, Kevin. II. Greenya,
John. III. Title.
E840.8.M49A37 1977   328.73'092'4 [B]   77-3833

PRINTED IN THE UNITED STATES OF AMERICA

To my mother and father

Contents

Acknowledgments

Writing this book was both a personal venture and one that could not have been undertaken without a great deal of assistance. I owe my thanks to many:

To the people of the thirteen counties of southeast Iowa that make up the First Congressional District for entrusting me with their voice in Washington for the 93rd Congress. The benefit of their counsel—whether through advice, encouragement, or complaints—bolstered my confidence that we were on the right path . . .

To my colleagues in the Judiciary Committee, among whom developed a special camaraderie as we worked on impeachment. The insight and dedication they brought to the inquiry are an important part of this book, and I am proud to have served with them . . .

To the talented and dedicated staff of the impeachment inquiry, whose tireless efforts can only be fully appreciated by those who had the opportunity to watch them work . . .

To the journalists who covered impeachment and reported the unprecedented happenings of 1974. Their penetrating questions occasionally caused me to redouble my efforts to find the answers . . .

To my congressional staff, whose advice and assistance were invaluable during the impeachment inquiry and whose help on this book, above and beyond the call of duty, was indispensable . . .

To all those who assisted in the writing and preparation of the book . . .

And, to all those who helped get me to Congress.

ONE: *The Election of '72*

When anything of public importance happens at the University of Iowa, it happens on the Pentacrest, a large grassy area atop a small hill. It contains five large buildings, four at the corners, and in the center is the Old Capitol, the historic stone building where, over a century ago, the legislature used to meet. That day, however, the Pentacrest was the site of a different kind of political gathering.

It was late October 1972, and the day was overcast. But from time to time the sun made an appearance, sparkled off the gold dome of the Old Capitol, and filtered through the last leaves to warm the friendly crowd of fifteen thousand.

I squirmed in my rickety wooden folding chair, trying to get comfortable. My turn at the microphone was past, and now I sat waiting, like all those in front of me clinging to trees, or window-sills, or rooftops, for George McGovern. Next to me sat Dick Clark, clad in his famous khaki safari suit, which after a thousand miles of trudging up and down and across the state had come to symbolize his uphill race for the United States Senate.

Clark stepped up to the mike for the final touches. "Okay," his voice boomed across the Pentacrest, "time for a little crowd check. I want everyone out there who is a Republican to identify himself."

He got what he'd expected: sprinkled applause, a few catcalls, and a good deal of booing.

"Now, I want to hear from the Democrats." The loud cheering was instantaneous and sustained, seemingly reverberating and amplifying among the five buildings.

Clark waited for the crowd to quiet. "Well, there are polls and there are polls. We've just conducted ours here."

Applause erupted again, began to die, and then was reignited as the door to the Old Capitol opened, signaling McGovern's arrival. I shot to my feet to join in the enthusiastic welcome for "the next President of the United States."

The cheers had to lift his spirits, momentarily belying the polls that predicted devastating defeat, and thrusting him joyously onward in his impossible pursuit of the presidency. As he stood a few feet from me, smiling and waving both arms, I wondered .whether he knew how the broad, shady lawns in front of him had rung for four years with the cries of war protesters. Surely he knew, if for no other reason than that's what advance men are for.

He began by talking of the war, ot Henry Kissinger's hurriedly called press conference that morning to proclaim, with exquisite timing, that peace in Vietnam was "at hand." With the suddenly solemn crowd, McGovern prayed that the announcement was true.

"But, the question that haunts my mind," McGovern told us, "is why, Mr. Nixon, did you take another four years to bring an end to this destruction?" He paused for an outburst of applause that passed immediate judgment on the suspect timing of the "peace at hand" announcement. McGovern supported his weary body on the podium as the students roared with the cynicism cultivated by so many years of the war.

He began to detail the horrendous toll of the war, in blood and money, and the insanity of it all. It was a familiar litany, similar, though more powerful, to the countless antiwar talks I had made.

Listening to McGovern's High Plains twang pierce the air, I thought of the bitterness and frustration I had encountered,

12

especially on this campus, in discussion of the war. For many in
the crowd the hatred of the war had been fused with a hatred of
Richard Nixon that had driven a few students and faculty members to suggest to me that Nixon be impeached for his Indochina
policies. I considered that proposal the height of both frustration and folly, and knew it was spawned by the same deep passions that were at that moment being transformed into cheers of
support for the man who promised to rid the nation of the war
and the Nixon White House.

"It is but a single step from spying on the political opposition
to suppressing the opposition and imposing a one-party state in
which the people's precious liberties are lost."

McGovern had suddenly shifted from war to the moral climate of the nation. He was calling for the wrath of the people to
bring down the wrongdoers of Washington, branding Nixon as
the ringleader of "the most corrupt Administration in the history of the nation." Earlier in the campaign the charge had been
"the most corrupt since Harding" but since then more information about secret Republican campaign funds and campaign sab-
otage had been reported.

He brought laughter from the crowd by apologizing because
Nixon had not joined him for the Iowa City rally. "There are a
lot of questions I was hoping he could answer for us," McGovern
said, launching into a series of questions aimed at Nixon's
knowledge of and involvement in the Watergate burglary, the
Russian wheat deal, the ITT controversy. The crowd exploded
with cheers that substituted for an incriminating Nixon response
to each question. He warned, "What's really involved in this
campaign is the decency and integrity of the political process."

The 1972 election was twelve days away and, listening and
watching thousands of people strain their voices and slap their
hands together to urge McGovern on to victory, I thought of the
incongruity of it all. On this day, in this setting, with this throng
of voters, McGovern was clearly a winner. Yet, I knew he was
doomed, and I suspected he knew it too. It was impossible to
know whether the cheers gave him hope or only a bit of deserved solace in the final days of his campaign.

Watching him, I remembered an editorial cartoon depicting
McGovern in a Don Quixote pose, atop a white charger jousting

13

with a windmill marked "Watergate." Through my thoughts I heard him calling me, saw his hand reaching out to pull me up alongside him, ". . . and here is your fine candidate for Congress, Ed Mezvinsky. I know you're going to send him to Washington where we need him . . ." and I struggled up as the cheers rose.

He grabbed my left hand with his right and we raised them above our heads. If he said anything to me it was drowned out by the noise, and by my recollection of a question on our poll of the First Congressional District. By a margin of three to one, the respondents had admonished Democratic candidates for any office to keep their distance from McGovern, lest the party's standard-bearer become a millstone. Surely, that did not apply to the voters gathered on the Pentacrest; I knew nearly all of them would be pulling both McGovern and Mezvinsky levers on election day. I smiled as I wondered what kind of reception my opponent, Fred Schwengel, would be receiving were it he and President Nixon embracing on the Old Capitol steps.

McGovern let go of my hand and raised both his arms to quiet the crowd. "I've got to go," he said. "The *Dakota Queen* is waiting to fly west. We want to win California, too . . ." For a few minutes the crowd refused to let him go, but then he turned away and quickly vanished into the tunnel of outstretched hands fashioned by his aides and Secret Service agents. Several hundred students broke into a run toward the other side of Old Capitol, where the motorcade was waiting, hoping for a last glimpse of their candidate.

Watergate. I knew that Kevin McCormally, my hard-working young campaign press secretary, wanted me to mention the break-in and the other charges of corruption in the Nixon Administration more often than I did on the stump. Actually, I did bring them up, but it was apparent to me that people in the First District of Iowa simply weren't interested in Watergate. I remember how exasperated Kevin had been when a poll we ran showed that Iowans equated Watergate, as an issue, with the question of how long liquor stores should be open. Occasionally, I raised the general issue of ethics, of dirty tricks in Washington, and of the rapidly waning trust in government. But I didn't

14

stress specific charges. Instead I stressed the need for changes i
the way government operated—and the immediate need for a
new Congressman from the First District.

After the rally we hurried back to our makeshift campaign
headquarters that were located (conveniently, for student volunteers) between two of the campus's most popular bars and directly above a third. Kevin put away the necklace of cameras that
seemed to have become part of his wardrobe.

Jon Kent and Pat O'Connor, who shared the title of campaign
manager, and Con Merker, my secretary, were next to return
from the rally. Kent told me that my driver, Tom Baldridge, was
getting the car and would be by shortly to carry me off for a
round of door-to-door campaigning in Lone Tree.

Smiling, Kent asked, "Have you got enough buttons, flyers,
and suckers to cover the town?" I walked over to a box of Mezvinsky lollipops, the latest addition to our name identification
efforts. MEZVINSKY was stamped on both the cardboard stick and
the cellophane wrapper. As I put a handful into my pocket, I almost cringed. I had just listened to George McGovern discuss
the weighty issues of the campaign and here I was, filling my
pockets with gimmicks.

Baldridge sprang through the door. "Let's move out. I'm dou-
ble-parked and this campaign can't afford another ticket." Spin-
ning toward the door, I stumbled over a folding chair, sending it
crashing to the dirty tile floor.

"Excuse me," I mumbled reflexively.

"Good God, Ed"—Con Merker looked up from her typewrit-
er—"you don't have to apologize to that chair. It can't vote!"

As the car sped along toward Lone Tree, I thought of the ut-
ter insanity of apologizing to a chair. My campaign stressed the
"new politics" idea of getting out and meeting personally with
the voters. However, when your political future centers on shaking hands and talking with people—at plant gates, parades,
luncheons, doorsteps, or anywhere else you can find a potential
voter—you can get paranoid about offending someone. But
apologize to a chair? It made me remember, for still another
time, the way my seventy-eight-year-old immigrant father
summed up the political life: "Who needs the aggravation?"
Sometimes, when he said that, I would laugh. But he was dead

15

serious. He thought I should go into his highly successful grocery business, or settle down to practice law, or at least do something that offered more security for my wife Micky and our four little girls.

There were days, and nights, when I wondered if perhaps my father was not right. The toll of the campaign, the "aggravation," was not lost on me. There was the demeaning scramble to raise the money that is all too synonymous with campaign success.

You could have a great candidate, superb issues, and organization, but without money—to pay for everything from bumper strips to television spots—you might just as well forget it. Money could not guarantee success, but in our 1972 system, which condoned and approved unlimited spending, without money you were doomed. And, to unseat an incumbent Congressman you needed a lot of money. By election day, my campaign had accumulated bills totaling more than $150,000 and while I personally contributed the $25,000 maximum allowed by law, I still had to find supporters willing to put up more than $125,000.

More disturbing than the money-raising hassles and the hoard of petty-to-severe campaign problems was the detrimental effect of the campaign on my family life. I was plagued by the feeling that my wife Micky and I were growing apart. Long-standing strains on our twelve-year-old marriage were aggravated as campaigning devoured our time and attention. Out on the campaign trail I often worried about the strength of our relationship and rushed through the schedule so I could get home.

Why put up with the aggravation? Because I wanted to be a member of the House of Representatives, the people's house, which John Quincy Adams had rejoined after his presidency. I believed I had something to offer as a Congressman and wanted to get into the House, where one could take an idea and transform it into a working policy that would affect—and, I hoped, improve—the quality of peoples' lives. For as long as I could remember, the credibility of government had been eroding, and I believed that one of the key elements in regaining the people's faith was for Congress to start doing a better job.

I wanted in. I wanted to be a member of the House and to help serve as a check on President Nixon, and to see that the sacrilegious amount of money and manpower spent on Vietnam would be shifted to domestic problems. (I had little faith in Kissinger's recent "peace is at hand" announcement.)

Back in December 1971 I had given myself the impossible assignment of reaching every voter personally. And ever since, I had tried to complete that assignment. One activity which had filled every daylight hour when there was no known gathering of voters I could attend, was door-to-door stumping. For eleven months I had been going from house to house in cities and towns—even stopping at the farmhouses in between—shaking hands and carrying the Mezvinsky campaign to the doorstep. I enjoyed it, and I considered it the most effective part of the personal contact campaign. A voter remembers a candidate who knocks at his front door.

The frenetic pace of the campaign, however, was getting to me. Catnaps stolen in the front seat of the blue Chevy did not make up for sleep lost to the schedule, and in the waning days just before the election I had the added problem of trying to disguise my physical exhaustion. As Baldridge stopped the car in Lone Tree, I told myself, "Just two more weeks."

By one of those political quirks, the 1972 Mezvinsky-Schwengel contest had attracted national attention. Both national parties were keeping an eye on the race because the 1970 results (when I had come within eight hundred votes of ousting Schwengel) proved that the southeast corner of Iowa had shifted from a Republican stronghold to a "marginal district." It could go either way. In fact, the *Almanac of American Politics* had predicted that a Democrat would win in either 1972 or 1974. Unfortunately, the *Almanac* didn't give any guarantees.

Our race also drew the television networks and the national press. It was supposed to provide the exciting spectacle of a squeaker. And—as an added attraction—the campaign pitted a sixty-five-year-old Republican against a thirty-five-year-old Democrat vying for the votes of a diverse electorate, a well-balanced mix of old and young, city and farm, Republican and Democrat.

Iowa ranks second only to Florida in the proportion of the population over age sixty-five, and the First District's high num-

17

ber of college students was a newly significant factor since the ratification of the 26th Amendment giving eighteen-year-olds the vote. The thirteen counties in the First District contain thousands of acres of the richest farmland in the world, and the rural complexion is complemented by the industry-based communities along 150 miles of the Mississippi River that hold more than half the district's population. Another 10 percent of the people live in Iowa City (where the University of Iowa is the main industry).

It was into this unique demographic jumble that I carried the message of my campaign: the need for change, the need for the First District to have a "fresh new voice" with "concern for the people" providing "dynamic and vigorous representation" for them in Washington.

The door opened quickly a few seconds after I knocked.

"Hi, what do you want?" a woman asked.

"I'm Ed Mezvinsky and I'm running for Congress." I spoke quickly, picking up on the impatience of her voice. "I wanted to drop by and introduce myself and . . ."

"Look, I'm trying to do some baking and have to get back to the kitchen."

"Oh . . . sorry to interrupt you. May I leave you a brochure?" Her hand shot out and grasped the flyer. "Thanks." "I hope you'll think of me on election day because . . ." The door was closed.

As the intrigue of Watergate increased with news story disclosures, so had the intensity of the caustic denials that anyone at the White House had anything to do with it. Each new charge stemming from the break-in was met with presidential press secretary Ziegler's heated assurances to the press and the people that it was "a collection of absurdities" or some similar comment indicating that the charge was too farfetched to merit serious consideration. Ziegler routinely said there was "no White House involvement in the Watergate incident" and angrily labeled stories suggesting otherwise as "hearsay," "fiction," or "the shoddiest type of journalism."

* * *

Having rapped on a screen door for the third time, I was almost ready to head toward the next house. But the door opened a crack and a young woman brushed hair away from her eyes and peered out. From the thin strap on her bare shoulder and the fact that the rest of her body was hidden behind the door, I knew she was still in her slip. Bringing half-naked women to the door was common when "door-to-door" was scheduled before 10 a.m.

She said good morning and I introduced myself. "Yes, I've seen you on TV. You look just like you do on the tube, but I didn't know you were that tall." Whatever the effect of my media campaign on the voter, it certainly provided a psychological boost for me. Our TV and radio ads were scheduled to peak the day before the election, and by this time watchers and listeners were being bombarded by Ed Mezvinsky for Congress spots. Because I was living and breathing my campaign, convinced that what I had to say, what I had to offer, was of utmost importance, it was always depressing to meet voters who had never heard of me. It was refreshing to find those who had.

"Don't worry, I'm going to vote for you," she said. We talked for a couple of minutes.

"Don't forget, Tuesday is the big day," I reminded her. "May I leave you a brochure?"

"If you stick it in the screen door," she suggested, "I'll get it when I'm dressed."

I knew that out in the Midwest we were getting a more thorough playback of the White House denials than of the Watergate charges that sparked them. But, there didn't seem to be much interest in the Watergate scandal in Washington, either. Wright Patman had ordered the staff of his Banking Committee to investigate the break-in and charges that it had been financed with funds laundered through Mexico. His committee, however, had voted in early October not to hold hearings. Another confusing element was that the *Washington Post* seemed almost alone among the press in having enough curiosity to dig into the Watergate story. If there was a scandal there, it seemed, the journalistic bloodhounds of the Washington press corps would have been out in full force digging for the facts.

*   *   *

"All right," the man at the door said after I explained what I was doing on his porch, "now tell me just why the hell I should vote for you?" He was almost grinning and I decided that it was a friendly challenge. He told me he'd just been laid off and we talked about the economy for a while. As I was preparing to go, he said, "I'll think about voting for you, Mr. Mavinsky."

"Mez-vin-sky," I said, stressing each syllable.

"Yeah, that's what I said, Mac-zink-ski," he imitated.

"Thank God you don't have to pronounce it," I said. "Just recognize it on the ballot. It'll be the longest name there."

Through the magic of television we had been successful in transforming my uncommon name from a liability to an asset. The goal was not to get people to pronounce it correctly, just to recognize it. My favorite media spot, put together by my friend Tony Schwartz, was a series of close-ups of people wearing Mezvinsky buttons. While no faces were shown, the clothes of the button-wearer were easily identifiable: a farmer, a nurse, a businessman, a plant worker. As the buttons were shown on the screen, a voice would mispronounce the name. After several variations, the deep voice of the announcer said, "People may not be able to pronounce Ed Mezvinsky's [pronounced properly] name, but we do know what he stands for." The visual then switched to a button on a housedress and a woman's voice said, "That's why I'm voting for Ed Mizzibinensky."

Nixon had not stopped at simply denying White House involvement in Watergate. In answering the suggestion that the investigation of the break-in might be short-circuited because of possible embarrassment to Nixon, the President told a press conference there was no cause for such suspicion because, "What really hurts in matters of this kind is if you try to cover it up." He assured the nation that there would be an intensive investigation. Attorney General Kleindienst promised "the most extensive, thorough and comprehensive investigation since the assassination of President Kennedy." When the results of the probe were in, and only seven men were indicted, Nixon praised the investigation, comparing it to the 1948 investigation of Alger

20

Hiss. Against the FBI's Watergate probe, Nixon asserted, the Hiss case had been a "Sunday school exercise."

As I walked across the street toward the next house, the skies opened, and rain mixed with snow began to fall. I always figured that door-to-dooring in the rain was a plus; and the same thing was true for plant gates. I had convinced myself that when people saw me drenched and shivering, they would think to themselves, "Now, that's the kind of dedication I'd like to have working for me in Washington." But maybe some thought I was simply crazy.

I approached a porch cluttered with bicycles, and noticed a NO SOLICITATIONS sign taped to a window. In an era when it was widely believed that candidates were peddling themselves like soap, I wondered if the sign applied to me. I decided not to find out. I turned around and walked toward the next house, thinking of the houses I had bypassed because of the BEWARE OF DOG signs.

A man opened the door after I had leaned on the doorbell a couple of times. Through a yawn, I made out, "Hi, what can I do for you?" I knew I had awakened him; he'd probably just made it to bed after a graveyard shift somewhere. He was pleasant considering the circumstances. After I introduced myself he told me, "You know, I think it's good the way you're getting out in the neighborhoods. You're the first candidate for Congress that ever came here." He tried to stifle a second yawn. We talked for several minutes and I told him about the results of our poll showing that 75 percent of the people in the First District felt pretty much left out of the political process, believing they had little or nothing to say about how their government was run. I handed him a flyer and shook his hand again. "I hope I didn't bother you." "Naw, good to see ya," he said. "Take it easy and don't get too wet."

Two weeks before election day Watergate seeped into the Oval Office. The *Washington Post* reported that H. R. Haldeman, Nixon's closest confidant and White House Chief of Staff, had exercised control over a $700,000 secret campaign fund. The fund's existence had been known—it was allegedly used to finance a massive campaign of sabotage—but for the first time the *Post* tied Haldeman, and through him the President, to it. McGovern seized on the report: ". . . it places the whole ugly mess of corruption, of sabotage, of wiretapping right squarely in the lap of Richard Nixon."

It could have been devastating. But it wasn't.

"Hi, I'm Ed Mezvinsky and I . . ."

"You a Polack?" the man staring through the screen door demanded.

"I'm an Iowan." My mother had immigrated from Poland, but I wasn't interested in discussing my family tree on somebody's porch.

"Well, I really don't give a damn what you are. You're running for something, I can smell that . . ."

"Congress."

"Hell, you're all a bunch of phonies. Don't waste your time here. I'm not voting for anybody this year." He slammed the door. His cynicism was not uncommon. His bluntness was. Up and down the district, in various ways, people were telling me I wasn't aspiring to a very noble profession. According to the polls, people had a hard time deciding if used car salesmen and garbage collectors were more or less trustworthy than politicians.

Maybe that helped explain the immunity to shock over the Watergate disclosures and charges. Maybe, I thought, people are already far too dubious of the men running their government to be surprised by such accusations; I realized that even those ready to believe the worst might consider it only confirmation of what they felt they had always known about politics and politicians. The people I met going door-to-door did not even mention Watergate.

By the time the polls closed at eight o'clock on the night of the election, I was resting at home, holed up with my emotions, my family, and a few friends. Dan Boyle, my long-time friend and confidant, sat with me throughout the evening. Boyle had been Johnson County Democratic Chairman when I moved to Iowa

City in 1967, was a partner in the law firm I joined, and had been instrumental in convincing me to run for the state legislature in 1968. I had won that race, and Boyle's enduring support and sage advice, both personal and political, had been indispensable to me during the years that led to this night.

Television's projection was that Nixon had a good shot at carrying almost every state, but, supported by the confidence of Boyle and other friends, I fought off the fear that our campaign might be overcome by a presidential landslide.

When the results were in they proved that our personal contact strategy and organization had made the difference. I won the district with 54 percent of the vote, defeating Schwengel by over 15,000 votes out of the 200,000 cast. The university community in Iowa City had turned out in force—over *90 percent* of the registered voters had voted—and had given me a 7,000-vote cushion in my home county. More surprising was Scott County, Schwengel's home, where 54 percent of the votes were for me. The best we had hoped for was to break even. I carried only six of the thirteen counties, but overwhelmed Schwengel in the urban areas.

At a victory rally at Iowa City's Knights of Columbus Hall, the Democratic workers were jubilant. The sting of McGovern's disastrous defeat—Nixon got more than 60 percent of the vote nationally and carried every state but Massachusetts and the District of Columbia—was muted by our local victories. A happy surprise was Dick Clark's upset victory over two-term Senator Jack Miller. (When Clark had first announced his plan to challenge Miller, nearly every politico in the state considered him a sacrificial lamb. Clark—well known across the state as a result of his thousand-mile walk—not only beat Miller, he did it handily, winning by more than 130,000 votes.) Clark's and my victories fit in well with the crazy maze of results across the nation as the Nixon landslide failed to filter down to congressional races.

At a Davenport victory rally, after midnight, a volunteer told me the national results supported the theory of a "conscience vote" playing a significant role in the election. The theory was that many of the voters who would pull the Nixon lever would do so with great reservations. Feeling somewhat guilty about voting for Nixon, these voters would salve their consciences by splitting their tickets to make sure that there would be a Democratic Congress to keep a close eye on Nixon. I agreed with the supporter that something had to be behind the unprecedented ticket splitting, but I really didn't think the theory applied to my race. I credited my victory to the voters' desire for change and to the hard work and organization, particularly among the new voters in the district. Several post-election stories, analyzing the national effect of the youth vote, cited its role in my race.

"What really did it," Schwengel told an interviewer in regard to his defeat, "was the youth vote. Johnson County and the University of Iowa did the trick."

TWO: *Beginnings*

I was the last of four children. I had two older sisters and an older brother. My father, an immigrant Jew from Russia, had settled in the Midwest in 1911 at the age of seventeen. But unlike so many others who struggled with the language and the culture of a new country, my father had prospered. He had built his horse and buggy produce route into a thriving business, and by the time he settled in Ames, Iowa, in the early 1930s he had saved the enormous sum of $50,000.

The business acuity that enabled him to succeed while so many others were failing never deserted him. By the time I was born, in 1937, my father was a very successful man. You would not know it to look at him, and his heavy, Eastern European Jewish accent might fool you.

He operated out of his main store in Ames, wearing the oldest of sweaters, using pencil and grocery-bag paper to add a column of figures, but Abe Mezvinsky was no ordinary man.

He was and is a smart man, a very smart man. The original peddler's cart long ago had turned into a grocery store, which turned into several supermarkets, which then turned into real estate holdings and a variety of other investments.

In addition to being smart, my father has always been generous. His charitable contributions are well known to many Iowans, and they are not limited to Jewish causes. One Sunday, the priest of the Catholic church across the street from our store preached a sermon about "Abe Mezvinsky's Christianity!" For several decades, hoboes who passed through our part of Iowa knew that they could get a stake—a full bag of food that would last several days—from Abe Mezvinsky's store. And the *meshullahim*, the bearded Jewish fund-raisers with their dark clothes and their foreign accents, came to our store and our house. They were never disappointed.

My father often said that if a good customer and a bum came into his store at the same time, he would take care of the bum first—because the bum would be hungry.

My father had wanted my brother Norton, four years my senior, to come into the business. And Norton tried, just as I did several years later. But my father, in a sense, had done too much for us, had exposed us to the best America had to offer. Once educated, degree-carrying members of the American middle class, we had little interest in the family grocery business, although we each, in our own way, tried.

By the time I began what my father hoped would be my apprenticeship, the memory of Norton's brief passage through the family business was all too vivid. Even though I had no more real interest in the business than had my brother, I did not want to disappoint my father. I only hoped that the fact I was now a college graduate would mean work of a more interesting and challenging nature.

That hope soon proved to be futile. My father's idea of how to begin in a business was "at the bottom," and within weeks of my graduation I was in the back of the store doing the same jobs I'd done when I was in high school. I cleaned out the produce bins, stocked the shelves, and when the old cash register in the front of the store would jam with a dozen people standing in line, my father would call out, "Eddie, Eddie! I'm needing you. Get up here!"

There was just no way that I could be content with that type of work. Perhaps that was why, at the age of twenty-three, I decided to oppose the elderly Republican state representative from our district.

Actually, I think the Democrats were happy to find a kid with a fresh face, some family money, and a relatively well-known name. (And my having been an all-state end in football didn't hurt.) I campaigned hard, and managed to overlook the startled reactions of my father's customers who were a bit surprised to learn that the tall young man who had just bagged their groceries was running for the legislature.

Unlike many of the people I eventually would serve with in politics, I had never been a very partisan political youth. I had taken part, and was elected to a political position, in the Hawkeye Boys' State when I was in high school. But I was far less interested in the politics than in the fun involved. In college, I stayed away from partisan political activities. My after-class interests centered on sports, women, and campus social and fraternal life. When I did get involved with a "political" cause in college it was strictly nonpartisan. A group of students wanted to have Pete Seeger, the folk singer, appear at the Student Union, but the administrators of the Union were cool to the idea. Ostensibly, they complained that Seeger would not be as big a draw as, say, a group like the Four Freshmen. However, some of us felt that perhaps the real reason Seeger was "undesirable" was that he'd been called before the House Un-American Activities Committee.

The "censure" bothered me, so a friend and I decided *we* would sponsor Pete Seeger. We would be producers! The Sol Huroks of Iowa City! We rented a hall off campus, promoted the show, and had a huge success.

Now, I think, looking back, that one of the reasons I ran for public office before I had been out of college a year was that I missed the excitement and feeling of commitment that had been such a big part of my days in school.

Because no one else had filed to run as a Democrat against the incumbent, there had been no primary. The general election in November was to be the only election. So, when I came back from the 1960 Democratic Convention in Los Angeles, where I had been a guest of the Iowa delegation, I plunged into campaigning. By trial and error I learned what it was all about.

On the eve of the election I still considered myself a long shot. And I was right. I lost. But I had led the Democratic ticket, JFK

27

included. I was pleased by my showing, but I told anyone who asked that I had no immediate desire to run again. Still, I was intrigued by politics.

I was definitely *not* intrigued by the work I was doing for my father. Finally, I confessed my unhappiness to him, and—true to form—he was both patient and understanding. Shortly after the election I told him I wanted to go to graduate school (to study political science) and he did not try to stop me.

Coincidentally, at the same time I thought that I wasn't hooked on politics, I also believed that I wasn't hooked on a certain young lady.

Myra Shulman walked into my life on the arm of a fraternity brother one night at a party when I was a sophomore in college. Micky—the name she preferred—was only sixteen at the time, and still in high school, but she had the face, figure, and poise of a much older girl. I couldn't take my eyes off her.

Within weeks I'd eased her away from my friend (so much for fraternity) and we dated on and off for the next three years. With dark brown hair and eyes, a lovely face, and a lithe build, she was unusually attractive. But her greatest asset was her mind. Her grades were straight A's, even though I rarely saw her studying. Micky was also an accomplished musician, both on violin and piano, and loved music with an intensity I would come to envy but not share. Many of her summers had been spent at the National Music Camp at Interlochen, Michigan.

In 1960, I'd completed my tour of duty in the family business and my race for the state legislature and had decided to go to graduate school. Micky and I were still dating. I had decided on the University of California at Berkeley, and in the early winter of 1961 I began school there. Micky was on the opposite coast, where she was attending Smith College in Massachusetts. We got together in Iowa during spring break and, afterwards, with both of us so far from home, we poured a lot of emotion into our letters and phone calls. In June, at the end of her sophomore year, Micky came to California for summer school.

Neither one of us wanted another year apart, and that August—with the blessings of both families—we were married. I was twenty-four and Micky was exactly twenty and one half.

28

Micky transferred to Berkeley with a near-perfect grade point average. It took her no time to adjust to California. If I liked it, she loved it. Student marriages, however, are rarely ideal. Ours was no exception. During that first year it became apparent that we really didn't know one another quite so well as we'd hoped, despite our four-year courtship.

In 1962 I decided that rather than pursue a doctorate in political science I would enroll in law school. To say we were busy would be an understatement: I wrote my master's thesis during my first semester in law school. Micky, who had received her B.A. one month after our first child—Margot—was born, had her hands full with graduate school and motherhood.

By the time law school was over, in 1965, we had another baby girl (Vera) and it was decision time again. I had a job during part of law school in the legal department of a large San Francisco corporation, but soon found out that it was not the life for me. In one way or another I kept getting involved in politics.

I had done some volunteer work in the campaign of a California Congressman, and when he got to Washington and learned that a colleague of his from Iowa was looking for a legislative assistant (an "L.A.," in the parlance of Capitol Hill), he gave me a good recommendation. By this time Micky had settled into a comfortable, if hectic, life as a young mother and was not delighted by the prospect of moving to Washington, D.C.

But she agreed. Our marriage had undergone some trying times, and I think both of us saw Washington as a "fresh start."

The Iowa Congressman who became my new boss was Neal Smith, whom I had met back in 1960. We all adjusted to Washington, and in late 1967 Elsa Mezvinsky was born. By the end of two years, however, I ran into a common Capitol Hill problem: I had learned about all I was ever going to learn about being a legislative aide to a congressman. I had also learned that I was eager to get directly back into politics. It would be only a matter of time before I ran for office on my own.

Micky was not pleased, but in late 1967 we moved again—back to Iowa. Lou Shulman, Micky's uncle, helped me out immediately. Even though I told him of my political ambitions, he paved the way for me to become an associate of his law firm in Iowa City. The other partners must not have been thrilled at the idea of hiring a young lawyer whose career goals were outside the law, but they could not have been more pleasant about it.

It had taken eight years for my political desires to resurface, but in 1968, after a vigorous campaign I was elected to the state legislature. This time (as opposed to my 1960 try) I ran from the district that encompassed our new home, Iowa City.

During that two-year term I gained—much to my surprise—a great deal of publicity. I even picked up a temporary nickname—"Rat Claw Mezvinsky." One of my constituents had shown me two rat claws that had been discovered by a student at the University of Iowa, who found them in his breakfast sausage at a dormitory one morning. This student had the foresight to send them to the university sanitarian. A short time later, I stood at my desk in the legislature and waved the "evidence" over my head, dramatic proof of what was happening under the state's existing lax meat inspection system. Within twenty-four hours I was Rat Claw Mezvinsky, and I had found a symbol that enabled us to defeat the meat-packers' lobby and pass a stringent meat-packing and inspection bill.

Being a state legislator entailed a great deal of travel, a lot of time away from home and our growing family, and a part-time salary. And since I wasn't interested in the day-to-day practice of law, in 1969 I decided to try the next year for the United States congressional seat held by Fred Schwengel (the venerable Republican incumbent who'd served in Congress ever since I had been in high school).

Everyone worked. Micky did a marvelous job, despite the fact that we now had four daughters (Eve having been born in June 1969) and campaigning was not on her list of favorite things to do. My friends, relatives, and supporters went all out. When the results were in and Schwengel had barely squeaked through with a victory margin of fewer than 800 votes, we were all desolate.

I had come far closer than anyone thought I would, under the circumstances, but I had lost. For a number of reasons, not the least of which was practicality, that would have been the ideal moment to give up my political ambitions. Or at least to shelve them for a decade or so. Not only would such a decision have pleased my wife and my father, it would have been an opportune moment to concentrate on the law practice and take advantage of the fact that my name was now well known in our part of Iowa.

But I couldn't stop. There had been 120,000 votes cast, and I had lost by a mere 765. Before anyone even asked me, I had made up my mind. I would defeat Mr. Schwengel in 1972!

THREE: *A Temporary Calm*

The days after my victory in 1972 were a time of unwinding, making phone calls of thanks, and receiving calls of congratulations, many from people I hardly knew or hadn't heard from in years. One day in the space of an hour, I heard from Congressmen Thomas (Tip) O'Neill of Massachusetts and Sam Gibbons of Florida. Both called to say hello, offer congratulations, and let me know that they were planning to seek the post of majority leader. The job was open because Hale Boggs, who had been majority leader since 1971, had disappeared in a plane crash in Alaska.

Now it was time to organize to be a Congressman. Much of my campaign staff would become congressional staff, and we arranged the establishment of district offices, which had been one of my campaign promises. We also planned a schedule that would get me back to the district a few times a month to hold town meetings and attend other forums designed to maintain personal contact with the people who elected me.

In late November, I joined newly elected Missouri Congressman Jerry Litton on a flight to Little Rock, Arkansas, to meet with Wilbur Mills. Mills was chairman of the Ways and Means

Committee, which controlled committee appointments. I hoped the visit would help in getting a good assignment, come January.

Flying south, I wondered whether, as a freshman member, I could make much of a mark in an institution that delegated power and responsibility on the basis of seniority. Throughout the campaign I had attacked the seniority system as being undemocratic, archaic, and a serious impediment to an effective, representative Congress. But now I found myself traveling eight hundred miles to visit, perhaps even to pay homage to, a man who more than any other epitomized Congress and whose power was partially a result of his having been in the House since I was four years old.

Mills was affable and busy. He had just completed a TV interview on the meaning of the election and the state of the economy, and he was entertaining the Reverend Oral Roberts when Litton and I were escorted into his office. We spent about thirty minutes talking about Congress. I put in my pitch for committees, letting him know that while I had no specific favorites—except of course his committee, on which he assured me there were no vacancies—I was most interested in tax issues, congressional overseeing responsibilities, antitrust law, and food issues. He said he would keep that in mind, and Litton and I left.

Despite the post-election time consumed by preparations for Congress, there was ample time to spend with my family. Finally, a chance to get reacquainted. Days and weeks with the girls were a pleasant contrast to the part-time father role I had played during the campaign, when I had seldom been around to tuck them in or share their problems and joys. Now I was waking up to the four girls jumping on the bed, watching smiles steal into their solemn faces when I kiddingly reprimanded them about having the audacity to climb into the bed of a United States Congressman, pouring orange juice for them at breakfast, taking their lunch orders at A & W Root Beer or Baskin-Robbins, carrying them around the house on my shoulders after dinner, answering their questions, trying to calm their fears about moving to Washington. I had missed moments like these during the campaign. There would be more time for the family from now on.

33

But, as we talked of the impending move to Washington, Micky suggested that she and the girls stay in Iowa City. I was very surprised, even though I shouldn't have been.

Ours was not a perfect marriage. In fact, we had even talked of separating at different times in our marriage, but I thought we'd passed that stage, and I did not expect the suggestion to intrude on the euphoria of victory.

Micky had given her all to the campaign, standing in for me at meetings I could not attend, riding in parades and tossing lollipops, dedicating endless hours to organizing volunteers, joining me in travels throughout the district for receptions and dinners, and campaigning door to door for months just as I did. She had wanted victory as much as I, and I was convinced that with the end of the campaign we would find the time needed to resolve our difficulties.

While her proposal to stay in Iowa City ostensibly stemmed from her lack of enthusiasm for uprooting the family again, it seemed to me that she preferred to face our marital problems through physical separation rather than a new start, devoid of campaign frenzy, in Washington.

For me to go to Washington alone, leaving the family behind in Iowa City, would not be all that unusual, nor would it be "politically embarrassing." Many members' families kept their homes in the district while the Congressman lived in Washington, commuting on weekends when possible and being with his family during congressional recess visits to the district. Such arrangements were, of course, far more prevalent among members from Eastern states, but Tom Railsback, the Republican who represented the Illinois district across the Mississippi from the First District, lived in Washington while his wife and family resided in Moline.

The prospect of being separated from Micky and the girls frightened me. I was convinced that our problems were solvable. But I knew a separation would seriously impede their resolution. We had to keep the family together for the girls' sake if for nothing more, I argued, and Micky, wanting what was right for the children, not too reluctantly agreed.

The momentous year, 1972, blew out in an Iowa blizzard, and the fury of the wind as we left Iowa City gave the girls earaches.

As our plane flew toward Washington, the President had ordered war planes over Hanoi, mocking the pre-election claims of
peace with murderous new bombing. Iowans had given Nixon
58 percent of their votes; but in the counties of the First District
I had outpolled the President, and I was sworn to try to end the
fighting. What did the people want? They had chosen a new
Congressman. Did they want a new policy? The plane vaulted
the cornfields and the Alleghenies, on its way from the Mississippi to the Potomac, bearing my doubts as well as my dreams.
When we landed, the sun was shining and there was no snow in
sight.

"Boy, is he short!"

I grinned, and then looked around the floor of the House of
Representatives to see if any other members had heard my
daughter Vera's all too accurate assessment of Speaker Carl Albert.

It was January 3, the day the House convened to begin the
93rd Congress, and I had bought my two older daughters, Vera
and Margot, onto the floor of the House chamber for my historic moment, the swearing-in ceremony. High above us, somewhere in the crowded gallery, sat their mother and their two
younger sisters.

Finally, after much searching in the poor light of the ancient
chamber, they spotted Micky's bright orange outfit, caught her
eye, and we all exchanged happy waves. It was the culmination,
the moment we had waited and worked for.

One of the girls heard someone say, "It's good to be back on
the floor," and asked me what that meant. "Well, if you should
ever call my office and they say your dad's 'on the floor,' it means
I'm over here, in this room working. It won't mean that I'm
crawling around on my hands and knees."

They both giggled, and several people near us turned and
smiled.

Soon it was time for the oath. Contrary to those familiar pictures of the new Congressman with his hand on the Bible taking
the oath of office in the sole presence of the Speaker of the
House, the actual swearing-in is an en masse affair. The hand-
some pictures are posed after the event.

35

I gave the girls' hands a squeeze and I rose as Speaker Albert solemnly intoned the time-honored words. I felt a lump in my throat as I heard myself swearing to support and defend the Constitution "against all enemies."

The Speaker broke the solemnity with his broad and contagious smile, and I looked up toward Micky as the applause filtered down from the galleries to blend with the vigorous hand-clapping on the floor itself. Then Speaker Albert said, "The gentlemen and gentlewomen are now Members of Congress."

The first weeks were a blur. There was the inevitable amount of wheel-spinning, but things eventually began to shake down to something resembling a routine. The mail was the first priority. Some members are diligent about answering each piece of mail that comes into the office, a practice I intended to follow. I also wanted to make sure that we were not sending out what were in effect "policy statements" before I'd had a chance to determine what my position would be on a given issue.

The problem is caused by the fact that a Congressman needs to have the benefit of hearings, staff briefings, leadership advice, in short, anything that will help to explain the issues. Then he or she can make an intelligent decision and take an informed stand. But the letters always want you to say yes or no immediately.

We wrestled with that problem and worked out a system whereby the letter writer was informed of my position on a bill at the time the letter was written, with the caveat that further study might conceivably change things.

There were also mechanical matters, such as the question of whether to buy one of the futuristic-looking devices that can sign your mail in your own signature, and do so with such fidelity that not even your mother could say it wasn't your own handwriting. But the device cost $1,000, which would have come out of the equipment allowance, and we decided that a perfect forgery was not worth it.

The sheer volume of the mail took some getting used to, even though I had worked as a Congressman's aide several years earlier. In addition to the requests for information and help, there was a flood of informational material, everything from newspapers to special-interest publications. And then there were the invitations, from individuals and groups representing every interest known to politics. There were invitations to receptions in committee rooms on Capitol Hill, to meetings in downtown hotels, and to select small gatherings in the glass-lined office buildings that comprised Washington's new business district. Parceling out my time became another of the main priorities.

Then there were the small niceties. The staff could not possibly know all of the letter writers personally, nor could they know which people *I* knew personally. So I had to screen almost all of the mail to make sure that "Harry," a friend of several decades, wasn't sent a letter addressing him as "Mr. Smith."

In the beginning it seemed that we spent most of our time figuring out what I could afford to do with my time. Would it be a mistake to miss this reception, or that meeting? Would the rest of the Iowa delegation be there? Would I appear to be the only member from Iowa who was so insensitive as to refuse? One day I finally asked Con Merker, my personal secretary, "When am I supposed to have time to really think about an issue?"

She smiled sympathetically, and reminded me that I had to rent a tuxedo for an affair that night.

Somewhere into the first month, I kept a breakfast date that I had been looking forward to for a long time. Back in 1967, when I worked for Neal Smith, I had the pleasure of meeting and then working with a young man who was to leave his mark on this country—Ralph Nader.

I wanted Ralph's advice on the question of committee assignments. There are, on Capitol Hill, all sorts of committees (in fact, there is a Committee on Committees) but every first-term Congressman dreams of being appointed to one of the important ones. Like everyone else, I had my preferences. And top on my list now was the Judiciary.

Over breakfast, that January morning, Ralph told me what I wanted to hear—that I should try hard to get an assignment to Judiciary.

You have to be a lawyer to be a member of the Judiciary Committee, and I was a lawyer, but that fact did not exactly diminish the competition for one of the thirty-eight slots. Almost half the members of the House of Representatives are lawyers.

I was aware that certain other new members, elected at the same time I was, had already begun "lobbying" for a spot on the committee. (Some months later I was told that Barbara Jordan of Texas had gotten former President Lyndon Johnson to intercede on her behalf.)

I made some calls, asking my old boss, Neal Smith, and a few other people to put in a good word for me. I consoled myself, in case I didn't get the Judiciary Committee assignment, with the thought that I would surely get my second choice, Government Operations.

Less than a week before the inaugural, the new committee assignments were made public. I was on the Judiciary Committee.

As the day of Richard Nixon's second inaugural drew near, I wrestled with a personal dilemma. A number of friends, both in Washington and in Iowa, were urging me to join in a planned boycott of the ceremony. Their point was this: If you are truly against the war in Vietnam, how can you attend the inauguration of the man who is continuing that war? It was suggested that, instead, I attend one of several antiwar demonstrations that were scheduled for the same day, January 20, in Washington.

After much thought I decided that my attendance at the inaugural would be simply part of my function as a government or public official, and could not be construed as an endorsement of Richard Nixon and his policies. I felt that I had an obligation to be there.

The day broke cold and gray. The members of Congress gathered in the Capitol Rotunda, and then filed out into the wooden bleachers to join the throng of some fifty thousand hardy souls.

I listened in vain for any specific mention of Vietnam, but the President spoke only in generalities, promising once again that he would lead us to "peace with honor." Somehow, the imminent peace that had been announced with such exquisite timing just before election day had not yet come about.

After his speech, the President was borne away on the crest of a fifty-band, forty-float parade down Pennsylvania Avenue. Micky and I met at the car and drove to a church in Northwest Washington to take part in an antiwar service.

Pete Stark, a newly elected Congressman from California who

was sitting with us in the balcony, and I were introduced as freshman members "who will help change things." How grand that sounded.

Three days later, on January 23, Richard Nixon announced that an agreement promising "peace with honor" had finally been reached. Hostilities were to end within the week. In two months all American troops and prisoners were to be out of Vietnam. My reaction was one of relief—and a strong hope that my instantaneous skepticism about the durability of the agreement was unfounded.

"On page 6, strike out lines 9 through 12."

Joe Addabbo's innocent sentence, so innocuous-sounding, was all the battle cry we needed. The Addabbo amendment had the power to end the bombing of Cambodia by pulling the purse strings shut.

It would do so by deleting an equally innocent-sounding sentence in the Second Supplemental Appropriations Bill of 1973, which read (lines 9 through 12): "Section 735 of the Department of Defense Appropriations Act, 1973, is amended by deleting '$750,000,000' and inserting '$1,180,000,000' in lieu thereof."

By early March, those who had been paying close attention knew that part of that "extra" $430 million dollars was to pay for the bombing operations in Cambodia. (Nixon's "peace with honor" plan applied only to Vietnam, not neighboring Cambodia. U.S. troops and POWs were home from Vietnam but daily bombing raids over Cambodia maintained a glaring American presence in Indochina.) The Pentagon was asking the Congress, through the guise of the requested change in the supplemental appropriations bill, for permission to shuffle its money around so it could spend more on the air war in Cambodia. Whether or not Congress would go along shaped up to be the first crucial test on the war for the 93rd Congress.

While $430 million is a staggering sum, there was more than that involved. The Pentagon had *already* spent $150 million of the asked-for-but-not-yet-approved money on the Cambodia bombing. Which meant that if the Congress agreed to the Pentagon's request, it would be handing the Administration and the military a blank check for waging war. And, in effect, Congress

39

would thereby abdicate its constitutional policy-making role and be just an unquestioning paymaster.

The people may not have been aware of the moves and the countermoves, but the White House clearly was. On May 7, Defense Secretary Elliot Richardson testified on the Hill that rejection of the Addabbo amendment would be evidence that Congress approved, or at least was willing to acquiesce in, the continued bombing of Cambodia. The battle lines were clearly drawn.

May 10 was the day. The appropriations bill was scheduled to be taken up shortly after noon.

Those who opposed the amendment used the tiresome—but, oh, so successful—argument that to stop the bombing would be to prolong the war; those of us who supported it viewed the Pentagon's request as tantamount to another Gulf of Tonkin Resolution, by which President Johnson extended the years of tragedy in Vietnam.

Early in the debate John Flynt of Georgia made a dramatic speech, warning us not to make the mistake he had made when he had joined in the House's unanimous passage of the Tonkin Gulf Resolution:

"I have regretted it almost from the very day I voted for it. When I face the Supreme Judge of the Universe, I shall ask Him for mercy—and to forgive me for voting for the Tonkin Gulf Resolution. I hope that the spirits of the 50,000 Americans who have been killed in Southeast Asia will not serve on the jury that tries my case."

The reporters in the packed press gallery were scribbling away, ready to record how the people's house voted this time.

I was too nervous, too excited to sit down during much of the debate. As Flynt spoke, I was standing near the back of the chamber, leaning against the brass rail. There had been no controversy in this place over whether to approve the Tonkin Gulf Resolution, but the chamber was alive with it today. Maybe the House had learned from that bitter mistake.

Addabbo's discussion of his amendment concluded with a plea to realize that more was at stake than whether bombs would continue to fall.

"It is time, I believe, that Congress send a message downtown

40

to the White House. And, that message should be pure and simple and easy to understand. The message I would send would say: 'If you want to bomb Cambodia, you come to Congress and detail just why you feel impelled to do so. You tell us how you would spend the money and where and what you will accomplish. Then the House will decide yes or no on that explicit request. But there will be no more covert going-along, no hiding of war funds disguised as innocent budget transfers. The House of Representatives is reasserting itself as a co-equal branch of Government.'"

It was time to vote. The buzzer system was activated, and throughout the House side of the Capitol, in the hallways and tunnels, and in every member's office, the buzzers began to sound and the small bulbs lit up—two "bells" meaning a roll-call vote. (They *are* buzzers, but everyone persists in calling them bells.) On the digital clocks at either end of the House chamber the lights flashed on and began to count down the 900 seconds during which time all votes had to be cast.

The name of every member appeared in lights above the Speaker's chair, and small green or red lights began to pop on to indicate whether the Congressman had voted *aye* or *no*. And to the side of the clocks a "scoreboard" kept a constant tally of the votes for and against the amendment. (This is the new computerized electronic voting system, initiated earlier in 1973, and it adds a special excitement to close votes.)

I stepped up an aisle to the small voting box fixed to the back of a bench and inserted my identification card. The series of small rectangular holes told the computer that Mezvinsky was about to vote. Glancing up at the clock, I noticed that there was only ten minutes to go and the Addabbo amendment was slightly behind.

I pushed the square button marked "aye" and watched the green light go on, instantly, beside my name.

Now there was nothing more I could do but watch to see the outcome. I remained tense as I stood off to one side, along with a group of other "ayes," oblivious to everything except the panel—which showed the vote as switching from one side to the other and then tied.

The numbers kept flashing, changing, flashing, and it looked

as if we were going to make it. We had a slight lead, and everyone stared fixedly at the scoreboard.

When the "ayes" reached 218—an absolute majority—cheers
rang out, and I found myself jumping up and down with glee.

The clock reached ten seconds, and spontaneously many of us
began to count down, out loud: ". . . six . . . five . . . four."
The chanting became shouts: ". . . two . . . one."

The clock stopped, and there was cheering, whistling, and
whooping on the Democratic side of the chamber. The Addabbo
amendment had passed, 219 to 188. Democrats were pounding
one another on the back and pumping hands. I was jumping up
and down, and I was hardly alone.

Up in the visitors' gallery, where a loud whisper often brings a
reprimand from the dour guards, the crowd joined in the clapping and cheering.

The Republican leader of the House, Gerald Ford, proclaimed it "a very sad day in the House of Representatives."

As far as I was concerned, the vote made everything worthwhile—all the door knocking, the picnic suppers, the pot-luck
dinners, and the speeches. It was worth it to stand on the floor of
the House of Representatives that single day, as a Congressman,
and cast a vote that helped the House raise its voice for the very
first time and say "No" to more bombs and bloodshed in Indochina.

Certainly it was long overdue, but it signified that Congress
was stirring—and willing to go after some of its lost authority. It
was a day I'll never, never forget.

Although the historic House vote did receive front-page coverage in most of the influential papers, it hardly received "big
play." Even the *Washington Post* squeezed it into a small story on
the lower left-hand side of page one. I was disappointed, but not
surprised. After months of neglecting Watergate, the papers
and newsmagazines were now treating it as topic A, partly out of
embarrassment at having been so outdistanced by Woodward
and Bernstein of the *Washington Post,* and partly because it was
the hottest subject of political and national gossip.

The denials of the President and his press secretary notwith-
standing, there *was* something to the Watergate story, and al-

though I didn't agree with the rabid anti-Nixonites who had already concluded that the President was the prime mover from the beginning, I sent out news releases to the district stating that the nation deserved to know the truth about the break-in—and what was now being called the cover-up.

Too much was happening that could not be ignored or even understood without more investigation. The Senate Select Committee on Presidential Campaign Activities, which everyone referred to simply as the "Ervin Committee," or the "Senate Watergate Committee" had announced that its public hearings would begin on May 17, amid rumors that James McCord was about to blow the whistle on some higher-ups and that John Dean had some stories to tell. McCord had written a letter to Judge John Sirica, who was in charge of the pending Watergate case, stating that he could tie the break-in directly to the Administration; and Dean had told reporters that he would not be a "scapegoat."

Other revelations plagued the Nixon White House. L. Patrick Gray, the acting head of the FBI, admitted that he had destroyed Watergate-related evidence; Nixon had accepted the resignations of Ehrlichman and Haldeman, his two closest and most powerful aides; and the Ellsberg case was dismissed by Judge Byrne because of "government misconduct"—the illegal entry into the office of the defendant's psychiatrist. It was a rough month, made rougher by the news that the White House had maintained its own secret security force, the "Plumbers."

The atmosphere was suddenly so charged with shock and indignation that one afternoon toward the end of the month I found myself in a meeting called for the express purpose of discussing the desirability of Nixon's *forced* retirement—through impeachment!

Representative Bella Abzug had called the meeting, and there were several of us sitting in her fifth-floor office in the Longworth Building. I looked at the others, wondering if they thought we were talking about a plausible happening.

Abzug had invited us to gather informally because she felt that someday, down the road, we just might have to talk formally and officially about impeachment as part of our constitutional responsibility. Bella felt that if and when the House had to begin an impeachment inquiry, it should not be totally unprepared. She wasn't suggesting a full-fledged move, a formal resolution of impeachment, but she wanted us to start thinking—just in case.

Never one to shy from controversy, Bella realized that she had to stay in the background, at least for a while, in regard to any impeachment moves. She was savvy enough to know that there were certain members of the House who would automatically oppose any cause she embraced. (Cloakroom wisdom had it that a number of conservative Congressmen, when unsure how to vote on a bill, would check to see where Bella Abzug stood and then vote the opposite.)

I had to agree with Bella that if she appeared to be spearheading any impeachment drive, a number of minds would suddenly snap closed.

We talked quietly—just the opposite of the old "smoke-filled room" cliché—and didn't accomplish a great deal. As I left her office, I felt that the House was not prepared for impeachment. I knew I was not.

As the Watergate scandal had grown larger, and closer to Nixon, I followed the story. It was impossible not to, what with the *Washington Post* on my doorstep and the *New York Times* in my office every morning, and the evening television reports filled with new developments.

I was troubled by what I was reading and hearing, but I was doing other things, too. I was wrapped up in the mechanics of Congress, the day-to-day existence, answering the mail, trying to keep up on the issues that I had to vote on each day. I had issued a few press releases on major Watergate developments, but in the same way that I made statements on my views on Nixon vetoes and reports that double-digit inflation was continuing to rob the public of its purchasing power. In the late spring of 1973, I didn't have the time or the inclination to become a serious student of Watergate.

During May, while Watergate was boiling, the House was voting on such diverse subjects as the private ownership of gold; whether to increase the number of seats in the Washington Redskins' football stadium; and the cutoff of funds for the bombing in Cambodia.

A bill I co-sponsored early in the month brought me more reaction from Iowa than any statement I made on Watergate. The bill involved a steamship, not a scandal. Its aim was to save the paddlewheeler *Delta Queen* from being scuttled by federal safety regulations that were not intended to apply to the steamship, but inadvertently threatened the last authentic stern-wheel riverboat still in overnight service in the nation. It might not have been earth-shaking legislation, but it was important to thousands of people in Iowa and across the nation who wanted to preserve this reminder of the past—the majestic beauty of the paddlewheeler plying the muddy Mississippi.

I simply could not conceive of Watergate leading to impeachment proceedings against Nixon. For that matter, I could hardly imagine how anything could lead to the impeachment of any President. The process itself seemed part of our past.

Back on April 30, John Moss of California had reacted to Nixon's Watergate speech by suggesting that the House open a formal inquiry into the possible impeachment of the President. (In that speech the President had announced: that his aides Haldeman, Ehrlichman, and Dean, and Attorney General Richard Kleindienst had resigned; that new information had come to his attention that suggested that there was a coverup going on; that, as "the man at the top" he accepted *responsibility* for any "improper actions" of the White House or his campaign organization; and that "justice will be pursued fairly, fully and impartially, no matter who is involved" because "there can be no whitewash at the White House.") Moss, a twenty-year veteran in Congress and a member of the Democratic Steering and Policy Committee, had the kind of credentials that ensured he wouldn't be written off as a fanatic if he suggested an impeachment inquiry. (When I met with Abzug in May she had told me she had been pressing Moss to push for a serious dialogue on impeachment.) But Moss didn't get anywhere. Majority Leader O'Neill publicly dismissed Moss's suggestion as "premature."

A few weeks later, at the end of May, Senate Democratic Whip Robert C. Byrd of West Virginia took the Senate floor to say that murmurings of impeachment were "at best premature and at worst reckless."

45

It was on June 6, however, that I got the clearest signal about how unprepared at least part of the House was for the sensitive topic of impeachment.

California Congressman Pete McCloskey had reserved a special order for that day, allowing him to control the floor at the end of the day's business. A special order is a routine device that allows members to debate issues not necessarily before the House at the time. McCloskey (a Republican who was something of a pariah to much of his party because his opposition to the Vietnam war led him to challenge Nixon in several 1972 primaries) planned to talk about impeachment, what he termed "the special constitutional responsibilities of the House with respect to investigation of matters revealed in President Nixon's public statements of May 22." He planned to deliver a speech on whether the House should initiate impeachment proceedings.

Unfortunately for McCloskey, the House worked late on June 6, and it was about nine in the evening when he walked to the well and adjusted the microphone to the proper height. Shortly after he began his speech, he was sabotaged.

Earl Landgrebe, a Republican from Indiana, effectively gagged his colleague. Rather than allow him to speak on the subject that many thought unthinkable, Landgrebe raised a point of order that a quorum—half the members of the House—was not present in the House chamber.

It was evident he was right. There's hardly ever a quorum present during debate on a bill and almost never during a special order. But a quorum call takes precedence over all business, and McCloskey was interrupted for the fifteen minutes that members are given to get to the floor after the bells ring three times—each ring about the length of a telephone's ring—alerting absent Congressmen to get to the floor from wherever they are.

Of course, at nine P.M., when the day's official business is over, most members are long gone, and after the fifteen minutes passed, the House was still far short of a quorum.

There was a motion made to adjourn, to close the House and thereby block McCloskey's planned debate. The motion lost. I— and just about everybody else—voted against it. The vote was 9–143. But the damage was done. Almost an hour was lost to the parliamentary maneuvering, and Landgrebe was still there, ready to demand another quorum call if necessary. This could go on forever.

McCloskey gave up. Under the Rules of the House, the sergeant at arms can be directed to search out and retrieve missing members. But McCloskey wanted a reasonable debate, which he knew would be impossible if Congressmen had to be dragged back to the Capitol from their homes, or restaurants, or from wherever they'd gone. So he moved to adjourn—that motion carried.

Although I hadn't planned to speak during the debate, I was disgusted at the way it had been prohibited. The Landgrebe incident confirmed my feeling that it would be a long time before the House of Representatives would seriously take up any impeachment resolution.

FOUR: *The House Is Not a Home*

The season wasn't even a month old and people were already calling it the "Summer of the Watergate hearings," or, as one young staffer dubbed them, "The Sam Ervin Show." May, June, July, August, the hearings rolled on—relentlessly and astoundingly. Senator Sam, his jowls shaking, quoted the Bible and Shakespeare and whatever down-home homily seemed to fit. He was the star, the grand inquisitor, but he shared the bill with a parade of past and present administration officials whose testimony fueled the fire of speculation.

The Plumbers were described in fuller detail, the Huston Plan to spy on dissidents was revealed, the enemies list made known, and any number of lesser evils were discussed on television and then debated in homes throughout the nation. Yet, for all the frightening specificity, no one truly and convincingly tied it all to the man in the White House.

Like everyone else in Washington, I was drawn to the television screen with a growing sense of morbid fascination. After the first few weeks of the hearings, the staff didn't even bother to ask if it was all right for them to be watching; they knew I was as intrigued as they were. Whenever we could steal the hours, we huddled in front of someone's tiny portable, and listened intently to the statements, the questions, and the answers. And our office was by no means the only one so occupied. All you had to do was walk down the hallway while Haldeman or Ehrlichman or Dean was testifying—especially while Dean was testifying—and you could hear the muted sound of the television sets seeping out from under the closed doors.

If the sound was fairly audible, it was usually the office of a Democrat. If the set was on very low, the suite belonged to a Republican.

Of all who testified, John Dean had the greatest impact. He brought the mess right up to the door of the Oval Office, but he couldn't get it through. He thought the President was probably aware of the cover-up, but he couldn't *prove* it. Yet he shocked millions with his carefully spoken litany of seemingly incriminating evidence, and he was clearly unflappable. His memory was prodigious, and his "image," so important an item in the Nixon Administration, was one of credibility, even if it was expedient credibility. I was surprised at the number of people in Washington who were talking about Dean as if he were a hero, one who had decided to save us from the worst excesses of Nixonism.

I held no brief for the President, but the lawyer in me cried out for something more tangible than John Dean had thus far provided. (And with his access to his own White House files cut off, it didn't appear that he was going to be able to come up with anything solid.) From my visits back to my district, and from conversations with other members, it was clear that as shocking as Dean's testimony had been, it failed to provide "the clincher."

Of greater interest to me was the revelation by Alexander Butterfield, in his testimony on July 16, that there had been a secret recording mechanism in use in the White House during all the period of time that Dean and others had spoken of—and that the tapes of these secret and obviously relevant conversations probably still existed!

The staff was as stunned as I. Kevin said, "My God, Ed, it has to be all there! That could be the end of it!"

I not only liked Kevin, I admired him. For a twenty-three-year-old, he had an unusual share of common sense. There were times, though, when he made me feel an old man at thirty-six. He was so sure the "smoking gun" would be included in one of

the taped conversations. I envied him that certainty, one I did
not share.

I simply couldn't believe that Richard Nixon, the consummate
politician of the modern era, would allow himself to be trapped
by a device of his own making. Yet there was a great streak of va-
nity in the man, not to mention the possibility of greed, and the
tapes could conceivably provide him with a record of history, a
record that would help him write his memoirs. Could the desire
for that record have lulled him into recording conversations that
might eventually be used against him in regard to the Watergate
scandal? It was an exciting possibility.

Within days of Butterfield's revelation, both the Ervin Committee and Archibald Cox, the Special Prosecutor, asked for the
tapes.

The President said no; it would violate "national security."
Neither Ervin nor Cox bought that argument, and subpoenas
were issued—the first for a President of the United States since
1807. And when Nixon ignored them, both the committee and
the Special Prosecutor's office took the matter to court.

Judge Sirica ordered the President to turn the tapes over to
him, on the principle that he could not rule on the dispute without hearing what was on the recordings. The President refused
and his lawyers appealed the judge's ruling. By late July it began
to look as if only the Supreme Court could resolve the stalemate.

The unfolding of the Watergate drama obsessed the capital
during the summer of 1973. You couldn't go anywhere in Washington without hearing the latest news, rumors, and even the
most blatant guesswork put forth as absolute truth. There was a
curious psychological force at work; the possibility that the corruption might reach all the way to the President fueled the anger of many people and the fear of others. It was unlike anything in the recent past.

I would have liked to study the whole picture in greater detail,
but I couldn't. For one thing I had a busy travel schedule—
which took me back to Iowa, where the Ervin Committee hearings had not generated the same kind of intense reaction as they
had in Washington—and the office demanded most of my time.

Of greater importance, however, was that while the Watergate case was building up, my marriage was disintegrating.

The bad news came in June. I was in my district for a weekend, and was about to enter the public library in Iowa City for a Friday night town hall meeting, when Lou Shulman (Micky's uncle) hailed me. He asked if I could meet him for breakfast the next morning.

We met at a restaurant in downtown Iowa City, ordered, and sat back. I was in a good mood. I knew I'd enjoy the visit with Lou, and I was interested in the series of meetings with constituents that had been set up for the day. I had seen too many older Congressmen lose touch with the people who sent them to Washington, and I had no intention of letting that happen to me.

Lou and I had been talking generally, but suddenly he leaned toward me and said, "Excuse me, Ed, but I have to lay it on the line."

I looked up, surprised by the change in his tone of voice.

"Micky has filed for divorce. She has retained me as her attorney, and the papers are already on file in Johnson County District Court."

I stared at Lou. All I could manage was a quiet, "No."

"I'm sorry, Ed, it's true, all right. Look, I don't have to tell you how I feel, but . . ."

I could hear his voice, but I barely paid attention to the words. I found myself growing angry with him. I knew he cared deeply about both of us, but he *was* the bearer of bad news, the unwelcome messenger.

Our food arrived, and it gave us an excuse to be quiet for a while. I was shook up, numb, even though most of our friends were aware that for the last five years our marriage was, as they probably described it, "shaky." There had been more than a few open, angry arguments that ended with the possibility of divorce. But I had never believed it, and we had always weathered the crisis. Yet here I was, faced with an irrefutable fact—and still refusing to accept this actuality.

We finished the meal, shook hands, and I got through the rest of the day, somehow. The raised voices, the many questions, the need for thoughtful answers, all helped to keep my mind occupied. I stayed up late, as late as I could, to make sure I'd be tired enough to sleep.

But on Sunday morning, stretched out in my bulkhead seat as I flew the "friendly skies" of United, I was forced to think about Micky's action. There was so much to remember. It seemed odd how the good times suddenly flooded my mind. But what kind of a life had it been for Micky, especially these last five years? Certainly not everything she'd hoped for on the day we took our vows.

Four children in quick succession surely limited her choices. Although she had been a superior student, I was the one with two advanced degrees while she still had not completed her master's degree in English. And her music, which meant so much to her, that too had to be curtailed if not given up outright. While we were in California Micky had played with the University of California symphony at Berkeley, but she had been too busy to join another orchestra in Washington. And even if she had, the four small children would have made it unlikely that she could perform very often, since she often had to be both father and mother in my frequent absences.

I had forgotten, in my haste to get ahead with my own career, just how much she loved music. She played and listened to it with a passion. I think she could have enjoyed a concert every night without ever being bored. But she had given most of that up.

And then there were the moves and the housing and all the decisions I had made without listening closely enough to her opinions. I remember how she felt about the much too big house I'd rented (with an option to buy) in Iowa City in a neighborhood where we were almost the only young couple.

Finally, there was her disinclination toward politics, especially the loss of privacy and the need for being "nice" to people even if they called in the middle of dinner.

Micky had put up with a great deal of loneliness and uncertainty, but it had always seemed to me that we were on a road together, and when it became clear that the road was leading toward Washington, I felt we could work out everything. There was, I thought, just a lack of time. And when and if I made it to the House of Representatives, everything would fall into place. Both in 1970 and again in 1972, Micky had worked like a trooper. And we had made it. I had really thought during the first few months in Washington that the situation had improved. That was why I was so stunned by Lou Shulman's news.

I had missed some signs, though. When I told Micky I would buy her a car for all the suburban Washington driving she'd be doing, she surprised me by saying, "Oh, Eddie, when you register the car, be sure you put it in *my* name."

As the plane began to circle Washington's National Airport, I realized that Lou Shulman had delivered more than divorce papers—he had also delivered my eviction papers.

I drove slowly up the George Washington Parkway toward McLean, thinking about how to leave my own home. When I pulled into the driveway, I wondered for a moment whether I should knock before going inside. I didn't. I walked in, the kids said hi, and Micky asked how my trip had been. It was much the same as before, but so different.

Micky and I went into the bedroom, and I told her I was moving out. I pulled out a suitcase and began packing enough clothes to get me by for a week or two and said I planned to come back later to get the rest of my things. I didn't say it, but inside I was hoping, praying that when I came back for the other clothes I would be accepted back.

As I was packing, Margot came into the room to remind me that she and Vera had a dance recital that afternoon at the McLean Ballet School. One reason I had not scheduled a Sunday meeting in Iowa was in order to be home in time for the performance. "Sure, I'll be there," I told Margot, and as I stared hard at the handful of socks I stuffed into the suitcase I held back tears.

We took two cars to the recital, and Micky and I sat together, along with Elsa and Eve, proud parents and proud sisters. With piano accompaniment, my daughters performed their brief ballet number and I found myself hoping it wouldn't end. But applause, and Eve's jerking on my sleeve, told me it had. It was time to say goodbye. I kissed Eve and Elsa and waited tensely for Margot and Vera. When they came we hugged one another.

When I got in my car, I realized I had no destination. I just drove around for a while in a state of semi-shock, wondering how and when I would get back together with Micky. I ended up at the Holiday Inn in McLean, checked in for the night, went to my room and tossed the suitcase at the foot of the bed. In the emptiness of my room I didn't know what to do. I kicked off my loafers, sat on the side of the bed, and broke into tears. Unable to control myself, I cried all evening. Sometimes I tossed in the bed, sometimes I stared at myself in the bathroom mirror. Mostly I thought about the kids, especially Margot, who at ten was the oldest. I knew I had let them down. Eve was only four, she probably didn't understand what had happened, but she would. The uncertainty made things worse. Finally, I fell into a troubled sleep.

I awoke with a dizzy, emotional hangover, showered, checked out, and headed for the office. When I arrived, I had Jon Kent and Pat O'Connor come into my office and, embarrassedly, explained what had happened.

They already knew. Micky had talked on Sunday evening with Con Merker, who had told the administrative assistants. They were good friends of mine and Micky's and had been through both campaigns with us. They were aware of the stormy character of our marriage, and were not shocked by the separation.

I told Kent and O'Connor that they would have to bear with me in the weeks ahead, because my efforts to put the marriage back together would undoubtedly mean that I wouldn't have the time or concentration to do all the things they'd probably think I should be doing.

When the House concluded its business that day, I drove to the Skyline Inn, a hotel about four blocks south of the Capitol. It was twelve dollars a night if I'd stay at least a week, so I signed in for seven days.

About a week later, I went back to the house in McLean, ostensibly to pick up the rest of my clothes but really to see Micky and the girls. I'd called Micky a couple times during the week, hoping for an instant reconciliation. I thought that being with her would help.

When I arrived at the house, it was empty; the lease had not yet run out, but Micky and the girls were gone. I knew she was planning to rent a place in Reston, Virginia, about fifteen or twenty miles west of Washington, for the summer. She picked Reston for the kids' sake—there were swimming pools and playgrounds within walking distance—but she hadn't told me she intended to move so soon. My initial anger dissolved into despair. I threw together the rest of my things, took one last walk through the house, almost as if I expected to find all of them in one room or another, and headed back to Washington.

On the first of July, I moved into a studio apartment on a monthly basis. I did not want to get locked into a long-term lease because I kept hoping that any day I'd be back with Micky.

On the weekends and whenever the House adjourned early, I'd drive out to Reston to see the girls. But, before each visit, I had to call Micky and arrange the time. We'd hit a fast-food place for dinner or go swimming or go to the park to play on the merry-go-rounds and swings. This was supposed to be fun, but I found that I could not stay with my daughters for more than a couple of hours. It was difficult handling all four of them by myself. Eve was so little, so demanding. And the emotional strain was difficult for me.

My visits to Reston usually included short chats with Micky but we seemed to be making no progress in getting back together.

In the office, the staff was understanding, but there was a nagging concern about whether and when and how we were going to make the separation public. As private a matter as a separation is, I was a public official. Because Micky had filed the papers in Iowa City, there was no problem that it would get out. Iowa's divorce laws are especially good at protecting privacy. Divorce petitions do not become public until they result in divorce. I knew, however, that the news would get around. Some of our friends in Iowa City knew, and the talk would spread very quickly.

It wasn't that I wanted to keep it a secret—although I was concerned about public reaction—but I figured it really wasn't anybody's business. I believed we'd get back together, so why tell the world we were apart?

The problem of how to announce the separation, if at all, was taken out of our hands when we got a call from my hometown paper, the *Iowa City Press-Citizen*, whose editor asked if we were separated and if I had a statement on the subject. I confirmed it and told him we would call him back when we had written a statement.

Kevin McCormally and Jon Kent were in the office with me, and Jon suggested that it should be a joint statement, from both Micky and me. I told Kevin what I wanted it to say and asked him if he'd type it up so we could check it with Micky.

A few minutes later he handed me a slip of paper that read: "Following a mutual agreement, we have temporarily separated and are in the process of trying to iron out our problems. We hope to get back together soon."

Jon went off to call Micky, but when he came back he had an odd look on his face. He showed me the statement. The second sentence—"We hope to get back together soon"—had been crossed out. Micky would agree to the wording of the first sentence, but the second had to go. I felt as if I'd been kicked in the stomach.

We phoned the statement to the *Press-Citizen* and then decided we should send it to all the other newspapers and radio and television stations in the district. A press release was still unpalatable to me. We concluded that the best way to handle it was for McCormally, as my press secretary, to write a brief memo to the news editors and news directors explaining that the *Press-Citizen* had called and asked for the statement. It was an FYI (for your information) memo and included the text of the statement.

The separation story made the front pages of several papers and sometimes was accompanied by an "in happier times" photo of Micky and me taken shortly after the election. I got twenty to thirty letters shortly after the story. Most either berated me for "abandoning" my wife and children, or were filled with biblical passages calling on me to renounce evil and turn to Jesus for salvation. The response was limited, and although it bothered me, it was harmless compared to an experience I had the first time I returned to Iowa after the separation became publicly known.

I went out for a weekend in late July, and Margot and Vera accompanied me so we could spend some time together and they could see some of their Iowa City friends. The biggest event on my schedule was the Coralville Centennial Parade. Coralville is a

suburb of Iowa City, and Margot and Vera joined me to walk in
the parade.

We were walking behind a float, all three of us waving, as we
passed a large apartment building. Suddenly, several voices
were yelling things like, "Hey, Mr. Ed, where's your wife?" and
"Mr. Congressman, Mr. Congressman, where's your woman today?" I tried, but I couldn't block it out. It was all I could do not
to stop and look at the hecklers. As the anger and resentment
welled up within me, I thought of the girls and hoped that they
had not heard it. They had done nothing to deserve being hurt.

My thoughts throughout the summer of 1973 were on my
day-to-day work as a Congressman and what, if anything, I
could do to change Micky's mind. I spent very little time worry-
ing about Watergate, about what it meant and where it might
lead. I was troubled by the scandal, but I didn't see anything I
could or should do about it.

The House reconvened on September 5 after our month-long
break and the first day back most of my conversations with other
members, especially other freshman members, concentrated on
sharing experiences from our travels among constituents.
Whether it was Barbara Jordan of Texas, Gerry Studds of Massachusetts, Pat Schroeder of Colorado, Andy Young of Georgia,
or Pete Stark of California, the assessment of the general mood
on Watergate was the same I brought back from Iowa. The scandal was coming in a poor second, or worse, to the cost of living.

Nobody I talked with had found much grass-roots agreement
with Nixon's description of Watergate as "water under the
bridge," but we'd all noticed waning interest in the scandal and
heard plenty of support for the President's pleas to leave Watergate to the courts and get the government to work on bread-
and-butter issues.

Leaving the case to the courts made a lot of sense, because
that's where the battle was being fought over the great unknown—the presidential tapes that held out the possibility of
finally resolving the crucial question of whether Nixon was involved in the cover-up.

The dispute over whether investigators would get a chance to hear the tapes was moving inexorably toward a resolution. By the time Congress reconvened, the case was before the U.S. Court of Appeals for the District of Columbia.

No matter how the Court of Appeals ruled, the dispute was sure to go to the Supreme Court for a final resolution. White House statements had made it clear that Nixon would obey nothing short of a "definitive" Supreme Court ruling ordering him to turn over the tapes. With that in mind, the chief judge of the Court of Appeals had ordered the case expedited in order to get it to the Supreme Court as soon as possible after its term opened on October 1.

At the same time, September brought the stunning news that Spiro T. Agnew, the Vice President of the United States, could very well be in serious legal trouble. This immediately diverted attention from Watergate and gave to Agnew the front-page headlines that had for so long been centered on his boss. From the first stories in August, reporting that Agnew was under investigation for allegedly taking kickbacks, the "Agnew case" quickly built to swirling rumors that he might be forced to resign.

By late September, when the Justice Department was preparing to take its evidence to a grand jury, the Vice President actually *asked* the House to open impeachment proceedings against him. He contended that the charges against him amounted to impeachable offenses and therefore the House was the proper forum for an investigation to "vindicate" him.

Speaker Carl Albert thought about it for less than twenty-four hours and said no. The Judiciary Committee would be the logical one to conduct such an investigation, and Peter Rodino called an informal meeting of the Democratic members to check our reaction to the situation.

"What Agnew's asking for," Rodino summed up, "is for us to get the grand jury off his back. It's not our job to do that and we're not going to." Nobody in the room tried to change his mind.

Turned away by the House, Agnew went to the courts (seeking to block presentation of evidence to the grand jury on the grounds that a sitting Vice President could not be indicted) and to the public. (He told a wildly cheering audience of the National Federation of Republican Women, "I will not resign if indicted. I will not resign if indicted.") It seemed that a long, nasty fight was in the offing.

On October 10, however, with dramatic suddenness it was all over. The Vice President resigned and pleaded "no contest" (which the judge quickly pointed out was the full equivalent to a plea of guilty) to a tax evasion charge. He was sentenced to three years probation and fined $10,000 and he was gone.

Late in the afternoon of October 18, the House adjourned, and, at Chairman Peter Rodino's request, most of the Democrats on the Judiciary Committee gathered in a private dining room in the Capitol. We were there because the 25th Amendment called for the President to choose and Congress to confirm a nominee to fill the vacancy in the vice presidency.

President Nixon had already done his part. Six days earlier, clearly relishing the suspense he created regarding whom he might pick, Nixon tapped Gerald Ford, Congressman from Michigan and minority leader in the House. Ford's nomination was disclosed during a prime-time, nationally televised White House event, an extravaganza saturated with perverse gaiety and devoid of any reference to the man who made it all possible: Spiro Agnew. The man twice selected by Nixon to be his Vice President was gone now, a disgraced felon, and his political corpse had no place in the gala debut of Gerry Ford.

With Ford's nomination before Congress, Rodino wanted to talk about the mechanics of the confirmation hearings in our committee. Somebody asked whether the pressure to expedite the hearing process would mean we'd be meeting on weekends and maybe during the congressional Thanksgiving recess.

John Conyers had been listening quietly, but his patience was evidently spent. He didn't care about the answer. He shifted in his chair and, interrupting, said, "I think it's absolutely ludicrous for us to even be talking about going ahead with Ford when the President who made this nomination is subject to impeachment."

He launched into a forceful argument on the illogic of considering the Ford nomination before initiating impeachment proceedings against the man who chose him.

Nobody in the dining room was stunned by the suggestion. Our meeting turned from a consideration of the "how" and "when" of the Ford hearings to a discussion dominated by arguments over whether we should proceed at all.

When the 25th Amendment was debated in Congress in 1965, one of the prime objections to it was that a President would be allowed to nominate his own "heir," thereby transforming the second-highest elective office in the land to an appointive post. The pitfalls of such a change had been widely debated at the time, but Congress never considered a set of circumstances such as it now faced: that a President, his credibility battered by a scandal that some considered basis for impeachment, would be nominating a replacement for a Vice President who had bartered away his office to avoid going to prison for felonious conduct. Had a member of Congress tried to bolster his case against the proposed amendment by presenting such a "theoretical" case in 1965, he would have seemed ridiculous.

But the 25th Amendment had been adopted and ratified and that was the flaw I saw in Conyer's argument. Nixon had not only the right but the obligation to nominate a replacement for Agnew. Similarly, Congress had to proceed with the confirmation process. Surely, we could reject as many nominees as the majority found unfit for the job, but we couldn't ignore a nomination.

Furthermore, I didn't think the public would stand for delay on Ford. Suggestions that the hearings be postponed until the President gave up the tapes (an issue that was still before the Circuit Court of Appeals) or appeared before the Ervin Committee for interrogation or made some concession on Watergate had already been dubbed schemes to "hold Ford hostage." Foot dragging by our committee would lead to more charges of congressional blackmail and playing politics.

The situation demanded that the question of impeachment and the nomination of Ford be dealt with separately. The public was pushing for prompt action on Ford, and there was little pressure on the impeachment issue.

Earlier in the week I had talked with fellow Iowan Neal Smith, and our conversation got around to the idea that maybe it was time for the House to begin to prepare for impeachment. After comparing notes on how little serious talk about impeachment we'd heard in Iowa, Smith said he considered it unlikely that the House would move on the issue.

An opportune time to have begun impeachment proceedings, he suggested, would have been during the summer, on the heels of John Dean's testimony before the Senate Committee. His hair-raising tales of White House-inspired burglary, bribery, perjury, and the harassment and intimidation of citizens whose "crime" was to disagree with the President had stunned millions of Americans. Their outrage, "at that point in time," might easily have been translated into support for impeachment.

But the dog days of summer and the Agnew shock had intervened, quieting the fury created by Dean's testimony. Smith reminded me that Congress moves where public pressure directs it. Impeachment did not seem a very probable destination.

I agreed with Smith's analysis and brought it up during our Capitol caucus. "Unless something dramatic happens, another bombshell, some overwhelming evidence or something like that, there just isn't going to be any momentum for impeachment. As long as there's no big support for it, there's no way to put Ford off," I said. "Unless something big happens to change things, I don't see that we've got any choice but to move ahead with Ford."

That had been Rodino's conclusion all along, that we had to proceed with the confirmation hearings. And as the meeting broke up, it was evident that was what he planned to do. Conyers was not dissuaded from his position, but a clear majority agreed with the chairman.

Father Robert Drinan, the Massachusetts liberal, was among the minority and, as we walked back to the office buildings together, he was steaming about Rodino's priorities. Since midsummer, Drinan's impeachment resolution had lain dormant in a committee file.

"I'm going up to Boston this weekend," he told me as we waited to cross Independence Avenue, "and if we go ahead with this nomination and don't move on impeachment, I'm going to blow the whistle on the committee. I'll call it what it is, a cover-up!"

When I realized he wasn't kidding, what started to be a smile turned into a mumbled, "Do what you have to do." Castigating the committee for not investigating Nixon's eligibility for impeachment before considering Ford's qualifications for Vice President would probably seem logical to a good many of Drinan's constituents. Just as surely, I thought as we parted, if he tried to make the same case in Iowa, where I was to spend the coming weekend, he would be called the "mad monk."

FIVE: *Saturday Night, Special*

The landing gear came up with a dull, metallic thud, breaking my concentration. I put down the sheaf of papers and stared out the little window as the 727 climbed away from Washington on its way to Iowa. As the lights along the Potomac became fewer and harder to distinguish, I was glad to be getting away from the Capitol.

It was Friday, October 19, 1973, and I was relieved to be heading back to Iowa for a weekend that promised nothing but work. Why? Watergate. Washington was overrun with rumors. I expected the trip home to provide a respite from this continual preoccupation.

Today had been a busy one in the can-you-confirm-this? and what-have-you-heard-about-that? department, with callers asking about the impending release of the White House tapes. Special Prosecutor Archibald Cox, a no-nonsense Bostonian, was determined to have those tapes. In fact, the Court of Appeals had just ruled in his favor. But the President, wrapping himself tightly in his cloak of executive privilege, was resisting.

The most recent White House ploy was Nixon's offer to let the aging John Stennis, Democratic Senator from Mississippi, listen to the tapes and report on their contents. Stennis may have been

a member of my own party, but he was known as a Nixon loyalist, and many viewed the offer as just another of the President's
famous "tricks." Before leaving I'd heard from Kevin McCormally that Cox had refused to go along with the Stennis compromise, and that the President was reportedly furious.

Ah, Washington. It *was* a relief to be heading back to the Midwest. All I faced was a battery of appearances the next day,
which happened to be Homecoming Day at the University of
Iowa. I had to be in my Iowa City outreach office in the morning
(where I'd be photographed signing a check for a local fund
drive), then the football game, and finally I was scheduled to
show up at receptions held in the Law School, the School of
Pharmacy, and the Engineering School.

It would be hectic. Again, I wouldn't eat properly. But it
would be Iowa, and I would get to talk to a few friends, such as
Kevin's father, John McCormally (publisher of the Burlington,
Iowa, *Hawk-Eye*). Even though I was intrigued with the mystery
of Watergate, I would not have time to think about it.

Saturday was busy. I made the receptions, but I missed the
game, and when I got back to my Iowa City office there was a
message from Kevin.

Earlier that day, Nixon had ordered Cox to stop issuing subpoenas to get the tapes and other materials from the White
House. Cox had refused, and had held a press conference to
state his reasons. He reaffirmed his opposition to the Stennis
plan, and he said he'd be in court on Monday morning to press
his search for the facts. My office had received a number of requests for a statement on my position.

I told Kevin to draft a brief message of support for Cox, and
before we could discuss the wording, someone reminded me
that I was late for a meeting where I was scheduled to speak on
the question of amnesty for draft evaders.

Several hours later, after dinner at the house of a friend, I
picked up the phone and called John McCormally. I wanted to
see if he had received my statement, and I also wanted to know if
he had heard any of the rumors that the President was getting
ready to fire Cox, something Kevin had mentioned earlier in the
day.

"We got the statement," John said, "but I think you're going to have to revise it."

"What do you mean?"

John's tone was not light. "Here's what's coming over the wire. Cox is out; the Special Prosecutor's office is abolished; Elliot Richardson, the Attorney General, has refused to fire Cox; Nixon fired Richardson; Richardson has resigned; his deputy, Bill Ruckelshaus, also refused to carry out the order and he's been fired; finally, Robert Bork, the third man on the Justice Department totem pole, discharged Cox. Bork is now the Acting Attorney General."

I could hardly believe it. I asked McCormally if he was sure the UPI story was accurate. It was, he said. He'd just seen a news bulletin on television that gave the same details.

God almighty! What was going on back in Washington? I thanked John for the information and promised to get back to him with a new statement in time for the *Hawk-Eye's* midnight deadline. I wanted to get right to a television set, but the schedule prevented it. If I was to make the Johnson County Democratic fund-raiser, being held at UI's MacBride Hall, we had to leave for the campus right away.

When I arrived, the raucous tone of the gathering told me that everyone had heard the news.

"Ed, I want you to hustle it back to Washington and I want you to impeach that son of a bitch" was one of the first greetings I received. Walking through the room, I heard the word "impeachment" over and over again. It was a partisan crowd, but it had taken this latest shock to bring that word to so many lips.

"Hey, Ed, did you hear Nixon sent federal marshals in to take over the Special Prosecutor's office? What the hell's going on back there?"

The uneasiness growing out of the unbelievability of what we'd heard found expression in grim jokes about "Banana Republics" and coup d'etats.

I made my way up to the front row and sat next to Senator Harold Hughes. The program called for me to make a short speech, and when my turn came I began with my own stunned reaction to the evening's events. I dismissed the President's high-minded rationale for the Stennis plan and suggested that Nixon's actions were an indication that "the greatest threat to the presidency is the President himself." There were cheers when I said that.

"Mr. Nixon kept telling us to leave Watergate to the courts," I continued. "But now he lets us know that he won't let the courts pursue the case. By firing Cox, the President has violated the will of Congress, the trust of the public, and his own promise to allow the Special Prosecutor to seek out the truth." More cheers.

"It is clear to me that Congress must step in, now."

Harold Hughes was the next to speak. Just the month before he'd surprised people throughout Iowa by announcing he would not seek reelection in 1974. Instead, when his term ended, he planned to devote full time to the lay ministry.

Hughes has an incredible presence in a crowd. When he rose to speak his grave demeanor seemed immediately transmitted to most of the audience. He spoke slowly, counseling restraint and urging that precipitous action be avoided.

"I know we've all had a stomachful of arbitrary actions by the President," he said. "But, I do not believe in mob rule. This case is still in the courts, and the courts must carry out their mission. Hopefully the tapes issue can still be resolved in the courts."

I was surprised by Hughes's restraint, his effort to tone down the crowd. He wasn't known for taking it easy on Nixon. When he returned to the seat beside me, I looked at him, searching for a sign of what was going through his mind.

He turned to me and, still somber, said, "Ed, you know, I've looked at this guy, and I know you've got to be careful. You never know what he might do." Hughes's expression was one of absolute seriousness. "Ed, you just can't tell about this guy," he said, "you could have tanks on your front yard."

Monday was Veterans' Day; the House was in recess and the Longworth building was quiet. Most of the offices were closed for the holiday. As I walked around the fourth floor, from the elevator to my office, I noticed piles of yellow Western Union telegram envelopes on the floor in front of every closed office door. The people were speaking.

When I walked into 1404, Doris Freedman, my legislative assistant, displayed a handful of telegrams addressed to me.

"Here's what they're saying, Ed," she said and began to read from the stack of messages:

"'We urge you to press for Nixon's impeachment. Preserve our liberty.'

"'Are we a nation under law or a nation under a President? If we're a nation under a President, we're screwed.'

"'I voted for Richard Nixon and am very sorry I did so. Impeachment proceedings should be begun against him.'

"'For arrogance and contempt of the people, impeach the President.'

"'Save the country. Impeach the President.'"

Doris paused and reached over to pick up a telegram that had been set aside. "I want to be fair, so here's the *one* that doesn't support impeachment: 'Please be patient with the President.'"

I picked up a few of these messages. They were from all over Iowa and the country, part of the "firestorm" of public reaction to what was being called the Saturday Night Massacre.

Cox had asked for a public judgment of his firing. "Whether ours shall continue to be a government of laws and not of men is now for the Congress and ultimately the American people," he had said in a brief statement after he was discharged. I was staring at the first ballots cast in that referendum.

"I've got to see Rodino," I said, almost to myself, as I put down the telegrams.

"Before you rush off, Ed, you're going to want to see what's coming over the telecopier," Kevin advised me. "Get this: a front-page editorial in the *Davenport Times-Democrat*, with a big headline you're not going to believe." He made me ask what it said. "'Impeach Now.'"

The telecopier is an amazing machine. I'd know soon enough if Kevin were kidding. A piece of paper is inserted into the machine, whirls around on a cylinder, and in six minutes a copy of the editorial would be transmitted over a thousand miles of telephone wires from our Davenport office to Washington.

"I want to see that as soon as it's done," I demanded.

I went into my office and called Rodino to let him know I was

67

on my way over. Nobody answered but I couldn't believe his office was empty.

Doris brought in the editorial and, with her leaning over my shoulder, I began to read it very carefully.

"This was on the front page?" I asked a couple of times. It was the harshest language I had ever seen in the *T-D*, a notably conservative newspaper, at least in its editorials.

After reading it twice, I walked over to Rodino's office in the Rayburn Building, with the editorial.

Rodino was there talking with a couple of his aides and Jerry Zeifman, chief counsel of the Judiciary Committee. I said my piece.

"Pete, I think we've got to look at impeachment, and if we don't do it right now, we're not doing our job."

The chairman nodded at the obvious. He pointed at his own stack of telegrams.

"You've got to see this," I said, pulling out the editorial. "Nixon probably thinks this firestorm is all a creation of the Eastern media. But here's a paper that backed Richard Nixon and endorsed my opponent in the last election."

He read it and handed it back with a smile. Rodino did not need convincing. He assured me that he was planning to move on impeachment.

I knew he was not unprepared. He had certainly been far more tuned in than I to the impeachment rumblings during the summer.

Two weeks earlier, on October 10, the day Agnew resigned, the committee had distributed a 700-plus-page book entitled *Impeachment: Selected Materials.* It was a monumental document, compiled by Zeifman and the committee staff, that brought together more about the subject of impeachment than had ever been printed in one piece before. The book had been criticized by some who thought it would be used by no one but history students; others complained that it was a cosmetic exercise, designed to mollify impeachment advocates by demonstrating the committee wasn't ignoring the issue.

I saw a copy of the light brown paperback book on Rodino's desk, and knew it was the beginning point. He knew the time would come for the committee to initiate an inquiry, and now that the time had arrived, at least some of the preliminary groundwork was done. (I made a mental note to find my copy and read through it.)

As I was leaving Rodino's office, I noticed that Joe Rothstein, one of his advisers, was sitting at a desk, writing. He told me he was working on a draft statement for the chairman, announcing that the Judiciary Committee would begin an inquiry to determine if grounds existed for impeachment of the President.

"You know the significance of this, don't you, Ed?" he asked pensively, pointing at the paper. "Once you start something in this place, there's no turning back."

The starting mechanism was activated the next day.

When the House convened at noon, the mood inside the chamber was wild. The talk was of the avalanche of mail and telegrams and telephone calls descending on Capitol Hill and demanding impeachment. Senior members assured me that the outpouring of public outrage was unprecedented. Several colleagues showed me the impeachment resolutions they were getting ready to introduce and asked if I'd like to join them. I saw Bella Abzug at the door to the cloakroom. Her broad smile seemed to be needling me, saying, "Boy, what did I tell you all along?" John Conyers had his reminder for me. "I was right," he said. "Why didn't you listen to me?"

I heard someone inside the cloakroom repeat the latest instant cliché, "Nixon is a Cox sacker."

"Did you drive by the White House and honk?" somebody else asked, referring to the demonstrators in front of the Executive Mansion displaying signs exhorting passing motorists to "Honk for Impeachment."

The two days that had intervened since the firing of Cox had done nothing to quell the angry reaction. Indeed, time to ponder the events of Saturday night had only reinforced the immediate, extreme response that getting rid of the Special Prosecutor was a desperate move to perpetuate the Watergate cover-up.

"The President's incredible and bizarre actions this last weekend have culminated a long pattern of pure and unmistakable obstruction of justice." Jerry Waldie, the tough-minded California Democrat, was at the microphone, introducing the first of

69

many impeachment resolutions. "His arrogance and lawless activity can no longer be tolerated."

He was followed to the well of the House by other members, a parade of emotional speeches demanding that the House take up impeachment. Abzug offered articles of impeachment charging the President with seven violations of the Constitution and the law.

Many of the speakers expressed sadness that it had come to this. Lester Wolff of New York said it was "with a heavy heart that I rise today" to call for impeachment but "the President's actions leave the Congress no alternative. . . ."

"I stand before you this morning agonized because I do not want, I do not desire to take this quantum step," said Parren Mitchell of Baltimore. "But, my heart, my conscience, my soul, all that is me, demands that this step be taken."

Ron Mazzoli of Kentucky called it "a painful day in my life. I have no desire to play any part, however slight, in bringing about the turmoil and upheaval of a presidential impeachment." He said his oath of office "requires that I move to force House consideration of that terrifying prospect."

I was standing at the rear of the chamber, leaning on the brass railing, when Lud Ashley of Ohio announced that his "great-granddaddy" had served in the House a century earlier, and had "introduced the impeachment proceedings against President Andrew Johnson." That was the only time in our history that impeachment had been brought against a President and it had given impeachment such a bad name that it had been consigned to the history pages ever since.

"That resolution of impeachment failed, as it should have, because it was introduced by my great-grandfather for purely partisan political reasons," Ashley declared. "The same cannot be said, Mr. Speaker, of the resolution that I have offered today."

Considering the intensity of public reaction to the Saturday Night Massacre, it was not surprising that the Republican side of the chamber was not the scene of battles among members fighting to get to a microphone for a chance to support Nixon.

As the session opened, Gerry Ford had announced that the Republican leadership had met and agreed to support the plan to refer impeachment resolutions to the Judiciary Committee.

70

Even Dan Kuykendall of Tennessee, who displayed a replica of a hangman's noose as he warned against "a legislative lynch mob," steered clear of any words of support for the President or even mention of Nixon by name. The noose, he explained, was a symbol for "those who would rush into this proceeding without going through an investigation."

A page tapped me on the shoulder and said I had a phone call. I started toward the cloakroom, but stopped when I heard, "In my considered judgment, history will record Richard M. Nixon as the greatest President this nation has ever had."

I heard it, but I couldn't believe anyone would be saying it, not on this day. As I turned around to see who was speaking, a disbelieving silence had fallen over the chamber.

My mouth dropped open when I recognized that it was Otto Passman, a Democrat from Louisiana. The seventy-three-year-old legislator was all worked up, his hands sweeping the air. "There comes a time when the fainthearted run for the showers; then, those with courage must speak up. I am taking my position on the side of the President," he blurted, red-faced, "because I believe he possesses unimpeachable integrity."

Referring to the firing of Cox and the defiance of the court order to turn over the tapes, Passman lectured, "Those with the brains of a juvenile moron know that the President is working within the framework of the law."

"Amazing," I said aloud, but to no one. In contrast to the relative silence coming from the Republicans, Passman took it upon himself to praise Nixon. He did so, he explained, as "a God-fearing and God-loving American."

I was nauseated. Here was one of ours, a Democrat, carrying the water for those in the President's party who didn't have the stomach for the task.

I didn't make a speech that day, but I did co-sponsor one of the many resolutions dealing with impeachment.

There were two distinct types of resolutions: those that proposed Nixon's impeachment; and those that called for an inquiry to determine whether there were grounds for impeachment. Some critics of any impeachment action lumped them together, arguing that the differences were only in semantics. I disagreed, and was deliberate in my decision to co-sponsor the resolution

71

offered by Phil Burton of California that would direct the Judiciary Committee to open an investigation of impeachment.

Impeachment is a privileged matter in the House—any member can call at any time for a vote on a resolution of impeachment. If the vote came soon, it would fail. While the sentiment might have seemed strongly in favor, I knew a case for impeachment had not been developed. It would take a strong case, hard evidence, to impeach the President. I still did not want to move too quickly.

The week following the Saturday Night Massacre saw a snowballing effect in the public—and the congressional—reaction to the Cox firing. On Wednesday, even more impeachment resolutions were introduced in the House, and Rodino had to call a special meeting of the Judiciary Committee Democrats to discuss how best to proceed now that "an impeachment inquiry is *likely*." One of the first decisions was that we had better hire a special counsel right away.

By Friday, the President knew that his precipitous actions had backfired. He went on television to announce, among other things, that he was determined to bring the Watergate affair to an "expeditious conclusion." He announced that he would name another Special Prosecutor, and that his lawyers were working with Judge Sirica in order to determine how best to "surrender" the nine tapes that had been asked for specifically in the original subpoena.

It was a strange situation. After all the excitement over the tapes, and we had all known of their existence ever since July 16, no one outside the White House had heard a one of them or read so much as a single transcribed word. Neither the Ervin Committee nor Judge Sirica had received a reel of tape or a page of transcript. But the nation and the Congress and the courts—and now the people—were all asking for them.

In the face of this rising crescendo of insistence, the White House lawyers had to announce in open court on Wednesday, October 31, that two of the nine asked-for tapes were missing.

How appropriate for Halloween! And one of the suddenly missing tapes included the conversation between the President and John Dean on April 15, 1973. That was the mystery meeting, the one that had so intrigued the Ervin Committee, and everyone else who heard Dean's comments.

According to Dean's testimony, during that meeting Nixon had asked him "a number of leading questions which made me think the conversation was being taped and that a record was being made to protect himself."

Dean claimed that during that session the President had discussed the idea of raising a million dollars for the Watergate defendants, and also admitted to Dean that he had talked about offering executive clemency to E. Howard Hunt.

What a prize that recording would be!

J. Fred Buzhardt, the President's special Watergate lawyer, told Judge Sirica that no recording had been made on that day because the system had "malfunctioned." Not a whole lot of people believed him. I certainly didn't.

The other missing tape supposedly covered a telephone call between the President and John Mitchell. According to the official line, that one didn't exist because it had been made on a phone that was not plugged into the White House taping system.

The charitable view was that both explanations were plausible and might even be true.

Reaction to the news indicated that a great number of people were not inclined to the charitable view. Within days, Senator Edward Brooke of Massachusetts became the first Republican Senator to call for Nixon's resignation, and *Time* magazine devoted the first editorial of its fifty-year history to call for the President to resign.

On November 7—the first anniversary of his landslide reelection victory—Nixon went back on television to say that he was instituting Operation Candor. But the candor went out of the operation two weeks later when the White House was forced to announce that there was an 18½-minute gap in one of the tapes it was getting ready to turn over to Judge Sirica. Despite Rose Mary Woods's admission that she was probably responsible for five of those missing minutes—she said she had accidently hit the wrong button on her Uher tape recorder—skepticism was running high. (And so was Watergate humor: Woods's mistake was quickly tagged "Rose Mary's Boo Boo," and people joked that to get a job as a secretary at the White House you had to be able to *erase* 100 words a minute, and that if Woods had worked for Moses, there would only be eight Commandments!)

The situation was so bad that a national poll showed that half of those questioned thought all of the tapes had been tampered with!

It came as no great surprise to any of the members that even though the Judiciary Committee was still holding its confirmation hearings on Ford, the full House voted on November 15 to approve a resolution assigning one million dollars to the committee to hire an inquiry staff to see if formal impeachment proceedings against Richard M. Nixon should be instituted.

In early December I fulfilled a promise I'd made to speak to my daughter Margot's fifth-grade class at the Franklin Sherman school in McLean.

I was still separated from Micky (and the girls) but maintained hope that we'd get back together. Less had happened with the divorce petition filed by Micky than with the impeachment resolutions introduced in the House. The petition was lying dormant in a Johnson County courthouse file cabinet. I viewed the fact that she was not pressing for prompt action as a good sign.

I got together with Micky and the girls once or twice each week and was happy to accept the opportunity to speak to Margot's class in my roles as father and Congressman.

My first surprise came when I was ushered into a large meeting room in the school and was introduced, not to twenty-five or thirty members of Margot's class, but to more than two hundred fourth-, fifth-, and sixth-graders.

I began with my standard presentation for grade-schoolers, which amounts to a quick civics lesson: Virginia has ten Congressmen and two Senators, and Iowa, where I'm from, has six Congressmen and two Senators . . . and so on. I also briefly mentioned that I was a member of the Judiciary Committee and that we were in the process of implementing the 25th Amendment to confirm a new Vice President.

"Okay, let's throw this open for questions," I said after about five minutes, a practice I usually follow regardless of the age of the audience. "Does anybody have anything they'd like to ask?"

Several hands shot up, and I pointed at a small boy sitting near Margot.

"Congressman 'Mazbiniskey,' do you think President Nixon should be impeached?" he asked in a clear voice.

Before I could respond, the auditorium exploded with cheers and *applause* that startled me. There were loud "hooo-rays" and ringing "yea, yea, get him's," and big smiles and kids clapping with their hands raised high above their heads. As the hostility poured out, my astonishment grew with the realization that these children were more antagonistic than the crowd in Iowa City had been in reacting to the Saturday Night Massacre. It was like reading *Lord of the Flies*, with children swooping down for the kill.

Silence came as suddenly as the outburst and I began to answer the boy's question as solemnly as possible, attempting to temper their emotions by impressing upon them the seriousness of what had been suggested.

"Do you understand what this is all about? Do you know what impeachment means?" I asked, almost incredulously. "It is a very serious thing."

The children listened quietly as I explained that the inquiry was designed to resolve the charges against Nixon, not to "get him."

Other questions followed, but as I responded I could not get over the excited cheering that had greeted the suggestion of impeachment.

After the assembly, while driving back to Washington, the eerie experience continued to nag at me. Nine-, ten-, and eleven-year-olds cheering at the mention of a word that the year before only Nixon's most ardent critics dared use.

Gerald Ford's nomination as Vice President of the United States came to the full House on December 6, nine days after the Senate had approved it on a 92–3 vote. There was absolutely no suspense as to how the vote would go. The television cameras from the major networks were already set up in anticipation of the swearing-in ceremony that was scheduled to begin at six that evening.

We convened at ten A.M., two hours earlier than usual, to ensure that the debate on the nomination could be completed on time. Charles Rangel of New York, a Democrat (and fellow member of the Judiciary Committee) who had opposed confirmation, made it clear that he was bothered by the obvious haste: "I feel somewhat superfluous in my role as a member of the House debating and voting on this confirmation. It appears that if we do not hurry, the ceremony will begin before we have a chance to vote!"

There were about five hours of debate on the nomination. I doubt if it had any effect on votes.

When the vote was ordered, I quickly moved to a voting box, stuck in my card, and pushed the "aye" button. I did not savor the moment.

I sat down next to Rodino and watched the tally board confirm that it would be "yes" by a landslide. I checked the names of the Iowa delegation; all six had green lights next to them. So did the overwhelming majority of names.

As the digital clock flashed off the final seconds of the voting period, Bob McClory of Illinois, the second-ranking Republican on the Judiciary Committee, came over and leaned down to talk with Rodino. He nodded his head toward the tote board—the final vote was 387–35. There was a lot of commotion on the floor, but I distinctly heard McClory whisper to Rodino, "I'm ready for the big one, now."

Deliberately, I did not look at McClory for fear that my expression would give away my surprise at what I had overheard. We took a one-hour recess after the vote and then reconvened for a joint meeting with the Senate for the swearing-in ceremony.

Once everyone was seated, the door at the back opened, and the doorkeeper announced President Nixon and soon-to-be Vice President Ford.

Everyone was standing, and the place erupted in tremendous applause. I had expected a royal welcome for good old Jerry, the likable man who had been a member of the House for twenty-five years, but the intensity of the cheering surprised me.

There was a brief pause in the standing ovation, just long enough for Chief Justice Warren Burger to administer the oath, then, when Carl Albert introduced Ford as the Vice President, the applause rocketed through the chamber again.

Ford looked almost embarrassed. Albert beamed a smile filled with happiness—and no doubt a good measure of relief at being another step removed from the presidency.

After a while I began to wonder how long the ovation would go on. I looked around the Republican side of the chamber and thought how long it had been since the Republicans had had *anything* to cheer about. It had been a bad year for them. Who could blame them for relishing their jubilation?

Then I looked up at Richard Nixon, who was standing a little to the side and behind Ford. He, too, was basking in the applause, but I knew he could never have enjoyed such a welcome if he'd come alone. I was sure he knew it too, but perhaps he hoped that at least some of the ecstasy being displayed for Ford as Vice President might magically rub off on the President.

"I am a Ford, not a Lincoln," Ford began his brief inaugural address. But as he spoke I had trouble paying attention. It was an unprecedented moment, but my mind was crowded with thoughts about what would happen next. With Ford sworn in as Vice President the excuse that had served as a brake on the impeachment inquiry was gone. The prerequisite had been met.

I stared at Richard Nixon and wondered whether picking a man so popular in Congress for Vice President might backfire, whether, instead of shoring up support for Nixon, it would make him expendable.

All I could think of was McClory's softly spoken but unmistakable, "I'm ready for the big one."

As we moved, slow step by slow step, into the impeachment inquiry, I thought more and more about Richard Nixon the man. In my brief career I had met a lot of politicians, but he had to be one of the stiffest and most unbending figures in all of American public life. I remembered the first time I had seen him in person, striding across the campus at Berkeley when I was a graduate student there and he was campaigning against Governor Pat Brown. Even just walking across the lawn he appeared to be rigid, all business.

77

When Micky and I had gone to the White House reception for the new members we'd had a momentary conversation with the President. He flashed the famous quick smile with the hint of nervousness behind it, and talked about the First District of Iowa. His conversation was all political. Not that I expected anything else under the circumstances, but I'm sure had it been Jack Kennedy there would at least have been some compliment for Micky's looks or a funny crack about Iowa weather.

I couldn't imagine Richard Nixon making small talk, nor could I imagine him dressed in anything but his careful, ten-years-behind-the-times banker's style. I was sure that when Nixon was a young Congressman, he must have taken his daughters for an ice cream cone or a soda, but I couldn't *picture* it.

And if that was the way he was, all business, what must the men around him have been like? Coincidentally, I had a chance to find out not long after.

During the Christmas holidays Micky and I were invited to a party in McLean, at the home of some neighbors. Because Micky and I were on friendly terms, we decided to go as a couple.

The party was pleasant, but halfway through the evening, I had an unsettling experience.

Our host introduced me to a man he thought I'd like to meet, a personal friend of his named Fred Malek. I had heard of Mr. Malek before. A staunch Nixon loyalist, he was the Assistant Director of the Office of Management and Budget. Apparently he knew that I was a Congressman, and after a few moments of polite small talk he asked what committees I served on.

When I said "Judiciary," his icy reaction as visible.

"Oh!" he said.

As offhandedly as possible I said, "Yes, we're looking at impeachment."

"You're wasting your time!" Malek snapped. "There's nothing there."

"Well, we'll have to see. I'm not quite as sure of that as you are."

He became furious. His face turned red.

Malek and I looked at one another, and it was obvious that so much tension had arisen that further conversation would be pointless. We parted without saying a word and headed for opposite corners of the room. Within minutes I'd lost all of my partying spirit, and Micky and I soon left.

The evening wasn't turning out the way I'd hoped, and it was about to get worse.

When we got to my car I discovered a rear tire that was becoming flat. The last thing I felt like doing was struggling in the cold to change it, so I eased the car onto Dolley Madison Boulevard in the hope we could wobble the few hundred yards to the nearest filling station.

I soon realized I was probably ruining the tire and maybe even the rim, so I pulled onto the shoulder. Just as I did, I saw the flashing lights of a police car. One of the problems of being a Congressman is that you get too used to the friendliness of the Capitol Police, and, forgetting that, I got out of the car and asked the young Virginia cop if he would help me change the tire.

He looked at me as if I were a runaway lunatic, and asked if I'd been drinking. By this time he had his ticket book out and was starting to write me up for unsafe driving. I started to get mad—I'd had two glasses of white wine at the party—and when Micky joined us she started to argue too.

Secretly, I was pleased to see Micky come to my defense so forcefully, but the police officer wasn't. I kept arguing, and a few minutes later I was in the back of the cruiser being given a breatholator test! I could already see the headlines in Iowa.

Fortunately there was nothing wrong with the equipment, and the little bag device told the cop I was sober. When he realized this, he became friendly, and he actually helped me change the tire. Micky was still fuming when I got back in the car, but I was trying to laugh off the experience. There is something exhilarating about *not* getting arrested. I dropped her off at her house in McLean and headed back to my apartment.

During the break between the first and second sessions of the 93rd Congress I spent as much time in Iowa as I could. I wanted to find out how my constituents felt about a variety of issues, but especially how they felt about the impeachment inquiry. In announcing the hiring of John Doar as special counsel on December 20, Pete Rodino had said that April 15 was the target date for completion of our impeachment investigation.

I was eager to talk about impeachment, and, contrary to reports that most people outside Washington were suffering a battle fatigue that translated into boredom, I found keen interest in the Judiciary Committee's inquiry.

I reminded listeners that positive House action on impeachment is akin to an indictment by a grand jury. It is only a finding that enough evidence exists to require that a trial be held. Explaining that a House vote to impeach did not mean removing the President from office—only a two-thirds vote to convict following a Senate trial could do that—helped relieve the concerns of some who had misunderstood the process.

I couldn't go into detail in describing the Judiciary Committee's inquiry because not much had been done; we had not held a single formal meeting on impeachment. But I discussed the appointment of John Doar and ran through a list of the areas that would be considered during the investigation: the Watergate break-in and cover-up; alleged misuse of government agencies, such as the IRS; the activities of the Plumbers; the President's approval of the Houston Plan sanctioning illegal acts; the secret bombing of Cambodia; allegations that the President raised milk price supports in exchange for campaign contributions from the dairy industry; impoundment; charges that Nixon improperly intervened in an antitrust case in behalf of ITT; and personal finances, including the President's taxes and the enormously expensive government-financed improvements on his private homes.

The one area that came up more than any of the others involved the President's taxes. During a brief meeting at Ft. Madison's Labor Temple, a stock clerk succinctly expressed why the President's tax returns were generating so much interest: "The average worker and his wife pay more taxes than Nixon does, Ed. Why don't you people do something about this?"

"We're looking into it," I assured him. "I've talked about it with Chairman Rodino, and the day I met John Doar I brought up taxes and told him I considered it an important area. I think the impeachment inquiry has to take a hard look at it."

I had raised the tax issue with Doar—it was the only specific area of investigation I had mentioned during our first meeting.

I knew that allegations that had received significant attention during the summer Watergate hearings would be scrutinized during the inquiry. But the tax issue hadn't arisen until the fall and, although it might not be a direct facet of the burgeoning Watergate scandal, I believed the questions raised by Nixon's tax returns demanded the attention of the committee.

Throughout the First District, I found widespread suspicion that "Nixon pulled a fast one on his taxes." Whether or not his low tax payments were legal, they drew a visceral animosity from the President's fellow taxpayers who felt he hadn't paid his fair share. The people of the First District were far more interested in the tax issue than the more abstract, constitutional questions to be studied during the impeachment inquiry. The President's nominal tax payments struck a raw nerve.

The celebrated Watergate tapes were another impeachment-related matter that came up often while I was in Iowa. The saga of the tapes was becoming curiouser and curiouser.

In mid-January, the experts appointed to determine what caused the mysterious 18½-minute gap on the vital June 20 tape reported to Judge Sirica that the obliteration of recorded conversation was deliberate. The gap was caused by at least five separate, manual erasures. If it had been an accident, an expert told the court hearing, "it would have to be an accident that was repeated at least five times."

There was little I could say when questioned about the experts' report, except to agree that a grand jury should investigate in hopes of determining who was responsible. The snide smiles I noticed in several audiences suggested that some people thought they already knew the answer.

Beyond discussing and answering questions about the matters under investigation by the Judiciary Committee, I explained to each group that, despite the month-long congressional recess, work was being done on impeachment.

The inquiry staff (which included more than forty lawyers) was in the process of gathering evidence that had been developed by other committees—most notably the Senate Watergate Committee—and by the time Congress reconvened on January 21, we hoped to be in a position to determine what further evidence needed to be developed. Efforts were also under way to define just what an "impeachable offense" was.

81

As I discussed impeachment, there was obvious interest in how this relic from the past would be applied. But the most common question was not about procedure or how I thought the committee would vote, but rather *when* the committee would make its decision. People from Davenport to Keokuk to Grinnell disagreed over whether Nixon deserved a clean bill of health or a bill of impeachment. But there was little discord over the importance of making the decision soon. The indecision was tiresome and maddening.

I answered by pointing to the April target date as a reasonable one and reminding my listeners that the pace of the inquiry would depend as much on the President's cooperation as the committee's efforts to expedite the investigation. The decision on impeachment would be based on the evidence and could not be made until that evidence had been accumulated and evaluated.

There were undoubtedly some who considered my stated dedication (to be guided by the evidence as to my ultimate vote on impeachment) a pious pronouncement, deceptively implying that politics would play no part.

I knew well that however I voted on impeachment, I would have to defend my decision to the voters of the First District. I would be judged at the polls, and that verdict would be influenced greatly by my judgment of Richard Nixon.

Out in Iowa, during my mid-winter visit, I couldn't forecast how the Judiciary Committee's inquiry would go, but I had a sense of the prevailing political climate—it was unfavorable to Richard Nixon. The economy was in rotten shape and the energy situation was making things worse. Domestic problems alone were great enough to arouse anger about how the nation was being run. Add to that the discontent caused by Watergate and it was easy to understand why, in all the talks about impeachment, I heard few voices raised in support of the President.

The second session of the 93rd Congress convened on January 21, 1974.

Conversations with colleagues fresh from travels around the nation revealed that they had found reactions similar to those I had discovered in Iowa. The impeachment inquiry would be supported, or at least tolerated, not so much as a vehicle to remove Nixon but as a process that might finally put an end to Watergate.

Disagreement over whether the President deserved impeachment or an apology was widespread, but there was a broad consensus that the decision should be made quickly, so Congress could turn its full attention to the people's more tangible concerns, particularly the energy shortage.

The longer the inquiry took, I was repeatedly reminded, the more susceptible the Watergate-weary would become to charges that impeachment was some sort of sinister political plot.

Vice President Ford had brought four thousand Farm Bureau members to a standing ovation the week before by lashing out at "a few extreme partisans" who he said were "bent on stretching out the ordeal of Watergate for their own purposes."

The way the Vice President saw it, there was a "relatively small group of political activists" who were scheming to "cripple the President by dragging out the preliminaries to impeachment for as long as they can and to use the whole affair for maximum political advantage . . . their aim is total victory for themselves and total defeat not only of President Nixon but of the policies for which he stands."

On January 22, Vice President Ford tried once again to help by announcing that the President had personally assured him that he was innocent and had evidence to prove it. But any advantage stemming from Ford's exuberant confidence in his boss was nullified when the Vice President, asked what the exonerating evidence was, explained that he hadn't had the time to look at it.

It was a ridiculous situation. If the President possessed such evidence, why wasn't he breaking his back to get it into print? If, as Ford said, Nixon offered to show him the evidence, how could it be that he wouldn't *make* the time to see it?

Maybe I was being overly skeptical. Maybe, after all these months of "stone-walling," the President did have evidence that could prove that he was being unjustly accused. If he had such material, there was no better time to present it than during his

State of the Union address to Congress. He'd be face to face with the men and women who were weighing his impeachment and his speech would be covered live by radio and television.

What a coup it would be if, after listing the actions he wanted Congress to take in the coming year, he could present evidence that could restore his credibility, shore up his popularity, and at the same time resolve the impeachment question that threatened to take up so much of the time and attention of Congress.

The State of the Union address was scheduled for January 30, and when the doorkeeper announced "the President of the United States" right on time at nine P.M., we rose from our seats in the packed House chamber and gave Mr. Nixon the first of three standing ovations. (We were, however, honoring House tradition, and not necessarily Mr. Nixon.)

The President's speech included a promise that there would not be an economic recession in 1974 and an indication that the Arab oil embargo might soon be lifted. As expected, he stressed the achievements of his Administration, most proudly the end of American involvement in Vietnam.

As he spoke of the accomplishments of the past and the challenges he intended to meet in the future, Mr. Nixon appeared to me to be eager for applause, looking for support in the chamber that might be transmitted to the nation by way of the television camera.

At one point, after saying he hoped his presidency would be remembered for establishing a structure for world peace, I watched Nixon stare at the Republican side of the chamber. I got the impression that his glance was demanding that they rise to their feet with cheers and applause that the folks at home could see. They did, and I realized that the speech I was hearing was part of his strategy to "fight like hell."

The message he was sending was that Richard Nixon had been and would continue to be a great President and therefore talk of removing him, for whatever reason, ranged from silly to treasonous.

For the moment it seemed that the President was not going to mention either Watergate or impeachment at all. He put away his notes, and the congressional delegation assigned to escort

84

Nixon from the House chamber rose and started toward the podium.

But then he began a postscript: "A personal word with regard . . . to the investigations of the so-called Watergate affair."

Suddenly everyone perked up. But what the President had to say was not earth-shattering: He wanted all investigations brought to an end.

"One year of Watergate is enough," he said, after telling Congress and the nation that, as far as he was concerned, he had already given the Special Prosecutor "all the material that he needs to conclude his investigation and proceed to prosecute the guilty and to clear the innocent."

Exasperation at the President's skewed perspective found expression in murmurs from a few of the Democrats sitting near me.

Although never using the word "impeachment," the President acknowledged that the Judiciary Committee had a "special responsibility in this area" and pledged to cooperate with its investigation. But Richard Nixon made it clear that the extent of his cooperation would be dependent on what "I consider consistent with my responsibilities to the office of the President of the United States."

Nixon's declaration unmistakably meant that his cooperation with the impeachment inquiry would be on *his* terms. It was a sign of respect for the office of the President that the pronouncement was not met with heckling, although there were a few hisses.

He concluded the 1974 State of the Union message by reaffirming that he "had no intention whatever of walking away from the job that the people elected me to do for the people of the United States."

That brought cheers, especially from the Republican side. We all stood up as the President left the chamber.

SIX: *Fits and Starts*

Spring is a marvelous time in Washington. Unfortunately, it doesn't stick around long, and it can never seem to make up its mind. From early March until the middle of May, there may be a week of such seasonal perfection that one could not imagine living anywhere else. But there is no way of telling just when that week will occur. One day it is winter again, with plunging temperatures and near-freezing rain, and then a day or so later the mercury rises and the humidity claims that it is early August. The weather, like the fortunes of the Nixon Administration, was unpredictable as we moved into the spring of 1974.

On March 1, as people were growing weary of the Watergate affair, a District of Columbia grand jury broke the doldrums with a fifty-page indictment. It charged that seven men, including H. R. Haldeman and John Ehrlichman ("two of the finest public servants I have ever known," according to Richard Nixon) and former Attorney General John Mitchell, had conspired to impede the investigation of the Watergate burglary. The grand jury listed forty-five overt acts as part of an elaborate plan to block the investigation. In stark black and white the indictment unraveled the cover-up.

Along with everyone else on Capitol Hill, I read the indictment avidly. It charged that the conspirators worked to obstruct justice by lying to the FBI, the grand jury itself, and the Senate Watergate Committee, and by paying hush money to keep others quiet. The seven were also accused of trying "by deceit, craft, trickery, and dishonest means" to induce the CIA to provide financial assistance for the original Watergate defendants. This conspiracy, the grand jury charged, began on June 17, 1972, the day the burglars were arrested at Watergate, and continued "up to and including the present time."

That was all included in the first of thirteen counts that made up the indictment. It was count eight, however, that intrigued me most. It involved a White House meeting that John Dean had discussed during his testimony before the Watergate Committee. At this meeting, Dean claimed, the President assured him there would be no problem raising a million dollars to help the Watergate burglars. Haldeman had followed Dean to the witness table, confirmed that the money discussion had taken place but added, under oath, that the President rejected the idea, saying "We can do that, but it would be wrong." Mr. Nixon had corroborated Haldeman's version but the grand jury, which had heard a tape of the session, charged in count eight that Haldeman was lying when he claimed the President had added the exculpatory words "but it would be wrong."

The day the indictment came down, I listened intently as Bernie Nussbaum, a top-flight trial lawyer who had been named to the inquiry staff by John Doar, said, "One thing it clearly shows is that Jaworski's people have material over there that we haven't got. And, it's material relevant to the involvement of the President!"

It would turn out to be a weekend full of surprises. The next day I had a lunch date with Larry Scalise, an old friend and former attorney general of Iowa. Our friendship dates back to 1960. We had shared a hotel room in Los Angeles when we weren't at the convention hall cheering John Kennedy on to the nomination. Those electric days in California had been my introduction to national politics, a glorious indoctrination for a twenty-three-year-old.

Larry was now in private practice in Des Moines and in Washington working on a case. I met him at a downtown restaurant, and he introduced me to the Washington lawyer with whom he was working. When I learned who that lawyer was I realized Larry and I wouldn't be talking about old times.

Scalise's colleague was Bob McCandless, John Dean's former brother-in-law.

After we ordered, I confessed to Larry that the reason I hadn't been very talkative when he'd called to set up the lunch was that I was becoming almost paranoid about talking on the phone.

The day before, Bert Podell, a Brooklyn Democrat who'd been in the House for four terms, took the floor and made a startling revelation. At least I was startled. Podell, who had been indicted in July 1973 for conspiracy, bribery, perjury, and conflict of interest, told the suddenly quiet chamber he now had proof that, as he had claimed upon indictment, the government had tapped his phones and broken into his home, his law office, and his office in Congress. His proof was in the form of a court order forbidding him to talk about the very details he was relating with obvious emotion.

Podell was taking advantage of the immunity from prosecution available to any member when he or she speaks on the floor of the House.

I was stunned by Podell's tale, but what surprised me almost as much was the casual acceptance by various members, such as Bill Hungate, that *of course* these things went on in this administration, this "law and order" administration. Many of us, they said, were probably "under surveillance" of one sort or another, and as I was on the Judiciary Committee, I shouldn't assume that I was not also being listened to and illegally recorded. As I told the story to Larry and his colleague, I saw that my hands were shaking a little.

"You know, it's really pretty eerie when you start feeling you can't talk on the phone," I found myself whispering across the booth. I felt a little silly, but McCandless told me that there was reason for concern.

"I want you to know it's very, very clear that down in the basement of the Executive Office Building are files on every member of Congress," McCandless said.

88

"Really?" Larry and I asked incredulously and in unison.

"No question about it." McCandless was in a position to know about such things, I assumed. After all, his former brother-in-law had been the architect of the infamous "enemies list." Before he decided to repudiate his activities in the Nixon Administration and turn government witness, Dean had served at the very heart of the Watergate cover-up.

At least twenty of the overt acts cited in the March 1 indictment appeared to be actions that could be substantiated primarily, if not solely, by John Dean. Apparently the grand jury believed his version of what had gone on and McCandless indicated that Dean was the source of his information.

McCandless said that it was one of the files from the EOB basement that had been pulled in the attempt to intimidate Senator Lowell Weicker during the Ervin Committee hearings. According to McCandless, it was only Weicker's public blast at the smear attempt that stopped efforts to discredit him.

"I want to alert you to something else," he said seriously. "They have been trying to get the press working on the 'Rodino-Mafia' connection . . . you know, 'If you're going to go after the President, why not go after Rodino?'"

"What are you talking about? There's nothing there," I said with a mixture of challenge and dismay.

Speculation that there was some skeleton in Rodino's background that could be used to induce him to go easy on impeachment had popped up time and again ever since the committee was assigned to the impeachment investigation. The most persistent rumors had Rodino tied to organized crime.

I didn't buy it, but it was easy to see where it got started. Rodino was Italian and he was from Newark. To a great many people, being Italian is viewed as being synonymous with Mafioso and the underworld. It wasn't surprising that someone would try to fit Rodino with the off-the-rack wardrobe.

In addition to his heritage and hometown, Rodino's friendship with Hugh Addonizio sometimes added to the smokescreen that was supposed to discredit the chairman.

Addonizio, also from Newark, and Rodino were both first elected to Congress in 1948 and had shared an apartment in

Washington. In the early sixties Addonizio gave up his House seat to become mayor of Newark; later he was charged, convicted, and sent to jail for corruption.

Despite firm denials (the U.S. attorney who prosecuted Addonizio has been widely quoted as saying, "There's never been an inquiry about Rodino, never the slightest anything. In my opinion, Pete Rodino is an honest man and a fine public servant"), the guilt-by-association mudslingers still surfaced occasionally.

"Bob, I've got a lot of faith in Pete. I talked with him about this when it came up during the Ford nomination," I said. "He's got nothing to worry about. And, anyway, if the White House had something on him like you say, why haven't they used it by now?"

McCandless seemed to have an answer for everything.

"The timing's not right," he replied. He offered this possible scenario: At some crucial point in the inquiry "out of the blue, you'll see some document pulled out of these files to discredit Rodino." He said it might come on some day when the committee released information damaging to the President "and that way, the front pages would be the arena for a balancing act—so much on the President and so much on the discrediting of the chairman of the committee."

I leaned back in the booth with an uneasy feeling. I was convinced that there was nothing seamy in Rodino's background, but that didn't eliminate the possibility that some fancy, official-looking document might turn up purportedly showing that there was. We'd learned during the summer that one of the Plumbers' activities was to fabricate documents, such as the bogus State Department cables implicating President Kennedy in the 1963 assassination of South Vietnam President Ngo Dinh Diem.

Maybe I was becoming too paranoid, but the talk of wiretapping, maintaining files on members of Congress, and attempting to influence some members of the committee and discredit others convinced me that the enemies list was all too real. It was sobering to realize that the people in the White House could be ruthless, and that they might consider me a threat to their survival.

Scalise and I never did get around to reminiscing about our sideline roles during the first act of Camelot.

By mid-March the impeachment inquiry staff had settled in. It was obvious to anyone who visited their offices on the second floor of the old Congressional Hotel across the street from the House Office Buildings that the offices had been chosen purely for their convenience, not for their class.

The first thing even the casual visitor had to notice was the tight security. No one got in who didn't have business with the staff, and then identification and a signature were necessary. Too many documents of a confidential nature were floating around those second-floor offices. With the Congress's reputation for leaks, the committee and the inquiry staff were going to have to be very, very careful.

Rooms that had once held beds, dressers, and night tables now contained typewriters, desks, and heavy copying machinery. In fact, the flooring had to be strengthened for fear that the heavy machinery would one day crash through to the premises of the Democratic Club, a popular watering hole on the floor below.

The staff numbered more than one hundred, forty-three of whom were attorneys, and whenever I visited, I was struck by their dedication and energy. Bernie Nussbaum was in charge of factual research. (His title was Senior Associate Special Counsel to the committee.) His counterpart was Joseph Woods, also a fine lawyer of solid reputation, who was in charge of constitutional and legal research. Both he and Bernie were considered "senior partners" in the impeachment law firm.

Working under Bernie and Joe were various task forces, each one studying well-defined areas. They were busy compiling, organizing, and analyzing a mountain of information relating to the scores of allegations under investigation.

Nussbaum told me, on one of my first trips to the offices, that he was already putting in fourteen- and fifteen-hour days, Monday through Friday. He also worked on Saturdays, but tried to knock off early so he could catch a shuttle flight to New York and spend Sundays with his family. And the staff worked equally hard.

91

The opportunity to take part in history is intoxicating, and apparently it more than made up for the spartan working conditions, long hours, and relatively low pay. (Top salary for staff attorneys was $36,000 per year, far less than many of these lawyers were used to making in private practice.)

When I met Smith McKeithen, a young lawyer three years out of Columbia, I filed his name away in my memory because he was working on the question of the President's taxes. The whole matter of taxes, and whether or not it might fit into the definition of impeachable offenses, had been much on my mind lately. To me, it had taken on the shape of a special interest.

Of course, all of the lawyers and staff members worked for the two "heads" of the firm, John Doar—the special counsel hired by Rodino—and Albert Jenner, the older, and extremely experienced trial lawyer from Chicago, whom the Republicans had added. They answered directly to Rodino and the committee.

The many staff attorneys and their aides and investigators, and the dedicated people who provided the clerical help were the part of the iceberg that few people saw. The members of the House Judiciary Committee were the tip. And that analogy was apt, in the minds of some people, for we seemed to be moving with all the speed of an iceberg.

However, as Chairman Rodino had said all along, we had to proceed with deliberate speed, but it could not be speed for speed's sake. Our task was too important, too sensitive, and too historic. It would not do for us to appear to be rushing Richard Nixon to judgment.

And then there was the matter of politics.

If the constitutional machinery to oust a President had been set in motion the day following the Watergate burglary, the House Judiciary Committee conducting the impeachment inquiry would have been a far different group. With the intervening election, the 92nd Congress had given way to the 93rd and nowhere in the House was the change more visible than in 2141 Rayburn, the committee's main hearing room.

The key catalyst for that change—no, the cause for that change—was the quiet, dark-haired Democrat from the Empire State, Elizabeth Holtzman. By her stunning primary victory over veteran Emanuel Celler of Brooklyn, and her subsequent election, she guaranteed changes within the committee that involved far more than personnel.

When I'd worked for Representative Neal Smith, back in 1965 to 1967, Manny Celler was one of the most powerful members of the House. He'd been chairman of the Judiciary Committee since 1959 and he'd run the committee like a benevolent despot. Along with William McCulloch of Michigan, the ranking Republican, Celler clearly extended the Judiciary's reputation as one of the most important and admired committees in the House. Committee members were fiercely proud of their assignment to it and bipartisanship was the order of the day. So closely did Celler and McCulloch work (and think) that some Republicans felt they were being led by two Democrats.

The Judiciary Committee I joined at the opening of the 93rd Congress bore little resemblance to its immediate predecessor. Not only was Celler gone, McCulloch had retired. Because the Democrats still controlled the House, the chairmanship passed automatically to Peter W. Rodino, a veteran of almost twenty-five years in the House. Quiet, by no means one to seek the limelight, Rodino was—despite his length of service—a relatively unknown quantity.

And, if the new chairman was something of an enigma, so was Edward Hutchinson, the ranking Republican and a fifth-termer from Michigan. Rodino was quiet; Hutchinson was silent.

Beyond the fact that the helm was in new hands, several other factors combined to strain the ability of even full-time Congress watchers to define this band of men and women who would determine the President's fate. Eleven of us—nearly a third of the committee—were serving our first terms. There was a striking cross-section of political attitudes, yet the committee did not reflect the politics of the full House. Voting records testified that, in general, the Democrats were more liberal than our counterparts and the Republicans more conservative than their brethren. At the same time, the pendulum swings within each party were well represented, the likes of moderate-to-liberal Republican Tom Railsback of Illinois and the conservative Southern Democrats Walter Flowers, James Mann, and Ray Thornton.

While the Republicans served up an all-white male cast, the Democrats included three blacks and two women. We represented twenty-one different states. We had five members over sixty years old, yet our average age was much younger than that of the full House.

Despite our brief introduction to the nation during the Ford confirmation hearings in the fall of 1973, the Judiciary Committee was still too new on the scene to have its direction accurately forecast. There was a 21–17 split along party lines, and we Democrats had the edge. But impeachment could never be as simple as that.

My distinguished colleagues:

The Democrats

Peter W. Rodino, Jr., the chairman, sixty-five, Congressman for Newark, New Jersey. Like me, the son of an immigrant. A kind and decent man whose raspy voice could command attention even when he spoke softly. Unlike Celler, "Pete" permitted other members to share authority, and he consulted with, and listened to, his underlings, even freshmen.

Harold D. Donohue, seventy-three, the ranking (most senior) Democratic member under Rodino. A quiet older man representing the area of Massachusetts near Worcester. Jokes about his falling asleep were often belied by his flashes of fighting spirit and pointed, critical questioning.

Jack Brooks, a fifty-one-year-old tough, cigar-smokin', blunt speakin' Texan. An outspoken and unashamedly partisan Democrat, Brooks could combine the twinkle in his eyes, a slow drawl, and devastating wit to make his feelings perfectly clear.

Robert W. Kastenmeier, fifty, representing Madison, Wisconsin, and the University of Wisconsin. Often referred to as the most erudite member of the House, Kastenmeier was chairman of a Judiciary subcommittee on which I also served.

Don Edwards, fifty-nine, a former FBI agent representing a California district primarily made up of blue-collar suburbs. A solid liberal and an intense civil libertarian, Edwards was softspoken and widely respected for his efforts to end the Vietnam War.

William Hungate, the white-haired, fifty-one-year-old representative who had Mark Twain's story-telling abilities and came
from Twain's hometown of Hannibal, Missouri. Hardworking,
perceptive, effective, friendly, and the guy to look to for needed
levity at the right time and in the right spirit.

John Conyers Jr., forty-five, from Detroit, Michigan. Often
called the "black firebrand" on the committee, John had pressed
Rodino to begin impeachment proceedings before the Saturday
Night Massacre. Articulate and politically astute, Conyers controlled his frustration at the slow pace of the inquiry to the surprise of those who expected constant raging from this man who
ranked high on the White House enemies list.

Joshua Eilberg of Philadelphia. Josh, fifty-three, was usually
quiet but he shared my intense interest in the questions raised by
the President's finances.

Jerome Waldie, forty-nine, from California, was not quiet.
An outspoken critic of Nixon, he was an early leader of the impeachment forces. He had decided to leave the House at the end
of the 93rd Congress and was a candidate for governor in California.

Walter Flowers, forty-one, from Alabama. A very able, conservative Southerner whose vote on impeachment would be especially crucial.

James Mann, fifty-four, of South Carolina, considered the
most conservative Democrat on the committee. His district had
given nearly 80 percent of its votes to Richard Nixon in the 1972
election. Jim was quiet during the early meetings and Democratic caucuses, yet when he spoke he was eloquent, demonstrating a
firm grasp of the evidence. Like Flowers, he was one of the
members whose vote would be critical.

Paul Sarbanes, forty-one, representing Baltimore, Maryland.
Also a first-generation American, Paul was a Rhodes scholar, a
solid liberal, and an intense listener. Sarbanes devoured the evidence, thoughtfully analyzed it, and, when he spoke, was listened to intently.

John F. Seiberling, fifty-five, from Ohio. A sharp antitrust
lawyer, devoted civil libertarian, and solid liberal.

George E. Danielson, fifty-nine, of California. A very decent
man who prided himself on his knowledge of the Constitution

and prosecutorial aspects of the inquiry. Like Edwards, George was a former FBI agent.

Robert F. Drinan, fifty-three, a Jesuit priest representing Boston suburbs. The good father, whose asceticism, suggested by his priestly garb, was enhanced by his near baldness, had a fiery temper and indefatigable energy. Father Drinan had introduced the first impeachment resolution against Nixon in July 1973.

Charles B. Rangel, forty-four, who took over the Harlem district once represented by Adam Clayton Powell. Highly respected, Rangel was the leader of the Black Caucus. He had a wonderful sense of humor, was never abrasive, and had a special talent for getting to the guts of a matter by asking penetrating questions.

Barbara Jordan, thirty-eight, from Houston, Texas, had a mind that was as sharp as her speech was articulate. Among the most politically savvy members of the House, Barbara would seldom speak unless she had something of significance to say and expected others to respect the value of her time in a like manner.

Ray Thornton, forty-six, represented a rural Arkansas district. Quiet and cautious, Ray was a former attorney general of his state. When he did speak up, he was one of the most eloquent and his Southern constituency added weight to his words.

Elizabeth Holtzman, thirty-two, representing Brooklyn. Tough, aggressive, and persistent, Liz was a thorough researcher and brought her serious demeanor to bear on the evidence that came before us. She was effective and especially good at raising sensitive questions.

Wayne Owens, thirty-seven, of Utah. One of the five freshman Democrats on the committee, Wayne was making his first term in the House his last. He was running for the Senate.

The Republicans

Edward Hutchinson, fifty-nine, from a mainly rural district in Michigan. Decent, conservative, and quiet. Despite his position as ranking Republican member, he was not a spokesman for the Republican members.

Robert McClory, sixty-six, of Illinois, was more vocal than

Sen. Harold Hughes (D-Iowa) and me during the '72 campaign

The posed photograph of my being sworn in by Speaker Carl Albert (D-Okla.) and Majority Leader Thomas P. O'Neill (D-Mass.)

MR. RODINO
CHAIRMAN

Chairman Peter W. Rodino, Jr. (D-N.J.) and Edward Hutchinson (R-Mich.)

Charles B. Rangel (D-N.Y.), Ray Thornton (D-Ark.), me, Paul S. Sarbanes (D-Md.), Harold D. Donohue (D-Mass.), Walter Flowers (D-Ala.), and Rodino

William L. Hungate (D-Mo.), me, and Jack Brooks (D-Tex.)

Robert W. Kastenmeier (D-Wisc.) | Don Edwards (D-Cal.)

Mr. EDWARDS

Robert F. Drinan (D-Mass.) and John Conyers, Jr. (D-Mich.)

Connie Chung interviewing Joshua Eilberg (D-Pa.)

Walter Flowers (D-Ala.) and Jerome R. Waldie (D-Cal.)

Conferring with James R. Mann (D-S.C.)

George E. Danielson (D-Cal.), Rangel, and Hungate

John F. Seiberling (D-Ohio)   Barbara Jordon (D-Te

Robert McClory (R-Ill.), Elizabeth Holtzman (D-N.Y.), Henry P. Smith III (R-N.Y.), Wayne Owens (D-Utah), and Charles W. Sandman, Jr. (R-N.J.)

Tom Railsback (R-Ill.) and Charles E. Wiggins (R-Cal.)

David W. Dennis (R-Ind.) and Hamilton Fish, Jr. (R-N.Y.)

William S. Cohen (R-Me.)

Wiley Mayne (R-Iowa)

Lawrence J. Hogan (R-Md.) and M. Caldwell Butler (R-Va.)

Trent Lott (R-Miss.)   Harold V. Froehlich (R-Wisc.)

Delbert L. Latta (R-Ohio) and Jerome M. Zeifman

Carlos J. Moorhead (R-Cal.)

Joseph H. Maraziti (R-N.J.

Meeting with Charles Colson

James St. Clair and John Doar talking with Hutchinson, Rodino, and Donohue

Samuel Garrison III, John Doar, and Albert E. Jenner, Jr.

Hutch and often seemed to take on the role of ranking minority member.

Henry P. Smith III, sixty-two, from upstate New York, was retiring from the House at the end of the year. Silver-haired and endowed with a beautiful voice, Smith was a courteous gentleman and orthodox Republican who said little during our committee meetings.

Charles Sandman Jr., fifty-two, of New Jersey. A stocky man who often seemed to view questions about Richard Nixon's conduct as personal attacks, Sandman responded emotionally and sarcastically. Occasionally during our meetings, Sandman would make good points, but their effectiveness was often diluted by his rough manner.

Tom Railsback, forty-two, my neighbor from Illinois. A moderate Republican, he was thoughtful and open-minded on the subject of impeachment. Tom was a highly respected leader among Republicans.

Charles Wiggins, forty-six, represented a California district that included much of the area Richard Nixon once represented in the House. Very conservative, one of the most able lawyers on the committee, and a defender of Nixon from the beginning, Wiggins was never strident and therefore was persuasive.

David Dennis, sixty-two, of Indiana. This short, bespectacled man could get me more riled up than any other member of the committee. Exercising his keen legal mind, feisty Dave Dennis sometimes appeared cocky and condescending, tediously raising point after point of minutiae.

Hamilton Fish Jr., forty-eight, of New York. A friendly, progressive Republican, his soft-spoken, well-reasoned comments during our meetings impressed me and gained him the respect of most members.

Wiley Mayne, fifty-seven, my fellow Iowan on the committee. Another former FBI agent, Wiley was conservative and very partisan. He had a talent for irritating others, but also for putting animosities behind him after the heat of battle.

Lawrence J. Hogan, forty-five, represented some of Washington, D.C.'s Maryland suburbs. An interesting guy, Hogan also had been an FBI agent and in our early sessions seemed to present himself as a strong Nixon partisan.

97

M. Caldwell Butler, forty-nine, of Virginia. A Southern gentleman serving his first term in the House, Butler's quick mind and sense of humor made him an articulate spokesman and a likable colleague.

William S. Cohen, thirty-three, of Maine. A former mayor of his hometown of Bangor, Cohen was tapped early in his first term as one of the rising young stars of his party. Articulate and determined to press the inquiry forward, Cohen proved to be one of the best questioners on the committee.

Trent Lott, thirty-two, represented a district of Mississippi that gave more than 86 percent of its vote to Richard Nixon in 1972. Extremely conservative, Lott seldom spoke up during our meetings.

Harold V. Froehlich, forty-two, from rural Wisconsin. Also quiet, but with a fiery temper that occasionally erupted, revealing a mind as conservative as it was sharp.

Carlos J. Moorhead, fifty-two, from Los Angeles. Very conservative and although he was usually silent, I concluded early that he had an almost closed mind on the subject of impeachment.

Joseph J. Maraziti, sixty-two, from New Jersey. A man who seemed to bask in the media attention brought to him by impeachment. His image would have been better served had he shared Moorhead's penchant for silence.

Delbert L. Latta, fifty-four, of Ohio, was placed on the committee solely for the impeachment inquiry, to fill a vacancy left by a retiring member. This fact, reinforced by his early outspoken support of Nixon and criticism of the committee, earned Latta the image as "Nixon's hit man."

Back in November, Peter Rodino had told the House that if the impeachment inquiry failed to be a bipartisan venture "it would be disastrous for the country."

He was going to great lengths to avoid such a calamity.

You could see it in his approach to the subpoena power, an authority routinely vested solely in the chairman of a committee. But, when we voted in the fall to grant Rodino that power, the move was met with harsh Republican complaints. Wiley Mayne charged that it was a "naked display of partisan power" that "leaves little reason for hoping for fairness in the future conduct of the inquiry."

The cries of partisanship made the committee look bad to the public. So, in January, when preparing to ask the House for special subpoena power for the impeachment inquiry, Rodino agreed to share the authority to subpoena with the ranking Republican member, Ed Hutchinson. There was still some grumbling (several Republicans complained that disputes between Rodino and Hutch would be resolved by the full committee where Democrats outnumbered Republicans) but the issue was effectively defused.

The impeachment inquiry staff itself was another testament to Rodino's intention to conduct the investigation in a manner that would rebuff, rather than invite, charges of a partisan witch hunt.

John Doar, the man Rodino's two-month search for a special counsel led him to, was a Republican. Doar had joined the Justice Department in the Eisenhower Administration and had become Assistant Attorney General for Civil Rights before leaving Washington in 1967 for New York City. He was serving as director of a community action redevelopment program in central Brooklyn when Rodino tapped him to lead the impeachment investigation.

When Rodino announced Doar's appointment in December, he emphasized that Doar was chief counsel for the full committee, not just the majority side.

But the Republicans wanted a chief counsel of their own and, in January, Hutchinson announced that the minority had selected Albert Jenner, a respected Chicago trial lawyer. I heard no grumbling from Rodino that the Republicans were trying to infect the staff with partisans, and I doubt if there were any private complaints since Jenner was one of the men whom Rodino had considered for the job that ultimately went to Doar.

The minority chose nearly a third of the attorneys hired for the staff, and Doar and Rodino applied a strict screening process to applicants for staff positions.

In early February, when the committee was presented with the résumés of our impeachment staff, Doar explained that one of the first questions asked every applicant was whether he or

99

she had taken a position on impeachment. If the answer was yes, that person was not considered further.

Rodino elaborated by relating that Doar once called him in regard to an applicant he (Doar) considered highly qualified. However, Rodino explained, "There was some question as to whether or not this individual had either signed a petition or had sent a letter or a . . . telegram advocating a position with relation to impeachment. When Mr. Doar learned that this was the case, he was advised that he was not to hire him and no other individual was to be hired who had taken such a position."

Another potential staffer, a lawyer recommended by Jack Brooks of Texas, was rejected. The recommendation of the third-ranking Democrat could not overcome the fact that the lawyer had at one time served as a consultant for the Democratic National Committee.

"I didn't think that would hurt his objectivity," Brooks announced, "but Doar did not even consider him and did not hire him, and this is the last we heard of that man."

The care being devoted to gathering a staff of investigators—not prosecutors or defenders of Richard Nixon—was a source of pride for me. And I was infuriated by signs that our efforts were being undermined.

On March 4, I learned (by reading a newspaper column by Rowland Evans and Robert Novak) that a special report on impeachable offenses had been prepared for Republican members of the committee. This was a sensitive area. In mid-February the inquiry staff had presented the committee with a memo on constitutional grounds for presidential impeachment.

The staff report was designed to illuminate the historical background and meaning of the amorphous phrase "high crimes and misdemeanors," and did not offer any fixed standard. "The framers did not write a fixed standard," the memo declared. "Instead they adopted . . . a standard sufficiently general and flexible to meet future circumstances and events, the nature and character of which they could not foresee."

While not setting out a specific definition of what constitutes an impeachable offense, the staff report did reject the notion, put forward by President Nixon and his lawyers, that an impeachable offense had to be a crime. The staff reported that fewer than one-third of the articles of impeachment adopted by the House in earlier impeachment proceedings had explicitly charged the violation of a criminal statute.

It was known, however, that some Republicans embraced the President's limiting definition. So, to avoid a political hassle early in the inquiry, Rodino had decided not to hold a formal meeting to discuss the memo or to move for committee adoption of the report. Instead, it was presented as a staff report simply for our consideration.

Now I read that the *full* staff report had been followed by a specialized report for the minority, one advocating a circum-scribed view of impeachable offenses. The second memo had been prepared by Sam Garrison III, a thirty-two-year-old lawyer (fresh from the vice presidential staff of Spiro Agnew) who served as Jenner's deputy minority counsel.

According to Evans and Novak, Garrison's memo was part of an effort to undercut Jenner, disputing the view he and Doar endorsed. Accompanying the Garrison memo, which was sent only to Republicans, the columnists wrote, was a magazine article about Jenner's "zeal to prosecute." Since he took the job in Janu-ary, Jenner had been an occasional target for harsh criticism be-cause he appeared to be more interested in developing the evi-dence (his job) than in defending the President.

During a briefing on March 5, I raised the issue of the minor-ity report and, as I knew I would, struck a nerve—the nerve of partisanship. No sooner had I asked Garrison if the column was accurate, than Hutchinson jumped to his defense.

Yes, there was a supplemental report and the minority had ev-ery right to ask for it, he said, and might very well do it again.

What about the magazine article? I asked. Hutch didn't know, so I asked Garrison. Before he could answer, McClory, the se-cond-ranking Republican, interjected that he'd seen a lot of newspaper and magazine pieces.

David Dennis declared that there was "obviously and absolute-ly" nothing secretive about the minority brief. (Even though Ro-dino said he was "completely unaware" that a request for such a report had been made.) Dennis added that he didn't think news-paper articles were very important.

Again, I tried to ask Garrison to explain what was going on.

Again, before he could answer, someone else came to his defense. Wiley Mayne testily suggested that I shouldn't waste the time of the committee discussing newspaper columns.

Frustrated, I again asked Garrison to respond to my question.

Walter Flowers, who sat right above and behind me, asked that I yield the floor to him.

"I'm trying to get an answer," I pleaded.

"I just want to join with you," Flowers said. "When I came in here I did not even know what you were talking about, but my curiosity has arisen now and I have got to know."

Finally, Garrison spoke. Yes, he had prepared the memo, at the request of the minority, and yes, he had included the magazine article on Jenner. In the same packet, the young counsel offered, ingenuously, he had also included a memo asking if any Republican member had a spare parking space to lend to the impeachment staff.

Rodino then entered the discussion. He said that he expected any request made of the committee staff to be made "for the purpose of furnishing the committee as such, and not the minority members or the majority members with views that are advocate views.

"I stated initially, and I am going to adhere to this," the chairman said sternly, "I have the power to hire and to fire. I stated that not one of the staff was ever to advocate a position one way or the other."

He noted that the staff report—the first one that was endorsed by both Doar and Jenner—was not the product of a request that the staff advocate either a broad or restricted view.

Rodino continued, "I think to suggest that the staff proceed with the writing of a strict position is something that I think frankly does not do credit to the committee."

Hutchinson again defended the propriety of the minority brief but the defensiveness displayed in response to my question indicated just how touchy an area I'd hit. I hoped that exposing the matter, and the stiff warning from Rodino, would serve to check what appeared to me as a drift toward converting some members of the staff from investigators to advocates.

After the briefing, when I was on the floor during debate on an energy bill, Jack Brooks commended me for "stirring things up" and lamented the obvious implications of the Garrison memo.

"Here, we've got Doar watering down the staff memo and doing everything to be fair," Brooks said, with patronizing emphasis on the word *fair*, "and what do we get for our trouble? For working to get a consensus? The Republicans come in and stab Doar in the back with the minority memo."

Problems with the staff soon faded into the background when we ran head-on into the White House itself.

Ever since the indictments came down, we had been hearing rumors that the grand jury had actually wanted to indict the President, or at least to name him as an "unindicted co-conspirator." The grand jury reportedly was forestalled from indicting Nixon by Jaworski's opinion that a sitting President could not be indicted. But they apparently had suggested that the evidence that led them to that conclusion and their report on it be turned over to our committee.

The White House was silent on the matter, but John J. Wilson, the lawyer for Haldeman and Ehrlichman, objected strenuously in court the day Judge Sirica heard arguments regarding whether he should grant the grand jury's request. Wilson contended that allowing the Judiciary Committee to have the report and supporting evidence would lead to leaks that would create pretrial publicity harmful to his clients. (I, and several other members, figured Wilson was shilling for the White House). At the hearing March 6, Sirica suggested that perhaps the impeachment inquiry should be put off until after the Watergate trials. The next day Bert Jenner, who had been present for the court arguments, told the committee the proper response should be to make a formal demand to Sirica that the material be turned over. A motion to do so passed unanimously.

But that was a small problem compared to what we had run into when Doar tried, through the President's new lawyer, James St. Clair, to get some material from the President. In late February, Doar had written St. Clair to request certain information considered pertinent to the inquiry. Rodino and Hutchinson had approved the request but, because of our strict rules of confidentiality, the rest of us on the committee had not seen the letter.

During our March 7th meeting, Doar read us a "sanitized" version of the request, which described in general terms what we were asking for. He then read us St. Clair's response and, even with the sketchy background, it was easy to see that the President's counsel's response was not exactly "responsive." It appeared, in fact, that it could better be described as evasionary.

St. Clair's letter announced that the President would make available to the committee all materials that had previously been given to the Special Prosecutor but made no reference at all to a key part of our request, for the tapes covering six specific days and events.

Furthermore, St. Clair said Nixon believed the "Watergate matter and widespread allegations of obstruction of justice . . . are at the heart of this matter" and therefore the material he was agreeing to turn over "should resolve any questions concerning him" and convince the committee there were no grounds for impeachment.

Jerry Waldie asked Doar if he considered St. Clair's response a refusal to turn over the tapes requested in the earlier letter.

"Well," Doar responded calmly, "he does not specifically deny that, but he does not give us that material." Doar offered this impression of St. Clair's letter:

"He seems to say to me: 'Mr. Doar, your case against the President is simply, purely, and only the Watergate cover-up.' And he seems to say second: 'Mr. Doar, the evidence that you need in your case is just the material that I gave to Mr. Jaworski.' And then he seems to say, third: 'that after you examine that evidence, and after you have considered just the Watergate cover-up, I am confident that you will find that the President was not involved.'"

What chutzpah! I realized I had ground the tip of my felt pen into the pad I was using for notes, smearing it all up. St. Clair was telling us how to run our inquiry.

I was not the only member who was bothered. Nor was the bother confined to the Democrats.

Drinan offered a motion to subpoena the material, but Doar

(and others) cautioned against it as being "too much, too soon." Tempers were high, especially after John Conyers repeated the President's televised remark of the night before, which characterized the committee's request as tantamount to asking that he "cart everything in the White House down to the committee and have them crawl through it on a fishing expedition." That, according to Conyers, was "arrogance." I agreed. Then Drinan, realizing that he probably didn't have the votes to pass a subpoena motion so soon, withdrew his motion.

Just before we adjourned, Charley Rangel asked a question that had to be on the minds of several people. He looked to the future when the committee might subpoena the President, and Nixon might defy the subpoena. Rangel said to Doar, "Do you have any problems in determining contempt of Congress as an impeachable offense?"

"No. I have no problem with that. None whatsoever."

The President was not to be our only antagonist, as it turned out. I was getting a lot of mail urging me, and the committee, to get it over with—either impeach or get off his back. But very few people seemed to think it was time for us to resort to our subpoena power. One afternoon I ran into Charles Whalen, an Ohio Republican I'd come to know and like. "Look, you can go slow," he said, "just do it right. You don't have to rush into a subpoena. Just go slow, so you can use the screws."

On March 12, I was sitting at my desk reading a newspaper when Doris Freedman, my legislative assistant, said, "Ed, I don't want to give you any grief about being late for your subcommittee meeting at nine-thirty, but the committee just called to suggest you better get over there because the chairman is so mad he's talking Italian."

"I'm going, I'm going," I said sheepishly. I had a feeling, as I ran, that Rodino's irritation was not caused entirely by my tardiness.

The day before, the White House had deliberately leaked the Doar letter of February 25 in order to embarrass the committee. What made it worse was that the committee members would learn for the first time the exact contents of the letter by reading it in their morning paper.

Rodino waited to respond until he had the full committee in front of him. He managed to restrain himself, as he told the members that everything asked for had been agreed upon by the Republicans, and we had asked for only what we felt would turn out to be pertinent.

Others were not so restrained. Jack Brooks was very angry, calling the leak "White House hucksterism" and "an affront to the committee."

Later in the day, we learned that Ron Ziegler had said our letter showed we wanted "carte blanche to rummage through every nook and cranny in the White House on a fishing expedition," and that we had no right "to back a truck up and haul off White House files." He added, without being asked, that we should adopt a definition of impeachable offenses before we asked for any more material.

When he heard that, veteran Harold Donohue from Massachusetts said, with a straight face, "I didn't know Ziegler was a member of the committee."

There were renewed calls for a subpoena, and some of them came from Republicans.

Railsback told me privately, "Maybe we should just vote to approve the staff report [on impeachable offenses]. Or, maybe we should just issue the subpoena." Even Trent Lott, a freshman from Mississippi who no one figured would ever vote for impeachment, said, "[The White House] is really making a mistake on this. We are entitled to this information and the President is making a mistake if he thinks that it's just Doar, and not the members, who think we are entitled to it."

Bob McClory went so far as to hold a press conference strongly criticizing the White House and reaffirming the committee's right to the requested material.

I was surprised to see him so vocal and also surprised to hear Rodino caution him to take it easy. It was the same advice the chairman had given me an hour ago in the cloakroom! Apparently, Rodino didn't want anyone, even a Republican, to give the impression we were hounding the President.

If the President and Ziegler weren't enough, Bryce Harlow, a presidential counselor, got into the act the next day. Referring to the fact that we had not examined all the material the White

House had given us already, he said, "The House committee is somewhat in the position of a lot of children at homes all over the United States. When you're at meals and you want seconds, you have to clean up your plates first."

He should have known better than to make fun of a House committee that way, especially one so fiercely proud of its power and standing. Rodino, however, refused to be ruffled. He said, "They're just trying to bait us into subpoenaing before we're ready."

Bit by bit, and after conversations with people like Doar and Bernie Nussbaum, I began to see what Rodino meant. A hasty subpoena could really be counterproductive, because it might make people think we were bullying or harassing the President. And it might give the President an excuse to cut off all cooperation with the committee, especially the flow of documents that were so essential to our doing a thorough and fair job.

Once again, Rodino's be-wise philosophy prevailed. I could see that Bernie was right, when he told me, "Look, we don't want to end up in a situation where we have a subpoena but we don't have any of the evidence."

Later that day, Rodino simply outfoxed the White House. He called a press conference to refute the charges of Nixon and his minions. But, wisely, he did not appear alone. He was joined by Edward Hutchinson, the ranking Republican on the committee, who not only backed up Rodino, but added, on his own, the strong comment, "There would be no inquiry if there were no suspicions about the President's actions in connection with the so-called Watergate cover-up." It was good for the people of the nation to see that united, bipartisan front.

I knew only too well that there would be all sorts of anguished cries from concerned citizens if all of the moves against the President were made by Democrats on the committee. One group that I feared would complain was the farmers of Iowa. Many of them had supported Richard Nixon for a long time.

Yet I was surprised, the very day after the Rodino-Hutchinson press conference, to learn that the White House tactic of trying to discredit the committee had not worked with a group of Iowa farmers who happened to be visiting in Washington. When I

107

told them that we were definitely not on a "fishing expedition," they listened patiently and thoughtfully. Apparently they (like a group of Iowa bankers I'd addressed earlier that same day) had decided to wait and hear the evidence. I hoped that their mature attitude was typical of the rest of Iowa's farmers.

Before I had any real chance to find out, however, Richard Nixon all but cut his own throat, as far as the farmers were concerned. The President made one of the most politically irresponsible statements of his entire long career.

On Wednesday, March 19, Conservative Republican Senator James Buckley of New York startled Washington by calling for the President's resignation. Our committee had not even begun to hear evidence, but a prominent Republican voice was asking the President to step down. It had to hurt.

Nixon wasted no time in telling Buckley what he thought of his suggestion. Speaking to a national television audience from Houston that very night, he said that it "takes courage to stand and fight for what you believe is right." If he had left it there, he might have been okay. But the President apparently thought that he was among friends because his audience was the National Association of Broadcasters. He opened the meeting up for questions.

The question that got him in so much trouble was asked by Grant Price, an Iowan—from Waterloo! It involved the Administration's call for all-out food production by farmers so that increased supply could combat rising food prices. What assurances could Nixon offer that increased farm production would not lead to a disastrous break in the prices paid to farmers?

In answering, Mr. Nixon chose to tell his audience that "American farmers never had it so good."

That comment tore open the heavens, and the criticism poured down.

For the most part, 1973 had been a pretty good year for farmers, but the outlook for '74 was not all roses. In the winter there had been a shortage of propane to dry corn, and now, in the spring, fertilizer was in short supply and cost up to 80 percent more than the year before. Most other costs of farm operation also registered staggering increases. The cattle industry was the

108

hardest hit. With feeding costs up and market prices down as much as $5 per hundredweight, cattlemen claimed to be losing up to $200 per head.

In response to Nixon's "Never had it so good" comment, the National Farmers Organization, headquartered in Corning, Iowa, called on Nixon to resign because of his "irresponsible statements." And if he didn't resign, he should be impeached, the NFO declared.

Iowa's conservative Republican Secretary of Agriculture Robert Lounsberry called the President's remark "a very repulsive statement."

Wiley Mayne, one of the President's staunchest supporters on the Judiciary Committee, fired off a telegram the next morning demanding that Mr. Nixon issue an "immediate retraction" and an apology.

I joined in the criticism with a speech in the House the next afternoon: "The only excuse for such a misleading statement is that Mr. Nixon must be so distracted by other matters that he is totally unaware of the agricultural situation in the country today."

Several farmers in the district must have drawn their pens within minutes of the President's comment, because by the end of the week I began receiving letters. " 'The farmer never had it so good,' " one handwritten note began. "It is regrettable that the Chief Executive of the greatest agricultural nation the world has ever known would make such a stupid, ignorant, and ill-timed remark. That in itself should be more than sufficient grounds for impeachment." The letter was signed, "A lifelong Republican," and came from W. C. Frame, rural route 4, Mt. Pleasant.

As I read Mr. Frame's letter, I thought about how far we'd come since the last planting season, when impeachment was a word used almost exclusively by historians—and writers of graffiti!

SEVEN: *A Matter of Taxes*

Congress is fond of precedent. Some would say too fond. But in regard to the impeachment inquiry, we really had no model to follow. President Andrew Johnson had been impeached, but that had centered on a single issue (his removal of one of his Cabinet members contrary to an Act of Congress) and there were many "extralegal" concerns. And that was a century ago.

In fact, throughout the nation's history, impeachment as a constitutional tool had been used only thirteen times—mainly against federal judges—and only eleven of those had been tried in the Senate. We were actually establishing precedent, at least for the modern era, every time we took a step.

The problem, however, was that most of our steps were being taken behind the scenes. The American people knew that the House Judiciary Committee was conducting an impeachment inquiry, but knew little more than that when it came to the details of what we were doing. The difficulty lay not just in the intensely political nature of what we were about, but in the nature of the process itself, at least insofar as that nature was recognized by Chairman Rodino.

Throughout the month of March most members were simply cooling their heels. We had caucuses and full committee meetings to discuss procedural matters, and we had our well-publicized fights with the White House, but for the most part we were simply waiting.

It had been agreed upon early that, as the evidence came in, it would remain in the hands of John Doar's people until it was all arranged and ready to be presented to the full committee in coherent fashion. Of course, the chairman and ranking member were privy to the essence of what was being learned but there was no wholesale dissemination of information to the rest of us.

This created some frustration, but by and large everyone agreed that because of the sensitive nature of our task—and the continuing danger of unfair and damaging leaks—this was the best way to proceed. So, even though some of the non-committee members of the House, and the journalists assigned to cover impeachment, thought we all knew plenty of deep dark secrets, that simply wasn't the case. We learned of certain matters from the news media.

This didn't mean, though, that we had no role. We could seek out John Doar or Bert Jenner or the staff attorneys and make suggestions. While some members decided to wait until hearing the formal presentation of evidence before getting involved in the investigatory process, others played an active role in order to make sure the right ground was being covered.

I belonged to the latter group, and my special concern was the matter of taxes. I'd become interested in Mr. Nixon's taxes weeks before he decided (in December) to have the Joint Committee on Internal Revenue Taxation review his returns. The key item was Mr. Nixon's half-million-dollar deduction for the gift of his pre-presidential papers. I had made several as-yet-unanswered requests to see those papers that nearly wiped out the President's tax liability for two years.

It was widely expected that the Joint Committee's investigation would determine that the deduction was improper because the gift hadn't been made in time to qualify for the tax benefits.

The President himself, in a news conference in late February, acknowledged that the "paperwork" on the gift "apparently was not concluded" until after the July 25, 1969, cutoff date for such deductions. Mr. Nixon tried to paint this issue as at worst a little mistake, an accountant's foul-up. But the deed for the papers

111

gift carried a date of April 10, 1969, more than three months before the gift deadline. There was little question in my mind that the deed was fraudulently backdated and, if the President knew about it, and was involved in a scheme to disguise the time of the gift to evade the law prohibiting deductions for such gifts, then that was tax fraud.

The specter of presidential tax fraud was surely a legitimate area of inquiry for the impeachment committee, and I had come to make regular end-of-the week visits to the staff offices in the old Congressional Hotel. I'd check in with Bernie Nussbaum, who was in charge of factual research, and John Doar to keep track of the progress in this area, and I usually found myself pressing for a more intense effort.

After one such meeting Nussbaum told me that Doar had confided that whenever he saw my face or heard my name, the word "taxes" popped into his head.

That was good.

The President's personal finances were one of six general areas being investigated by the staff, but I knew that work on this particular issue was more or less in a holding pattern awaiting the findings of the Joint Committee.

Concerned that this delay and the understandable and proper emphasis on Watergate-related activities might result in short-changing the tax investigation, I gave myself the assignment of becoming part of the investigative staff as well as a member of the committee

I met with Sheldon Cohen, former director of the IRS, to discuss Mr. Nixon's tax returns and particularly the suspicious gift-of-papers deduction. The President had often said that it was Lyndon Johnson who had advised him to take such a deduction. Cohen, who had advised LBJ on tax matters, told me that he'd advised Johnson against claiming such a deduction in 1969, the year of the Nixon gift. Knowing that Congress was moving to eliminate the tax benefits for such gifts, Cohen said he told LBJ, "You don't want to be the last one out of the station."

I'd also spent nearly four hours talking with Larry Woodworth, the head of the Joint Committee staff that was going over Nixon's tax returns. Woodworth thoroughly discussed the staff's efforts and, on the question of whether fraud was involved, told me he was disturbed by committee chairman Senator Russell Long's public comment that while the President would probably be required to pay additional taxes, fraud was not involved.

"He should have said that we have no *proof* of fraud, not that there was no fraud," Woodworth told me and added assurances that the staff report would leave the question of fraud open for the Judiciary Committee to consider. Fraud was the key and, as John Doar often reminded me during my routine pilgrimages to his office, fraud is tough to prove because you must show intent.

I expected that when the Joint Committee issued its report in April, the President would be shown to have greatly underpaid his taxes. I also expected that the President would respond by saying, "I'll pay the tax, just as I promised I would. I'll abide by the decision made by the committee." Then, I was almost certain, Mr. Nixon would explain that it wasn't his fault, that he'd just followed the advice of his accountants. I could hear the President saying, "They put the tax return in front of me and, like other Americans who have tax advisers, I accepted their counsel." Subordinates! That's the same argument he used in regard to Watergate. But if there was a delinquency, it would be on Nixon's part—a direct, undeniable link to the President.

For this reason, the fraud investigation had to be pursued vigorously. As I once told Nussbaum: "You don't impeach a President for taking the wrong deduction—you'd have to show fraud. I want to know if there was fraud."

There were other reasons adding to my intense interest in the tax question. One was that I perceived that the White House was trying to avoid the issue. In arguing that the Watergate cover-up was all that was involved in the impeachment inquiry, St. Clair obviously ignored the personal finance aspects. I considered that a glaring, and telling, omission. And another factor in my decision to take an activist role in this area was that taxes are a subject the public would readily understand.

On March 17, I learned that Wilbur Mills, the powerful chairman of the House Ways and Means Committee, agreed with my reading of the public's mind. Mills told viewers of *Face the Nation* that Nixon would be out of office by November. He predicted that the President would be forced to resign and one of the strongest factors in that decision would be the pending report of

113

the Joint Committee. Mills said the report would show that Nixon substantially underpaid his taxes and that this would be too much for the American people to take.

While I didn't think the report would result in Nixon's resignation, I agreed with Mills that it would be devastating to the President's standing with the public. In Iowa, I had spent a lot of time over several weekends talking about the tax situation and hearing question after question about how could it be fair that the President paid less taxes than my constituents whose annual income was a pittance compared to the President's salary.

While the people I met were surely concerned about the charges of illegality growing out of the Watergate cover-up, interest in that aspect seemed to be waning. On the question of taxes, I found a real and growing bitterness.

The banner headline slashing across the front page of the *Washington Star* was blunt:

NIXON TAX DUE: $476,431

It was April 3 and the results of the review of the President's taxes were finally out. Four months of pouring over his returns had produced the sorry finding that the President of the United States had vastly underpaid his income tax in every year of his first term in the White House.

"Jeez . . . us!" I heard someone exclaim as I walked into the Democratic cloakroom, "half a million bucks!"

One member said, almost in awe, that the figure totaled more than ten years of congressional salary. I told them, without mentioning the name, that on the floor a Republican had said to me, "Boy, that would just about wipe me out!" *Just about* wipe him out! That would put me in the deepest recesses of the poorhouse, with no release in sight.

When I got back to the Longworth Building, the autopsy on the President's taxes was sitting on my desk. *Examination of President Nixon's Tax Returns for 1969 Through 1972* was an imposing document, 1,000 pages long and almost two inches thick. It was quite a contrast to the thin stack of tax forms sitting on the edge of my desk and awaiting my attention before April 15.

I started paging through, and there, on page four, was the bottom line. Total deficiency: $444,022.00 plus interest in the amount of $32,409. And, according to a footnote, because 1969 was now beyond the statute of limitations, the interest charge of an additional $40,000 was not included in the final tab. The President could pay that if he felt like it.

I went through the document carefully, after telling our staff to hold all calls for a while. After an hour and a half, I had the general picture. It was devastating.

The Joint Committee staff had recommended disallowing $560,000 in deductions, and although the gift of the papers took a major portion of this (and the backdated deed affair was laid out in all its glory) there were other embarrassing revelations. One of them was that the President should have paid a capital gains tax when he sold his New York City apartment; he hadn't because he had claimed that he had put the profits into his "principal residence" (a perfectly legitimate deduction) which he listed as the estate at San Clemente. However, on his California tax form, he had avoided taxes there by listing the White House as his principal residence.

Okay, concluded the report, have it your way. But now you owe for the gain on the apartment sale. It was like an Alice in Wonderland argument, but the report stayed on this side of the looking glass.

There was more, much more, right down to petty deductions that were ruled improper. It was a disillusioning document.

Of course, as the report stated, it was not a "due bill," but it was the reasoned opinion of the tax body that the President had chosen to "arbitrate" the matter.

The next day President Nixon said that he would pay up, and to my astonishment some members of Congress praised him for that statement. Senator Wallace Bennet, a Utah Republican and a member of the Joint Committee, called Nixon's decision to pay his back taxes a "wonderful example for the American taxpayer." The same logic, I guessed, would heap praise on a convicted felon who "agreed" to serve a prison term.

A White House statement said the President felt that he could "make a very strong case against the major conclusions" of the report, but would pay so that no one would question his promise to abide by the Joint Committee's findings. Also, the statement laid the blame for any "errors which may have been made" on those who prepared the returns, not the President himself. That sounded familiar. Another point that bothered me was the White House claim that the Joint Committee's report offered no evidence of fraud.

That last point was not entirely true. In the introduction, the staff wrote that it made *no attempt* to draw any conclusions about fraud because to do so "would be inappropriate . . . in view of the fact that the House Judiciary Committee presently has before it an impeachment investigation relating to the President."

The report truly damaged Mr. Nixon's credibility, but beyond that I worried about the questions it raised in regard to the IRS, and *its* credibility. It had not only audited several of the returns in question, but had complimented the President on the way he handled his taxes. That sounded almost sarcastic, in view of the Joint Committee's report.

Following the original audit, an IRS official wrote to the President informing him that the returns were being "accepted as filed." That's standard IRS language and there is a second sentence that officials, at their discretion, can send along to taxpayers. The President received the discretionary touch: "I want to compliment you on the care shown in the preparation of your returns."

How could the IRS be so blind?

The week after the tax report was made public, Senator Lowell Weicker helped shed some light on that question. On April 8, he revealed a series of documents that had been uncovered during the Senate Watergate Committee probe. Taken together, as the *Washington Star* noted, the memos "showed that former members of the Nixon Administration had no compunction about using agencies of the government, particularly the Internal Revenue Service, to do in political enemies and help their friends." Weicker himself charged that use of IRS files to compile dossiers on Mr. Nixon's political opposition meant that the agency was "acting like a public lending library for the White House."

By the time the memos were released, picturing the IRS as having been annexed to the White House for the political purposes of helping friends and harassing enemies, my daily mail was full of letters referring to the chief executive as the "chief tax cheat" and urging me to "impeach the tax dodger." Weicker's revelations weren't going to make Americans any happier as they sat down with their pencils to fill out their own 1040 forms.

Checking over tax forms is never a pleasant task and this April 15 was especially frustrating. I had to keep reminding myself that it was not crazy to forego perfectly legitimate deductions so I could pay about $4,000 *more* in taxes than I owed.

Jon Kent, who helped prepare my tax return, had discovered that I'd accumulated enough deductions in 1973 to reduce my tax liability to zero. (I didn't have a gift-of-papers deduction, but items like spending nearly $10,000 of my personal income for office expenses in order to keep the congressional offices running and paying the interest on my $130,000 personal debt were deductible.)

I did not think it was proper, however, for a U.S. Congressman to pay nothing in taxes. So Jon refigured my taxes, arbitrarily deleting deductions, and came up with a figure of $4,020.15.

Admittedly, my generosity was not purely altruistic. I believed I had a responsibility to pay something in taxes, but I was also going to make my returns public. Paying zero in taxes wouldn't look too good. I could wrap myself in the Internal Revenue Code, but that wouldn't convince skeptics that I hadn't pulled a fast one if the bottom line on my tax form read $0.

And I was certain that my tax returns would receive close scrutiny, particularly because I was pressing the investigation of the President's taxes. I had not forgotten my luncheon conversation with Bob McCandless.

I kept hearing how sensitive the tax issue was, how difficult it was to prove fraud. I sometimes wondered if the sensitivity surrounding this issue had anything to do with anxieties that engaging in a thorough investigation of Mr. Nixon's taxes would invite similar scrutiny of the tax returns of the investigators.

I felt I had no choice but to keep pushing the tax issue. Bernie Nussbaum had told me the week before that the Joint Committee report convinced him that fraud had been committed in the

117

preparation of the President's returns. He mentioned the lawyers who prepared the returns and said it would be tough to "pin it to the President."

But he also told me, "Ed, if it were you, you'd be in jail."

EIGHT: *Mr. Hays Objects, and Other Problems*

Change rarely comes easily to Capitol Hill. Nor does it often come quickly. And the substance of the issue has little or nothing to do with how long it takes for something to be changed, a situation that sometimes causes students of government to throw up their hands in despair. But on March 20, as we filed into the hearing room for a morning meeting, we discovered a change had been made.

Our seating arrangement had always seemed to me and several of my colleagues to be backwards. The traditional arrangement in the Judiciary Committee was to have the chairman in the middle, with the Republicans to his left and the Democrats to his right. And the location of the staff offices (where members caucus, make and take phone calls, and do quick research during a hearing) corresponds to this setup. Yet in 1973, when I joined the committee, it was the other way around. When members needed to go to the staff offices, we had to go to the opposite side of the large room. The inconvenience aside, it invited disruptions.

Today, however, Rodino had ordered a switchover and we were now seated according to House tradition and common sense. I asked someone why we had previously been "out of order," and I received an answer that is perfectly acceptable—to people who have spent years on the Hill: Manny Celler, for thirteen years the previous chairman, had a bad ear. The afflicted ear was on his right side, so that's where he put the Republicans. The chairman, a Democrat, wanted to be sure that during debate he did not fail to hear and recognize a member of his own party. Peter Rodino's hearing was unimpaired.

That day we faced a request from the President's lawyer, James St. Clair. He wanted permission to "participate in any prehearing discovery as well as in any hearing conducted by the Committee," and he wanted to sit in while the inquiry staff took depositions from witnesses, and, finally, he wanted the right of cross-examination. Never, in any previous congressional investigation, had such rights been granted. The inquiry was, after all, just an inquiry, and if impeachment ever came to trial in the Senate, St. Clair would be able to employ the full complement of legal procedures. The request was outlandish, but instead of being rejected out of hand, it set off a full-fledged partisan debate.

Democrats Brooks and Flowers made the most powerful statements in opposition to St. Clair's request, and I was in agreement with them. But after an hour and a half of debate, I could not get the chairman's attention so that I could join in denouncing the proposal.

When I did gain the floor the next day, I was still mad. "If the President is impeached," I said, "Mr. St. Clair will get his chance to demonstrate his renowned trial techniques . . . and there is no useful purpose in permitting Mr. St. Clair to give us a preview during the inquiry stage."

Had St. Clair and his client in the White House been displaying even a modicum of cooperation with our inquiry, I probably would have been better able to control my temper. But the constant stone-walling hardly deserved rewards. I was also irked that St. Clair was working behind our backs. He had been meeting privately with key Republicans in the House in what the *New York Times* called "an apparent effort to win support for President Nixon's refusal to give Watergate evidence to the House Judiciary Committee."

During the hearing, I angrily wondered aloud whether St.

120

Clair was "practicing law or playing politics, and is he the President's counsel or is he the President's lobbyist?"

My voice became louder as my speech quickened. "I really resent the thought of what's happening because we are trying to be objective, we are trying to run a fair investigation, and now I think we see a political stormtrooper coming in here to represent him [Nixon]."

My comments were clearly unpersuasive to those who supported St. Clair's request, which they said had to be fulfilled to be *fair* to the President in this historic and unfamiliar process. John Doar said he knew of no situation in which counsel was allowed to be present during "the questioning of witnesses preliminary to presentation to the committee." Only Rodino's assurance that the request would be considered and an announcement that a search for precedents was under way seemed to mollify the most vocal of St. Clair's supporters.

Following the hearing, and after being gently admonished by Paul Sarbanes for my use of the word "stormtrooper" to describe St. Clair (an admonition I knew I deserved), my anger subsided. I knew St. Clair's maneuvering was a political ploy to divert us from the evidence. It was becoming clear that we'd have to mix in some politics of our own in order to get the evidence that the White House was so reluctant to supply.

Jim Mann of South Carolina, who was considered, next to Flowers, the least likely Democrat to support impeachment, told me, "I'm starting to think that we've got to begin thinking like P.R. men and not just lawyers." It might prove wise, he suggested, to give in on appearance of counsel. "Remember, the soundest legal principles could be lost on the American people if the President continues to charge that he's being unfairly treated."

The next day, Clark Mollenhoff, the Washington Bureau chief of *The Des Moines Register*, sounded a similar chord. As we discussed the St. Clair participation question, Clark advised, "Look, Ed, you can afford to be magnanimous on this. You can afford to lean over backwards to be fair because the President is fighting a losing battle.

"Be magnanimous," he repeated, "you've already got four aces in your hands."

During the next week Rodino purposely did not hold any committee meetings on impeachment and avoided more partisan wrangling over St. Clair's role. In caucuses and private conversations Rodino urged several of us to follow a low-key approach, to punctuate our public statements by stressing that our inquiry was not the place for an adversary proceeding but at the same time avowing that whatever was worked out would be fair to the President.

The controversy over St. Clair's request was muddying the water and distracting us from the evidence. It had to be put to rest. And whatever arrangement was finally reached with the President's lawyer had to be one that would belie the impression that the committee was trying to railroad Richard Nixon.

This was a critical matter, as Jerry Zeifman, the committee's general counsel, noted one afternoon when he told me he saw no choice but to "give ground" on St. Clair's participation. Otherwise, he argued, the issue could present the President's partisans with a reason, totally removed from the evidence, to vote against impeachment.

The opinion of Dave Dennis confirmed Zeifman's observation. "You know, as far as I'm concerned, my vote has to be to a great extent based on how fair we are with St. Clair," he told me. "There is no way I can go along with any vote [for impeachment] if we do not allow cross-examination."

While efforts were being made to move the St. Clair issue to an acceptable resolution, much of the press attention focused on the turnover of the grand jury material to the committee. The U.S. Court of Appeals for the District of Columbia had upheld Sirica's ruling to fulfill the grand jury's request that its secret report and briefcase of evidence be given to the Judiciary Committee.

Doar and Jenner had picked it up at the U.S. Courthouse at the foot of Capitol Hill on the morning of March 26. Rodino told me that he had deliberately not gone along, explaining that he didn't want to "make a big deal out of this or give the appearance that this is the end-all."

Despite the chairman's efforts, a big deal *was* made of the transfer of material that was widely assumed to show the President's role in the cover-up for which his former aides were indicted. Cameras recorded the event, stories were written (*Newsweek* let its readers know that the briefcase had cost $37.95!), and one of the most frequently seen pictures across the nation showed only the briefcase and John Doar's hand.

So we knew a lot about the briefcase itself. But we knew nothing about its contents. Doar and Jenner had taken it directly to the inquiry offices in the Congressional Hotel, where tight security and our rules of confidentiality meant that only Doar, Jenner, certain selected staff members, Rodino, and Hutchinson had immediate access to the material.

Rodino told me the next day that he had already spent several hours reading the grand jury's report and going over the backup evidence. He didn't elaborate on the contents, beyond saying that it was *not* just a rehash of material that the White House had turned over to the Special Prosecutor's office (most of which the committee had already received).

Rodino changed the subject to that of the quality of the White House tapes, which the grand jury had sent to the committee via Judge Sirica. He said that they were so poor that it usually took ten hours to listen to a single hour of tape conversation. Although the committee had a lot of very sophisticated audio equipment, including a device that helped filter out extraneous noises, the "cleaning process" was tedious.

A new consultant had been added to the staff, a listening specialist to help with the transcribing of the conversations. A professor at a Midwestern university, and an acknowledged expert in deciphering tapes, he was blind.

The sensitivity of his hearing was attested to by a story about another staff member who walked into an office and began to stretch the muscles in his neck to relieve soreness. Our new consultant turned from his work and asked, "Are you having some trouble with your neck?" What better person to have listening to the Nixon tapes?

My conversation with Rodino whetted my appetite to know what was in the report, and I was not alone in feeling frustrated at not having access.

On April 10 a subcommittee of the House Administration Committee was considering H. Res. (for House Resolution)

1027, a routine resolution that would give the Judiciary Committee an additional $979,000, mainly to fund the impeachment inquiry from April 1 to June 30. The latter date was when we hoped to be finished.

Most of the members at the meeting thought they had read the mood of the House, and the country, as approving the request without much opposition. But no one had read the mood of Wayne Hays, the all-powerful chairman of the full committee.

Rodino began the presentation, assuring the subcommittee that the money originally delegated was being well spent, that not only was the committee's normal work getting done, but all the inquiry staff members—clerical as well as professional—were working up to seventeen hours a day, and that included Saturdays, Sundays, and holidays.

I didn't anticipate any objections, so I was not really listening to the chairman. Instead, I was gazing around the marvelous old room on the third floor of the Capitol, so different from 2141 Rayburn. Then my appreciation of the artwork and the fine decorative scrolls that lined the walls was interrupted by the sharp voice of Wayne Hays. He had asked for permission to question Rodino first. (Though chairman of the full committee, Hays was not a member of this subcommittee.) It was more a demand than a request.

He began by announcing that it would be "very difficult" for him to support any recommendation from the Judiciary Committee for impeachment, "and I will probably oppose it on the floor, because I have an extremely low regard for Mr. Doar or the veracity of the staff under your direction."

Heads snapped around, and Hays explained why he was so worked up. There were quiet groans from the back of the room as his story unfolded.

It turned out that Hays had been insulted by two staff members of the inquiry. (Hays was famous for his temper. He once told me, matter-of-factly, "I don't suffer fools gladly, and there are a hell of a lot of them around here.") For some reason, Hays had been in the Congressional Hotel, and he had rung for an elevator. As he stepped on, he found two young men holding soft drinks.

Apparently they didn't look as if they were working very hard, so Hays asked them where they were going. They replied, "What's it to you?"

"What are you doing, just riding up and down this elevator?"

"That's right, buddy," they said to Hays, "just riding up and down the elevator."

I could imagine Hays's mood at the moment, because he was recreating it now, if not reenacting it. He glared at Rodino and Doar and recounted how the boys had proudly told him, in response to his demand, they worked for the impeachment inquiry.

"That's interesting," Hays said he had responded, since the committee was soon to be before *his* committee to ask for more money.

The boys had tried to apologize, but it was too late.

The incident had happened a while back and an earlier Hays speech about it had been reported in the papers. I thought it had all been smoothed over, but his venomous performance proved the incident still smoldered within him.

When Hays finished, he left the room and left the funding request up to the subcommittee members. They didn't share his anger. But the topic led to all sorts of speeches, partisan speeches on impeachment (and even a long discussion about why the committee wasn't holding hearings on proposed constitutional amendments to ban abortions). It wasn't until later in the afternoon that the subcommittee got around to voting on our request. Then there was a motion to cut the amount by a third (which lost by only one vote!). But the subcommittee finally gave its okay.

I couldn't believe that anyone would want to cut off the impeachment inquiry in midstream. I didn't think the full House would ever do it, but I was concerned about Wayne Hays. I hoped that when it came to the full House he would not oppose it. Perhaps Pete Rodino could work his magic on him by then.

Hays was a gruff, tough man, but there was also something special about him. He was almost a paradox. I saw him later that afternoon, after his scene before the subcommittee, and he repeated his complaint about the elevator incident and voiced his opinion that a newspaper article about it had tried to put him in a bad light.

But suddenly he grinned broadly and said, "Ed, look, you gotta see this." He stretched out his arm to show me his new wristwatch: It bore a caricature of Richard Nixon on its face. His eyes shifted back and forth with the seconds and, printed below it was the line, "I am not a crook."

When I entered the hearing room on April 11, I almost stepped back in surprise. The room was packed, and the counsel tables had been pushed forward to make room for several rows of now-occupied folding chairs. It looked as if all the spectators were reporters because everyone seemed to have either a notepad or a camera.

Someone pointed out Teddy White, the author of the *Making of the President* books, and I heard a voice behind me say, "Do you *really* think he's calling it "The Unmaking . . . ?"

The crowd expected something big.

The stage had been set the week before when Peter Rodino declared that "the patience of this committee is now wearing thin" in regard to our still unanswered February request for materials from the White House. After weeks and weeks of waiting and putting up with dilatory tactics, we had decided on April 4 that we'd give Mr. Nixon a deadline in writing. That deadline had been April 9. It had come and passed, and still what we had asked for had not arrived.

Instead, we had received a letter from St. Clair, a letter I considered patronizing and offensive. He said he was "pleased by the progress . . . toward providing additional specifications we felt were lacking in your original request." St. Clair told us that a review of the requested material was under way and that sometime after Congress returned from its Easter break on April 22, material would be furnished "that would permit the committee to complete its inquiry promptly."

Still refusing to tell us whether we were going to get what we asked for, St. Clair incongruously closed his letter by saying that the President wanted to "reiterate . . . his desire to cooperate. . . . If any problems develop," St. Clair wrote as though from another world, "I, of course, stand ready to meet with you in an attempt to resolve them."

Another stall.

126

It was not just the Democrats who were tiring of this White House game. Ed Hutchinson did not disguise his displeasure when he said, "I cannot understand why there would at this late date still be any doubt in anybody's mind as to what it is we are after. We are not after irrelevant material, we are not after a state secret. We are simply after information that is going to bring this matter to a conclusion."

Waldie told me that the feigned innocence of St. Clair reminded him of the manner with which one goes about avoiding paying a bill. "First, you send in the bill but *forget* to enclose a check," Waldie explained. "So you get word back from the creditor saying he didn't get your check. And you say, 'Oh, gosh, I'm sorry' and promptly send off the check—but *forget* to sign it. That'll give you two, maybe three more weeks of delay."

The tactics behind St. Clair's letter were just as obvious—a little more brinksmanship to see just how far the committee could be pushed. Our meeting today would provide the answer—perhaps in the form of a subpoena for the President of the United States.

Rodino opened the session with a statement designed to heal the partisan split that had developed over the question of St. Clair's role in our inquiry. The subpoena could wait a little longer.

We'd discussed St. Clair's participation in meetings and Democratic caucuses earlier in the month. Even those who were initially opposed to permitting the President's counsel an adversary role were becoming resigned to letting St. Clair in at some point to avoid being branded a lynching party.

Now the question was at what stage St. Clair would be allowed to participate. Bill Hungate raised one of the most graphic arguments against letting the President's counsel take part in the prehearing investigation: "When I think of the problems with Mr. St. Clair, I think of an obstetrician," Hungate told the committee wryly. "For an obstetrician to be helpful and competent in delivering a child, it is not necessary for him to attend the conception. Indeed, his presence at that stage may hinder the expeditious completion of the project." He earned a good laugh.

Rodino announced that he would support permitting St. Clair to attend our meetings when the staff presented evidence to the

127

committee, and St. Clair could receive the same materials given members. The President's counsel would also be allowed, at the end of the presentation, to comment on the evidence and recommend that certain witnesses be called; and, if witnesses were examined by the committee, St. Clair would be allowed to ask questions which the committee deemed appropriate.

We'd vote on the procedures later, but Rodino wanted to let the committee know his thinking to allay fears that St. Clair was to be locked out.

We then moved to the question of our six-part request. Doar read the letter from St. Clair and then told us that about an hour earlier he'd received a phone call from the President's counsel. St. Clair wanted to know whether, if in the next day or two he furnished material requested in the first four categories, the committee would agree not to issue a subpoena.

Donohue had the privilege of suggesting the proper response to that eleventh-hour plea. "I move that the committee on the Judiciary authorize and direct the issuance and service upon Richard M. Nixon, President of the United States, a subpoena" demanding that our entire request be fulfilled by April 25.

It was evident that it would take a subpoena to wrest the tapes and other material from the White House so there seemed little need to debate Donohue's motion. The Massachusetts Democrat asked for unanimous consent to limit debate to one half hour. But there was objection so we had to take a vote, and, splitting right down party lines, agreed to the half-hour limit. Twenty-five members asked for an opportunity to speak on the motion, and we were each allotted one minute.

Charlie Sandman of New Jersey ended up spending a good part of his time grumbling that he had such a short time to discuss "one of the most important subpoenas ever issued in the history of mankind."

Most of the half hour was spent on an amendment Dave Dennis offered. Dennis wanted to delete from the subpoena the two categories of conversations that St. Clair had *not* included in the package he was dangling before us in an attempt to divert us from the subpoena.

I agreed with Kastenmeier, who said he thought it was "a little too late to make a deal," but it was clear that many Republicans were in favor of the Dennis approach.

To those worried that the subpoena would precipitate a confrontation with the White House, Rodino pointed out that there would be no confrontation if the President complied.

"I am not seeking a confrontation," the chairman said, "I am seeking evidence to make a determination that is fair and honest to the President, and, most important, to the American people."

Father Drinan declared that "the conversations that would be deleted by the Dennis amendment are absolutely urgently required and those who vote for the Dennis amendment will be unconsciously voting to cover up the cover-up."

Most Republicans seemed unmoved.

Jim Mann asked for any information that supporters of the Dennis amendment had about the evidence they were so willing to forego. In responding to a question from Hamilton Fish, Doar noted that St. Clair had never argued that some of the items requested were more or less relevant than others.

When the half hour was up, we voted. The outcome surprised and somewhat sickened me. The amendment was rejected, but only one Republican, Caldwell Butler, joined the Democrats in the 22-16 vote to retain the integrity of the subpoena.

I was ready to vote on the subpoena and if the Republicans wanted to make it a party-line vote, so be it. Let them feel the consequences.

But Del Latta wanted to offer an amendment that would make the last two items requested more specific. He hadn't drafted his amendment, and Rodino would have been well within his rights to ignore Latta and call for a vote on the subpoena. The chairman, however, agreed to recess for lunch and reconvene later in the afternoon to permit Latta to offer his amendment.

I thought the break was a mistake. But I was proved wrong. During the luncheon recess several Republicans led by Bob McClory attempted to get St. Clair to put his hypothetical suggestion about providing part of the requested material into a written promise. But they couldn't, and the lack of any assurances restored the resolve to subpoena that had been diluted by St. Clair's vague compromise proposal.

129

When we reconvened, Latta's amendment, which simply made the subpoena more specific, was adopted by voice vote, indicating that the bipartisan spirit had returned.

Then, with dramatic speed, the subpoena itself was approved on a 33-3 vote. For the first time in the nation's history, a President was subpoenaed in regard to an inquiry investigating impeachment charges against him.

What would happen was unclear. Mr. Nixon's dealings with the Special Prosecutor had taught us that it was not unthinkable that the President would defy a subpoena. There was no way we could force him to comply.

Earlier in the month, several committee members were discussing this subject and it had been suggested facetiously that if the President refused to comply with the subpoena, "We'll go down there, arrest him, and bring him back and lock him up in some room down in the basement of the Capitol."

Hutchinson, who was one of the three Republicans who opposed the subpoena, facetiously suggested, "If you have the Sergeant at Arms go to the White House to arrest him, make sure he carries the mace"—the symbol of authority in the House.

There did seem, however, to be several viable alternatives if Mr. Nixon ignored our subpoena.

We could hold him in contempt of Congress (or, as Rodino suggested would be more appropriate, contempt of the Constitution). Or we could simply take the noncompliance into account as we deliberated impeachment and include it as an article of impeachment. Six senior Republican Senators had warned the President on April 11 that "The first article in the bill of impeachment very well could be contempt of Congress," if Mr. Nixon withheld evidence from the committee.

Refusing to supply subpoenaed evidence might also be the basis for the committee's drawing "adverse inferences," to the effect that the material had to be incriminating or he would have turned it over. This was another factor to include in the impeachment equation.

It was possible, some members suggested, that we could sue to force compliance, but I didn't think resorting to the court system was the answer, not with the Constitution so clearly vesting impeachment power exclusively in the House. Perhaps the President would relieve us from these worries by cooperating. I truly hoped he would comply.

He had until April 25 to decide, and we had a ten-day congressional recess I was eagerly looking forward to.

On Friday, April 12, the first day of the recess, I forgot about impeachment. Joyous noise surrounded me—the screams and oo-aahs of a circus crowd. As I sat there with my four daughters, I didn't look for parallels with Watergate or impeachment—not even when the man put his head in the lion's mouth!

Ringling Brothers, Barnum and Bailey (or whoever owned it now) put on a wonderful show, but the real fun for me was watching the kids. Margot, Vera, Elsa, Eve—each one had a special reaction to the clowns, the high-wire daredevils, and the animals. Watching them was its own kind of special circus.

The drive back to McLean featured a nonstop debate as to which was the "absolute best" part of the circus, with an occasional side comment to the effect that Mother had made a big mistake by staying home.

Micky and I had dinner together, a relaxed and pleasant evening. It was late when we got back to McLean, and Micky let me sleep over, on a couch in the den. It had been against her better judgment, but I almost begged her. For the first time in months I thought that her firmness might be giving way, and that she might consider making one more try. I felt odd, settling in to sleep on the couch, but it beat the lonely apartment back in the District of Columbia.

Saturday morning was a repeat of the slightly madcap family scenes I remembered so well. We all had breakfast together, the girls looking pleased yet slightly puzzled to see me.

It was glorious, and I was ready to move back in for good, but my illusions soon faded. Micky was not ready to forget the separation, and when she realized that was the drift of my thoughts, she became upset and asked me to leave.

I resisted, we argued, and her request turned into a demand.

Frustrated, mad at myself, at her, at anything and everything handy, I picked up my raincoat and walked out the door. It was a mile to the gas station where a mechanic was adjusting the brakes on my car and, as though planned to add to my misery, huge raindrops began to pelt down on me.

I struggled to get my raincoat on, trying to figure out why I seemed to be driving myself to run into a stone wall, time after time. As usual, I had tried to force the issue. It was never Micky. I kept forgetting that all recent signs (save the good time we'd had the evening before) pointed in only one direction: final divorce. Micky had retained a new lawyer (a Republican no less) after her first attorney, her uncle Lou Shulman, asked to be released from the case because he believed he could not be objective.

As I walked along in the rain, a passing car seemed to swerve, purposely, to hit a puddle and drench me even more. I started to curse, but I noticed the two bumper stickers. One read VIRGINIA IS FOR LOVERS and the other shouted IMPEACH NIXON. I almost laughed. Nixon! The man seemed to be dogging my footsteps.

As I was being chased out of what I still thought of as *my* house, I was trying to chase him out of his. I thought of his lifelong struggle to get where he was and the hell he now found himself in. Just then I felt sorry for him.

I got the car, tossed the soaked coat on the floor, and headed back to Washington.

People say that Washington's weather is perverse, terribly unpredictable, and that day was a perfect example.

As I drove across the Francis Scott Key Bridge, into Georgetown, the sun broke through. The weather and the weariness of the morning seemed a part of the past. I turned on the radio and heard Elizabeth Drew tell her listeners that we should all be focusing on pleasant things. Spring, for example. Look around, she advised, and see all the colors and other signs of new life, and realize that Watergate is not everything. It cannot stop spring.

I smiled. In a few minutes M Street would become Pennsylvania Avenue, and I would pass the White House and turn toward the Capitol and the dome would be shining with the rain-drying sun. It was a beautiful city.

* * *

132

During the week of April 22, the Judiciary Committee met and agreed to grant Nixon a five-day extension of the due-date on our subpoena. We were "going the last mile" with the President.

Several days later, while we were still awaiting the President's response, the full House was debating the funding resolution for the Judiciary Committee. There had been reports that Wayne Hays, still miffed about the elevator incident, would oppose the resolution. But, to my relief, he took the floor expressly to deny such reports and to urge approval. He also defended the Judiciary Committee against charges that our new April 30 deadline meant that the committee was dragging out impeachment.

"There has been foot dragging. There has been stalling," Hays said. And he knew where to lay the blame: "The President's attorneys have used every trick in the book to keep from giving the evidence."

He then referred to reports that White House sources believed the tapes would prove the President innocent. He concluded by declaring, "If I were President and the tapes would prove my innocence, I would not only give them to the committee, I would do better: I would give them to television, and sit there grinning while they were being played on TV."

Our funding resolution passed on a voice vote.

NINE: *Under Way . . . at Last!*

"1. On December 2, 1971 Gordon Strachan reported in writing to H. R. Haldeman, Assistant to President Nixon, on activities relating to the President's re-election campaign. In his Political Matters Memorandum of that date Strachan reported:

> *John Dean*—The Attorney General discussed with John Dean the need to develop a political intelligence capability. Sandwedge has been scrapped. Instead, Gordon Liddy, who has been working with Bud Krogh, will become general counsel to the Committee for the Re-Election of the President, effective December 6, 1971. He will handle political intelligence as well as legal matters. Liddy will also work with Dean on the "political enemies" project.
>
> Jack Caulfield will go over to the Committee when the Attorney General moves. Caulfield will handle the same projects he currently does. In addition he will assume responsibility for the personal protection of the Attorney General.

1.1 Memorandum from Gordon Strachan to H. R. Haldeman, December 2, 1971 (received from White House).
1.2 Gordon Strachan testimony, 6 SSC 2448-49.
1.3 President Nixon statement, May 22, 1973, 9 Presidential Documents 695.

1.4 John Dean testimony, 3 SSC 924-25.
1.5 John Caulfield testimony, 1 SSC 251-52."

John Doar, looking slightly less rumpled than usual, cleared his throat and began the presentation of the evidence. It was May 9, and we were finally making progress. Impeachment had begun.

Chairman Rodino had called the meeting to order forty-five minutes earlier, so that the television cameras could record the historic moment before the committee went into executive, or closed, session. (The evidence we were about to hear, some of which came from secret grand jury materials, would include mention of numerous people who had committed no crime, and some mention of several who might have; confidentiality had to be maintained.) Everyone in the room was introduced, including the President's lawyer. Rodino went over the rules of confidentiality very carefully. When he asked St. Clair if he realized that he was also bound by those same rules, the lawyer said, "I do, Your Honor." Catching his slip, he immediately corrected: "Mr. Chairman, excuse me." There were several smiles.

John Doar explained that every day we would receive a black notebook containing the condensed items of importance that the staff, after four months of work, felt to be of evidentiary value. Each item was headed by a separate tab that was numbered and even sub-numbered for careful reference. At the bottom of the page were notations giving the sources of this evidence, such as "SSC," for the Ervin Committee (Senate Select Committee), or the number of a White House document. In simplest terms, the arrangement of the huge books showed what we had and where we had gotten it.

So cautious was Doar that he would do nothing at this point except present the facts. No conclusions would be drawn until all of the material had been presented; then Doar and Jenner would sum up the evidence for the committee and tell us what they thought it proved. Doar would *not* be a prosecuting attorney presenting a case to a jury, at least not until the time came to sum up (and even then, some members feared, he would resist advocacy). His method was to make sure we had *all* the pertinent facts.

135

Before beginning to read from the tabbed pages, Doar had given a careful background statement covering all the principals in the drama that was about to unfold, telling us—for the record—where they came from, how they got to the White House, or what their specific connection was. It was unusually thorough. I resisted a slight urge to smile when he said that Mrs. Butterfield and Mrs. Haldeman "were good friends and fraternity [sic] sisters in college."

Using charts and diagrams, he had shown where everyone of importance was located on the first floor of the White House, and where the "bugs" were (differentiating the few that had to be turned on from the majority that were "voice-activated"). And then he had begun his long, dry recitation of who said what to whom and when.

Three hours and some minutes after he'd begun, his voice showing signs of strain, John Doar finished with the first book. We were on our way. As I walked back to the office, I suddenly remembered Joe Rothstein's comment that "Once you start something around this place, there's no stopping it."

The first day of the committee hearings was only eleven days after the President's latest—and perhaps his most seriously miscalculated—gamble, the release of the tape transcripts. Nixon had gone on television to proclaim that even though the tapes were going to make him look bad in some ways ("Never before in the history of the Presidency have records that are so private been made so public") they would exonerate him in the long run, and would show that he, not John Dean, was to be believed.

His high-risk ploy blew up in his face almost immediately. When I read my copy (each member of the Judiciary Committee received a personalized copy from the White House, which was the President's way of responding to our subpoena for the tapes themselves) I was stunned by the language, the mock-tough-guy air, and the whole aura of a bunker mentality within the White House. The frequency of "expletives deleted," in place of obviously crude words and phrases, actually made the tone *worse*. Nixon and his top aides sounded like a bunch of thugs.

If the people at the White House thought the tapes would help the President's case, they had sorely miscalculated.

136

The *Chicago Tribune*, a staunch Nixon backer for decades, published an editorial calling for the President to resign. Senator Hugh Scott, the Republican leader in the Senate, said that the tapes revealed a "shabby, immoral, and disgusting performance."

I didn't have the heart to ask my daughters Margot and Vera what their classmates out in McLean were saying. I didn't because even before the release of the transcripts a teenager from Iowa had been visiting my office and asked me if I could get him an autographed picture of President Nixon. I knew the boy came from a family of Democrats, so I was curious about why he wanted it. I asked him, and he looked sheepish for a moment, and then told me that his friend had one—and all the kids got together and threw darts at it!

The mail in my office was overwhelmingly negative, and the angry reaction only intensified as paperback copies of the President's words hit the bookstands. Readers were sadly convinced that the portions that had been reprinted in newspapers or read during the nightly news had not been taken out of context.

The nation reacted vehemently to the printed word but, by mid-May, only a handful of people had actually *heard* any of the conversations. (These favored few included some people at the White House, the Special Prosecutor's staff, the Watergate grand jurors, Rodino, Hutchinson, and selected members of the impeachment staff.) When the time finally came for the committee members to listen to the tapes, in the secrecy of the hearing room, there was great curiosity. There was also an air of resignation, as if no one really expected to be shocked anew. After all, we had read or heard about the most shocking items. We were growing used to shocks in Washington, weren't we?

Apparently not, for listening to the tapes proved to be an emotional experience.

Before we actually began listening there was a lot of good-natured kidding. The press wanted pictures of us wearing the headphones (that had been set up in Room 2141, all connected to the master tape recorder) but most of us shied off, mainly because we realized we looked pretty silly in the cumbersome earphone sets. Rodino had said no, but to the surprise of many, Harold Donohue agreed to have his picture taken, a decision he must have regretted the next day when scores of newspapers carried a shot of him looking like an elderly rabbit. Finally, the photographers left, the doors were closed, and John Doar started the tapes.

I looked around at a few of the members as the machine began to whir and the first recorded snippets of talk started coming through. Rangel caught me looking at him and grinned, like a big kid. Others looked grim. Many members had an expression that was close to awe, for we were about to "eavesdrop" on our President talking to his aides in the privacy of the Oval Office. Certainly this was a historic first!

Some members, I learned later, felt like children who were listening to their parents through a bedroom window or open door in the dead of night.

This awesome feeling was also mixed with incredulity, as if we couldn't really accept the fact of what we were about. God, I thought to myself when I recognized the voice of Richard Nixon and realized that he, Haldeman, and Dean were discussing the "problem" of attorney Edward Bennett Williams, who represented *The Washington Post,* and how "to fix the son-of-a-bitch." This was the President of the United States, and what he was saying was never intended, obviously, for outside ears!

Nixon was not speaking loudly, and his words came out in a hesitant and halting manner. As the tape wound on, and the talk turned to other people who had to be "dealt with," there were occasions when Haldeman or Dean or the President—or all three—would begin to laugh. I felt my stomach tighten.

The laughter was cruel, almost sick. It had an eerie quality that I found scary. The things they were saying about people were bad enough, but the laughter was frightening. They could have as easily been a gang of criminals plotting an elaborate revenge.

The more I listened to the tapes, the more depressed I became. This was my President, our President, and he was sounding like some evil dictator, or some crazed ruler who probably viewed himself as a benevolent despot.

No wonder so many people back home had reacted with outrage to the transcripts. No wonder the conservative *Chicago Tribune* decided to print the entire set. But those reactions stemmed

138

from the printed word, and hearing the words was worse, so very much worse.

The speakers discussed people as if they were animals, and their ideas for dealing with them came across as callous and cold. Expediency was the only goal. I couldn't help but think of Nazi Germany.

I looked around the room. Most of my colleagues seemed to be subdued, as the tape played such phrases as "modified, limited hang-out" with no mention whatsoever of truth, only how to avoid the release of damaging information. Some looked upset, and a few seemed to be flushed with either embarrassment or anger.

Ironically, Nixon's once-private scheming was now being heard by several people from an America far different from that of the rich bankers Nixon so admired. Here were, for example, three very different Americans—Rodino (Italian-American stock), Sarbanes (Greek), and Barbara Jordan (black and female)—who truly understood the Constitution of the United States, and knew what it meant to minorities, listening to the President disparage some of the fundamental principles of the nation.

Rodino and Doar (in what I eventually came to see was their wisdom) had exercised a degree of "censorship" over the tapes. If Nixon, or someone else, made a particularly disparaging or racist remark, it was not included in the tape that was played for the full committee. Their reasoning was that it might so annoy the members that it would become difficult to be objective about the evidentiary value of the material. However, Rodino said that if any member wanted to listen to the excised portions, he or she could do so in the offices of the inquiry staff.

I went up there several times, as did at least half the members on the committee. And although I was shaken anew by what I heard, I had to agree with the chairman that he had been right in excluding it as "irrelevant to the inquiry."

There were Richard Nixon and his men making jokes about blacks and Italians (Rodino must have fumed), calling some of the Justices of the Supreme Court "clowns," and the President not even being able to remember the name of Justice Rehnquist, whom he had appointed to the court!

139

One thing that came across clearly was that Nixon had no particular fondness for Jews. He may have set up a "Jewish arm" in 1972, and he may have had Rabbi Baruch Korff's committee for "fairness to the President" out fronting for him at this very moment, but his prejudice showed. His very tone of voice gave him away.

The racial and religious slurs may have distorted the actual evidence, but they were there, and they bothered me tremendously. All along I had been trying to look only at the evidence, to be objective, but now I was bothered by a rising feeling of dislike for the man, Richard Nixon. Each day I had to remind myself that I could not vote to impeach the man simply because I couldn't stand him personally.

One of the problems for the Southerners on the committee (of either party) was that they stood in such awe of the presidency. My background and upbringing had also stressed the wonderful importance of that office. As I grew up, I tended to see the man and the office as one and the same. Eisenhower, Kennedy, Johnson—the Presidents of my adult years—and certainly Truman and Roosevelt before them had *been* the presidency as well as the President.

Hearing the tapes completed the process by which I was finally able to look at the man inside the symbol. What had begun was the growing realization that Richard Nixon, *the man*, had a lust for power and perhaps also for money.

It isn't hard to understand a man's desire for financial independence, but in Nixon's case independence didn't seem to be enough. He wanted real wealth, like that of the Republican businessmen and bankers he'd known in Orange County, California, and in New York City, where he'd practiced law. There's nothing illegal about that. There is, however, something illegal about not paying your taxes.

In regard to almost all the other allegations against the President, it was possible to give him some benefit of the doubt and accept for the time being his defense that everything had been done for reasons of national security. Certainly there had been occasions when Nixon's Democratic predecessors in office had used the CIA, or other arms of government, for questionable ends, offering the same excuse.

But there was no way Nixon could twist his personal tax she-nanigans to make them fit under the umbrella of national securi-ty. When it comes to cheating on your taxes, it is personal. You are out for your own financial gain, and the presidency cannot be used as a defense. It is a simple situation: If John Q. Citizen did it, he would be committing a crime—and so would the President of the United States.

That inescapable fact continued to gnaw at me, forcing me to differentiate between the man and the office. It came down to this: If he wasn't honest in his tax returns, how could you trust him to be honest in other areas?

I also began to look askance at some of Nixon's other financial dealings and to pay more attention to the rumors about wealth hidden away in foreign bank accounts and "Bahamian trusts." Richard Nixon had not been an unusually wealthy man when he came to office, but in five years' time he'd accumulated some im-pressive real estate holdings. In five years in office the President of the United States had made so much money that when he was forced to compute his taxes fairly, his back-tax bill came close to half a million dollars!

The tax and personal finance issues epitomized my fears about the overall conduct of Richard Nixon, and they enabled me, finally, to separate the man from the office. Although some people felt we were involved in a battle for power between the legislative and executive branches of government, I didn't feel that we, the committee, were "attacking the President." What we were doing was investigating charges against the man who held that august office.

On May 15—after only two full days of hearing the evidence presented by John Doar and his staff—the Judiciary Committee voted 37-1 to subpoena more material. This time we asked for tapes and for the President's daily diary in regard to Watergate and also in regard to the ITT case and the milk money affair.

We did not have high hopes of getting a positive response. St. Clair had been putting up stop signs for days, and the indica-tions were that the White House would prefer to let the courts settle the matter. But the near unanimity of the vote was heart-ening.

Not that the problem of partisanship had gone away. If anything, it intensified during the first weeks of May. The Republicans on the committee seemed, in a sense, to have the tactical advantage, because they were more privy to White House thinking. And some of the majority members began to talk of our somehow hiring a special prosecutor, or a kind of task force, to make sure that the "case" against Nixon was vigorously pursued.

What bothered people like John Conyers, and even those of a more calm demeanor like Barbara Jordan, was that John Doar's low-key presentation was so slow and careful that he would never get around to "making his case." For days, that phrase was popular. Several members also expressed concern that the "faceless forty," the lawyers on the inquiry staff who were gathering the material that eventually made its way into our big black books, were too research-oriented, and not sufficiently experienced in the kind of investigation that builds toward a strong showing of guilt, such as in the preparation of a criminal case—or, as in this situation, a bill of impeachment.

I suffered the same frustrations about the tedious pace of the presentation, but my continuing close contact with Bernie Nussbaum reinforced my faith in our staff. Once, in early May, Bernie patiently heard me out as I went over my concerns that we were not developing the kind of strong evidence that would be needed. Then he looked at me for a moment and said, "Don't worry, Ed, we've got a case." I knew I couldn't press him on the point—there had already been a big flap over leaks to the press from someone either on or with the committee—but I thought about his comment a lot in the next few weeks.

One thing I knew was that many of us were getting tired. The pace and the amount of work were taking their toll. John Doar in particular was working very hard. It was common knowledge that he and most of his people were staying in the office until one and two in the morning, and then were back at it by seven or eight the next morning.

It became a standing joke to ask other committee members when they'd last been in their offices. A single hour each day, devoted to normal office business, seemed to be about average.

Being temporarily (or so I hoped) without a family to go home to each night, I probably had more time than others. But even I felt myself growing more and more tired. One Saturday, Micky brought the girls, plus a friend with her children, down to the Capitol, and I took them all to lunch in the House cafeteria. Afterwards, I led them through the empty House chamber, and when one of the kids saw the lounge chairs on the balcony off the Speaker's lobby, she said, "Is that where the Congressmen get their suntans?" I laughed, but I had a sudden vision of the comfortable old sofa in the cloakroom, and I'd have given a lot to flop down on it that very moment.

Micky was understanding. She knew what kind of a toll these long days and nights could take. I'm sure she avoided bothering me with family details that needed my attention simply because she knew how much I had on my mind.

On the few nights when I did see the kids, the hardest part was putting Evie to bed, because she would invariably say, "Daddy? When are you coming back to live here? Why don't you live here anymore?"

Clearly my answers had not been satisfactory. For one thing, I didn't know how to explain separation to a four-year-old. And, as to when I was coming back, well, that possibility was growing more remote with each day.

On May 22, the President let us know how he felt about our subpoenas:

. . . Thus, it is clear that the continued succession of demands for additional presidential conversations, has become a never-ending process and that to continue providing these conversations in response to the constantly escalating requests would constitute such a massive invasion into the confidentiality of presidential conversations that the institution of the presidency would be fatally compromised.

The committee has the full story of Watergate, in so far as it relates to presidential knowledge and presidential actions. Production of these additional conversations would merely prolong the inquiry without yielding significant additional evidence. More fundamentally, continuing ad infinitum the process of yielding up additional conversations in response to an endless series of demands would fatally weaken this office not only in this administration but for future presidencies as well.

Accordingly, I respectfully decline to produce the tapes of

presidential conversations and presidential diaries referred to in your request of April 19, 1974 that are called for in part in the subpoenas dated May 15, 1974, and those allegedly dealing with Watergate that may be called for in such further subpoenas as may hereafter be issued.

It was an amazing letter, and it made two things "perfectly clear": One, we had the most unusual question of the legality and efficacy of our subpoena; and two, St. Clair was no longer calling the shots; his client had just demoted counsel to the status of a go-between.

I'd had different feelings about St. Clair from time to time, but this was the first instance in which I felt a bit of sympathy for him.

TEN: *One Step Forward, Two Steps Back*

"I realize the importance of what we are all about, but I can't help feeling that we are going much too slowly in the committee. You know, if my wife makes a magnificent dinner, but we have to sit around drinking cocktails and eating appetizers for three hours before we get to the main meal, well then you just don't enjoy the meal as much."

There were smiles in response to Paul Sarbanes's analogy. It certainly underlined what was bothering most committee members in the last weeks of May. Somehow we were going to have to speed things up.

We all, Democrats and Republicans alike, knew the necessity for proceeding cautiously. But did the country understand what we were up against? I had my doubts.

Admitting the risk to his vocal chords, John Doar had turned over the reading of the daily material from the black books to several of his assistants, and occasionally Bert Jenner would lend a hand. (I found it interesting that Jenner was far more formal than Doar. He invariably said, "Ladies and Gentlemen of the Committee," as if he were back in court.) But it was a laborious process.

145

Jack Brooks complained, "Damn, I could read all this stuff for myself a lot faster. Having all of it read to you is like being back in the fourth grade." Although this was becoming a familiar complaint, I didn't see how the process could be speeded up much, unless it was decided that we really didn't need all the detail read into the record. But at the same time, we had to studiously avoid any unnecessary delays.

I had really gotten annoyed when a couple of reporters buttonholed me after a hearing and asked if I didn't think we should adjourn the hearings while the President was out of the country. (He was making a trip to the Middle East.)

"I thought," I told them, "that the President himself said that one year of Watergate is enough." I was about to say more when Chairman Rodino came by and, in response to the same question, snapped, "We're not even considering it."

There had also been a suggestion that we recess on June 4 because there were primaries being held in several states. But Jerry Waldie, who was on the ballot for governor in California in a tough primary fight against a field that included the son of former Governor Pat Brown, spoke sharply against the proposal.

"To be perfectly frank with you, Mr. Chairman, I do not think that we ought to adjourn for any primary for any state including ours. I think that we are so damn far behind on this committee that we ought not to adjourn. We ought to stay in session."

There was a bit of applause, which I joined gladly. It was heartening, perhaps even amazing, to see a Congressman who would pass up such an important day because of the work of the committee.

All of these sentiments were in evidence on May 30 when we began the business meeting. The regular meetings were closed to the public and the press—because we were still dealing with confidential material—but there was a growing feeling that they would soon be open. In fact, public hearings were anticipated. The television people had built platforms, installed extra lights, and I noticed that the man who controlled the volume of the microphones in the hearing room now sat in a smart enclosure covered with expensive-looking draperies. There was also a conspicuously large hole in one wall, that we were told was necessary to make room for even more equipment.

Media coverage seemed inevitable, much like a self-fulfilling prophecy.

Walter Flowers made his feelings clear on the need to open the hearings. He had drafted a proposed letter to the President stating, among other things, that the committee would look upon continuing refusals to honor the subpoenas as possible grounds for impeachment. In explaining the reasoning behind his letter, he touched on the open versus closed issue:

"Now, this committee is moving forward thoroughly . . . and, above all, fairly. I for one think it will be good when the American people can come into our sessions through the eyes and ears of the news media. I believe that this process that we are undergoing serves to affirm the strength of our system and the manner in which this process is going forward gives me confidence in the future, whatever the outcome of our deliberations might be."

I agreed with Flowers, but I couldn't help wondering how the public would react if it had to watch Doar and his staff reading page after page of the notebooks. It had already put a few members to sleep, and was hardly prime-time material. There were, however, good reasons for our not going public yet, the chief among them being that the release of certain materials might prejudice cases that were still to be tried involving a host of Watergate figures, both major and minor.

A shortened version of Flowers's letter was offered by Don Edwards, and after very little debate, it passed by a vote of 28–10. This surprised and pleased me, because it looked as if we might be putting partisanship behind us. On the first of May, when we had voted by the narrowest of margins to send a similar letter, only one Republican (Bill Cohen) had joined the Democrats; this time we had seven more (McClory, Railsback, Smith, Fish, Sandman, Hogan, and Butler).

A bit later Railsback made a motion to in effect turn the question of the committee's subpoena power over to the courts, but it did not pass. The vote against it was 32 to 6, the exact same tally by which a related measure offered by David Dennis was defeated. The committee was for the most part confident of its own subpoena power. Both Doar and Jenner, when asked, stated their strong views that the viability of our subpoena power would be reaffirmed in any ultimate court test.

147

Many different viewpoints got aired in that meeting, and the quality of the debate was unusually high. Perhaps the highest point was reached when Ray Thornton began to speak, slowly and carefully, about where the basis of our power really lay. The room grew quiet.

After explaining why he felt it wouldn't be necessary to go to the courts for help on the subpoena question, he said, "It has been implied that the need is to muster enough support of public opinion to convince the President to comply with our subpoenas. The suggestion is that a ruling of the Supreme Court would give us much more credibility and increased public support. But I submit, Mr. Chairman, that the question is not whether either the House or the Supreme Court or the weight of public opinion can convince a reluctant President to honor a subpoena . . . the real question is of authority and compliance with the rule of the law as distinguished from power. The standard is what the Constitution requires, not what public opinion would support."

Ray Thornton was putting into words, eloquent in their simplicity, what I'd been straightening out in my own mind for weeks. And I could see from the looks on the faces of the members around the room that I was not the only one he was impressing. He spoke for only a few minutes, but he mentioned John Marshall, two important constitutional law cases, several Presidents, and above all the Constitution. When he finished, there was a round of applause.

During the lunch break two different reporters told me that after hearing Thornton, they'd changed their minds and decided that the Judiciary Committee needed lawyers on it after all.

That afternoon I found myself in the odd position of moving to table a contempt motion made by a fellow Democrat, Jerry Waldie, with whom I usually agreed. My motion carried, 27 to 11, but I did not feel pleased. I believed Nixon *was* in contempt, but I made my move in an attempt to keep the family together.

I knew that certain Democrats would be upset with me. I squirmed a bit, but I felt better when Jack Brooks, in a brief statement, agreed with me. After the vote, he looked over and flashed me the "thumbs-up" sign.

* * *

148

By the first week of June, the slow pace inside the hearing room and the furor outside were not our only problems. We had a definite "leak" in our boat, and the White House was gloating over it. Until the hearings went public, everything we heard— unless specifically exempted by the committee or previously made public elsewhere—was to be considered confidential. After each session our black books were carefully shepherded away to our offices, and we locked them up for the night. The tape transcripts prepared by the staff, after listening to the tapes, were returned to the staff offices. But somewhere, tongues were wagging. And it did not make the Judiciary Committee look very judicious.

Both the *Washington Post* and the *New York Times* had run stories in May that apparently could not have come from any sources other than the committee—because they were based on material that we were hearing (either documents or tapes) at the time. It was a bad situation.

And it was not much better for the press, oddly enough. Because one or two newspeople had been the recipients of the privileged material, the others were forced to try and get it too. I had several obviously embarrassed reporters hint around to me that they would love to know what was in certain of the pages we had in front of us, or on certain tapes. I said no.

Everyone seemed to have his or her own particular "suspect." Naturally many people thought the leaks came from one of the harsh anti-Nixon Democrats. (When somebody suggested Drinan as a possible source, another Democrat made a face of mock horror and said, "If he's the one, then I'll never tell him *my* confession!") But there were also those who thought the leaks could as easily have come from the Republican side, as an underhanded way of discrediting the inquiry. It was an unpleasant thought.

The committee had managed, by the end of the first week of June, to make some visible progress. We had been aided by several developments outside the committee, developments that could conceivably speed up the inquiry.

On May 31, the Supreme Court had agreed to hear the tapes dispute. If the court did make it a special matter and render a quick decision, our position might be greatly strengthened. And on June 3, former Nixon aide Charles Colson (who had once said he would walk over his own grandmother to help reelect Richard Nixon) surprised the nation by pleading guilty to all the charges against him in the cover-up and the Ellsberg break-in cases.

Colson's plea must have shocked the White House—not to mention his co-defendants. I heard that he made up his mind after a prayer meeting with Harold Hughes, the man responsible for Colson's much-talked-about religious conversion.

Already reeling from the Colson surprise, the White House suffered another blow two days later when the *Los Angeles Times* broke the story that *all* the grand jurors in the Watergate cover-up case had voted to name President Nixon as an unindicted co-conspirator, and that had it not been for Special Prosecutor Jaworski's legal opinion that a sitting President could not be indicted on a criminal charge, Nixon would have found himself a defendant along with the rest of his crew.

For a few days I thought that these developments would force the President to cooperate with the committee, but, as had happened so often before, these setbacks only intensified Nixon's efforts to "rise above Watergate." On June 10 the committee learned that the President flatly refused to comply with our latest subpoena. He also rebuked us for suggesting we could draw adverse inferences from his failure to comply. To do so, claimed the President, "flies in the face of established law."

"Mr. Mezvinsky. Congressman, please, just a couple of quick questions?"

I was on my way into a caucus of the Democratic members on the committee, trying to get through the phalanx of reporters who were crowding the hallway, when a woman reporter called out to me.

"Okay. But only a minute or two. We're supposed to start at five-thirty, and it's twenty-five after now."

"Thanks. I wanted to ask, because of the President's letter, are you going to ask for contempt?"

"I don't know."

"But don't you think you have to be strong, especially now that the President is on the upswing?"

That surprised me. "Who says he's on the upswing? I don't feel that way."

"Joe Alsop said so in a column this morning, and you hear it a lot. And the President's off on a foreign trip and attracting huge crowds and everything. You really don't feel that way?"

"No, I really don't."

Once inside, I relaxed a bit. It bothered me that people seemed to be keeping score, one for the committee, two for the President, one for . . . I suppose it looked that way from the outside, though, because (except for the leaked material) no one really knew just what evidence the committee was hearing, and the White House was certainly waging a vigorous public relations campaign on the President's behalf. We had to end the closed hearings and get to the public debate.

I spotted Jerry Waldie off to one side, talking with Liz Holtzman and a few others. I felt bad about Jerry. This was the first time I'd seen him since his loss in the California primary. Jerry may have lost the election for governor, but he hadn't lost his special sense of humor. I told him I was sorry, and he said, raising his hand, "The people have spoken. God damn the people!"

During the meeting Rodino read the entire letter from the President, and it was very quiet in the room. At one point, when he meant to read the statement from Nixon that said turning over the material we'd requested would be "a strain on the Constitution," he mistakenly called it a "stain." There was a brief moment of laughter all around, and several members said "Freudian slip," but it was soon quiet again so that Rodino, noticeably bothered by what he was reading, could finish.

The discussion that followed centered around whether we should again respond with a letter. Rodino said, "No, I don't think that would have any effect whatsoever."

The letter was an affront. It was very strong, as if Nixon were some kind of king who was telling us what we could and could not do from his position of supreme power. Hungate cracked, in reference to the letter, "Give him a 'D.'" But I didn't laugh.

Then John Doar made a statement reaffirming the right of the committee to ask for what it had, and refuting the President's legal and constitutional arguments.

It seemed to me, as I sat there listening, that we were building

151

up to a whopper of a partisan fight on the committee. Rodino told us that there had been a hot and heavy Republican caucus and that there was a good chance that the Republicans would side with the President, at least on the basis of what they had heard so far.

John Conyers was downright angry.

"We just can't countenance it," he said, referring to the President's refusal to comply. "We are affected by this stone-walling, and the most serious element is the obstruction of justice. This would set a precedent for all future Presidents."

I thought John had made a good point, and I was surprised when Rodino said, rather sharply, "You know, the people don't give a damn about obstruction. They have to have the rest of the package. They need the substantive counts."

"Yes," added Barbara Jordan, "that's right. The people won't support impeachment unless we give them the real goods."

Several others spoke up, making the point that we had to produce evidence to show, for example, that Nixon approved payment of hush money to the Watergate defendants, or some clear violation of the law, as with taxes, or a solid example of perjury, because obstruction of the committee would never be enough by itself.

After the meeting broke up, a few of us drifted back to the table where the coffee was set up to find the price of a cup had just been raised a nickel. A new sign, taped to the wall, read COFFEE NOW 15¢. I thought the laughter was caused by the evidence of inflation, but when I got closer I saw that someone had scribbled, just above the price, "Republicans free."

Well, if that's what it took to get them out from behind the stonewall, so be it. It would be the smallest of the compromises we would probably have to make.

I ran into a reporter I knew on the way out of the meeting, and after one look at my face he decided not to ask me any questions. Finally, after we'd walked the length of the hallway, he said, "Look, Ed. I won't ask you anything for the record. But what's eating you?"

"Oh, it's just that I think the Republicans are asking for too much. They want to be able to put on the earphones and hear Nixon say, 'I *am* a crook!' before they will ever vote for impeachment. Then they can tell their constituents that they voted for it with a clear conscience. But it's just not going to be that way. It's like Perry Mason. They're expecting someone to stand up in open court and say, out of the blue, 'Okay, I did it.'"

What was also bothering me, although I didn't mention it to my reporter friend, was that we were on the verge of a real battle with the Republican members of the committee over the question of how many witnesses to call. The Democrats wanted to call five key people, and the Republicans at least twice that many. I was becoming convinced that there were certain Republican members who viewed delay as their best strategic ploy.

The rest of the week was a blur of meetings, arguments about rules of evidence, leaks of information, and lists of witnesses. I was greatly relieved, on Sunday morning, to be driving out to Micky's to see the girls.

It was Father's Day, and although the weather was disappointing, the day certainly wasn't. I got several gaily colored rocks from Evie, and some pictures ("suitable for framing") from the older girls. We went to Farrell's ice cream parlor for lunch and sundaes, then to the movies for *The Sound of Music.*

The girls were enjoying the picture so much, so obviously happy, that it started me thinking about myself and whether I was happy at that moment in my life. After a while tears came to my eyes, and I was glad we were in a dark theater. For some reason, the tears had been very close to the surface lately.

On Thursday of the week before, we had celebrated Flag Day on the floor of the House. I had been sitting near Speaker Albert and next to Peter Rodino. There was a color guard presentation and the Army band played "You're a Grand Old Flag." I was feeling the usual rush of emotion that comes over me when I see the flag displayed in formal ceremonies, and I looked at one of the young soldiers who was holding a flag and shaking a bit.

I guess he was nervous, with all the pomp and circumstance, but for whatever reason he was making the flag shake too. That made me think of Richard Nixon and the committee and impeachment. All of a sudden I was almost crying. I couldn't resist the thought that Nixon had somehow stained the flag.

Everything seemed turned around. I looked over at Henry

153

Aaron, the baseball great, who was being honored in the program, and it made me wonder if we had run out of heroes in all areas except sports.

Watergate, and all that it represented, was almost constantly on my mind. That same night, I had taken Micky to see a special showing of the fine old film *All the King's Men,* about a Southern politician whose career closely resembled that of the late Huey Long. Within a half hour I was thinking of Nixon and the crowd around him. Certainly I wasn't alone that night in drawing the comparison, but I wished that I could at least go to a movie without thinking of the President and the impeachment inquiry.

Micky sensed my mood as I drove her home, and we talked quietly about the girls, and Micky's classes (she was finally finishing her master's and was getting certified to teach English as a foreign language) and such weighty topics as whether I was eating properly. We didn't talk about Watergate, and we didn't talk about divorce, but there was an unstated realization that both topics were headed for their resolution. At that moment the President's chances looked a lot better than mine.

"Hey, Mezvinsky"—Wayne Hays was waving to me as I walked onto the floor on June 18—"I saw your ad in *Time*!"

Standing next to him, Phil Burton, another important member with years of service and accomplishment, also had a comment: "I guess you don't have to worry about getting reelected, now."

They were referring to Hugh Sidey's *The Presidency* column in a recent *Time* magazine that was devoted to me and my activities on the committee. I had spent several hours with Sidey and found him to be insightful and sympathetic. When his article appeared, and I saw that he had written only about me, I could hardly have been more flattered. He had closed his piece with a quote from me:

> Mezvinsky knows the issue may be with him the rest of his life. "There is an eerie quality to it all," he says. "This is no carnival. . . . We are all on trial. . . . We have to understand the strategy being used by the White House. We must understand

154

better our own role. We cannot run away from this now. It is on us."

In response to Hays's and Burton's good-natured ribbings I felt like assuring them that I thought I'd be in the committee room for the rest of my life and they wouldn't have to worry about my getting any more attention from the press.

After registering my vote on a measure that had provided a break from the presentation of evidence, I did an about-face and headed back to 2141 Rayburn. At five minutes to six that afternoon we were still at it, and we were tired. Most members had their coats off, cigarette smoke hung in the air as if it too could hardly move, and several members had their eyes closed. We'd had only an hour's break during the day, except for calls to the floor. Bert Jenner was yawning.

We took a five-minute break, but it didn't appear to refresh anybody. Yet, as tired as we all were, we were still listening with care. Or at least John Seiberling was, for he caught something that most of us had missed.

We were listening to evidence relating to the White House taping system and what the President might or might not have known about certain matters. We were hearing about a Nixon trip to Key Biscayne in October 1973. Steve Bull (the White House person in charge of access to the tapes) and Rose Mary Woods had accompanied the President, and we were told that some tapes were delivered by Bull to the President.

Suddenly, Seiberling said, "Mr. Doar, do we have any explanation by Bull as to why the odd hours?"

There was a quick exchange as to the actual testimony and soon it became clear that Bull had delivered tapes to the President, in his villa, at two o'clock in the morning.

Now that impressed me. Why was Nixon, who had so often professed his lack of interest in having anything to do with Watergate, asking for tapes to review at two A.M.?

A few minutes later, after Jerry Waldie had chased down and confirmed the two o'clock tape delivery that Seiberling had caught, we came across another matter that bothered me even more. Doar was reading from an Elliot Richardson affidavit, in

155

which Richardson recalled a conversation with the President shortly after the plea arrangements had been worked out in the Agnew case. Richardson testified that as they were walking toward the door, at the end of their meeting, the President said, in substance, "Now that we have disposed of that matter, now we can go ahead and get rid of Cox."

That burned me. Maybe I was losing whatever objectivity I thought I'd developed, but it sounded like the *real* Richard Nixon, and it struck me as very cold, and very hard.

The growing frustration of the members was evident the next day, both in the hearing room and at a Democratic caucus that evening. I was standing next to Barbara Jordan, just before the hearing began, when David Dennis walked in the door. "Well," Barbara said quietly, "we can tack on another ten minutes." Jack Brooks nodded his agreement.

Caldwell Butler walked up and joined the small group of us who were speculating as to the source of the leaks from the committee. Hungate said, "If you ask me, I think the Butler did it." Caldwell groaned and shook his head.

Late in the hearing, James Oliphant, one of the inquiry staff counsel, was demonstrating the Uher 5000 tape machine in order to explain to the committee why the Stanford Research Group had concluded that the 18 ½-minute gap could not have been an accident. It took him quite a while to get both the necessary buttons down in order to simulate erasing, and when he finally made it, the committee gave him a round of applause. He went on for a long time, answering questions as to what could and could not have happened, and then Rodino said that we would spend only ten more minutes on the tape-gap issue.

Seiberling cut in with a quick question: "I just wondered if among the alternatives, the panel considered a sinister force?"

Rodino, smiling, told Oliphant that he didn't have to answer that one, but Oliphant replied, deadpan, "I am sure they did."

The question of the White House tapes came up again that evening at the caucus. Rodino had been talking about releasing some of the material that had been presented to the committee, so that when it came time for St. Clair to make his defense that would not be the only information available to the public.

I suggested that we release the actual sound tracks, the tapes themselves, so that the public could hear what Nixon and his lieutenants really sounded like—which was a much more impressive experience than simply reading the transcripts. Holtzman agreed and went one step further by suggesting that we not delete some of the "sensitive matters," like the racial and religious slurs that were on some of the tapes but not included in the transcripts (which, thanks to the mysterious leakers, the public had already heard about).

Rodino quickly disagreed, stating that this would surely lose us the moderate Republicans on the committee. Rangel said maybe we could use that as a bargaining lever, but Barbara Jordan, speaking very seriously, said, "That would be a mistake, and we would live to regret it."

I thought Jordan was right. We had to proceed with great caution and certainly with "clean hands." A bill of impeachment would have a tremendous impact on the nation and we should not be accused of having used thumbscrew politics to get it out.

The discussion shifted to the question of an impeachment timetable. Earlier in the day, I had been talking to Tip O'Neill, and he told me that Rodino had mentioned to him that we had to get impeachment to the floor by August 15 so that it could be in the Senate by September 1. I thought that was too long.

Apparently, John Seiberling felt the same way because in the caucus he said, "If it's not in the Senate by August 1, then it's all an academic exercise."

The point was that the closer we got to the fall elections, the less likely it would be that the process would be concluded. Few Republicans were going to want to vote for impeachment just before the election. And many politicians of both parties would prefer to postpone a decision on such a volatile issue until after the voters had spoken.

Someone raised the possibility of working nights and weekends, and Brooks cracked, "Okay, we'll be good little boys and girls, but not Sundays. My wife locks me in the house on Sundays." A few minutes later, though, Jack was serious. For months, he'd been complaining that Doar was not "aggressive" enough, that he didn't have enough "political savvy." Brooks put it bluntly: "I can't ask John Doar how to screw Republicans."

157

This discussion, which was taking place off to one side of the room during a break, attracted Jerry Waldie, who agreed with Brooks that Doar was not "enough of an advocate" and that he was too low-key. Wayne Owens disagreed, saying he felt Doar *was* an advocate, but "in his own way." My mind was not entirely made up, but I tended to agree with Owens.

John Doar spoke in his own defense, pointing out that the committee needed, in his opinion, a "firm foundation of fact, so that we'll have a solid basis with which people cannot argue." He went on to point out—for the first time— that his staff was already busy preparing drafts of four alternate articles of impeachment.

This raised heads all around the room. Doar said that the four areas would include: a broad-based Watergate article, one on abuse of power, one on taxes (and I thought he smiled in my direction), and another on the President's refusal to answer or comply with our subpoenas.

There were some low whistles, and a few members clapped quietly. We'd come a long way from those first halting days in the autumn of 1973 and there was a certain relief in knowing that the committee would soon complete its historic task. With articles being drafted, the time would soon come for each of us to judge whether the evidence called for the impeachment of the President.

That night, just before dozing off, I listened to the late news. According to the commentator, Nixon had just left for Key Biscayne and would go to Russia from there. Following his return from the Middle East, he had spent all of one day in Washington. Perhaps it had something to do with the climate.

ELEVEN: But No One Ever Said, "This Is My Country"

The Fourth of July celebration in Muscatine, Iowa, was a welcome return to old-fashioned politics. Elections of all sorts and sizes were coming up—mayoral, gubernatorial, state, and congressional—so the early morning parade saw a large number of office-holders and office-seekers swelling its ranks, in and out of convertibles, waving banners and grabbing any loose hand to shake.

Later that day in Mount Pleasant, we had Governor Robert Ray, Senator Dick Clark, Congressman John Culver (who was running for the Senate seat that was being vacated by Harold Hughes so that he could pursue his religious work), and so many others that we all walked instead of riding. I looked around at the crowd and almost laughed out loud—there appeared to be more people *in* the parade than watching it! Of course the rain, which had pounded down overnight but let up during the day, hadn't helped, but the ratio of crowd to candidate was hardly inspiring. Someone later told me that there were forty-one different celebrations that day throughout Iowa, and that although there were only two hundred people on hand to watch the candidates in Mount Pleasant, the small city was visited by all the major candidates.

159

That night, after having visited six different cities, I watched the late news and witnessed the media event (which had apparently been timed to make the prime-time news shows) of the President's landing in Maine on his return from Moscow. How interesting, I thought, that Nixon should just happen to land in the middle of Bill Cohen's congressional district, at a time when Cohen was being talked about as one of the possible Republican swing votes on the impeachment panel. I suppose some people viewed the arrival as symbolic of Richard Nixon's continuing quest for peace in the world. I viewed it as a gross example of impeachment politics.

The next day began with a seven A.M. private airplane flight over Lake Odessa, where a group of people calling themselves Ducks Unlimited were concerned with preserving the natural habitat as a feeding and resting place for ducks and other waterfowl. There were stops in Donnellson, in Columbus Junction for the big parade in honor of its centennial (where I was picked up by an NBC camera crew and followed around for a while), and in Burlington's Autumn Heights, for a discussion of housing and the problems of the elderly, where someone suggested that fishing licenses for older people should be reduced because "We don't catch as many fish." The last stop was Fort Madison, where a town meeting was scheduled for the next morning.

For the most part the problems brought up were local issues— sewers, low-rent housing, landfills, rights of World War I veterans, erosion, the draft, amnesty, civil rights, farmers' problems, trees, wheat, Russia—the whole spectrum with emphasis on the economy.

But when Watergate did come up, which happened almost everywhere without my raising it, I was surprised by the vehemence of many people, especially the older Republicans. One old-line Republican mayor said, heatedly, "We don't want King Richard. If I were in your place I'd kick him out right now!"

At several stops I got questions about the milk money that had been contributed to my 1972 campaign. This was a new, sensitive, and, I thought, sidetracking issue. The committee was investigating Richard Nixon's motives behind a surprise 1971 decision to raise dairy price supports contrary to a USDA decision. Three dairy associations had pledged $2 million to Nixon's reelection effort, and the question was whether this amounted to a bribe.

This was surely a relevant area of inquiry for the committee. The problem was that sixteen members of the Judiciary, myself included, had also received contributions from the same dairy cooperatives. We'd all reported them publicly at the time but in the midst of impeachment there were charges that we should all be investigated, or that we shouldn't pursue the inquiry about Nixon.

A couple of my colleagues, including my neighbor Tom Railsback, had returned the money they had received. And there were calls for me to do the same. This annoyed me. Dairy farmers were my constituents, and they had every right to contribute to my campaign, and I had every right to accept as long as the contributions were publicly reported and had no strings attached. I decided not to give in to political pressure by making what I considered the phony gesture of returning the money. However, realizing the sensitivity of the matter, and the fact that the issue was detracting from the committee's work, I chose not to accept any dairy contributions to my 1974 campaign.

Each time the milk money question arose, my explanation of the critical difference between my situation and Richard Nixon's was usually accepted as a satisfactory answer to the conflict-of-interest accusation. (But I couldn't talk to everyone personally, and there were some people whose minds I could never reach. During one Independence Day parade a man shouted from the curb, "Howdy, Mr. Milky Moosvinsky!")

Flying back to Washington on Sunday night, I was tired from all the traveling and all the talking, but it was a good kind of tiredness. I had run into some people, here and there around the district, who didn't like what the committee was *doing* to "our beleaguered President," but they represented a small minority. Most people, Republicans as well as Democrats, told me that the process had to go on, that the committee had to finish its work. And they would accept the outcome as being in the best interest of the country.

About halfway through the testimony of the witnesses, I began to wonder if it was worthwhile. The Republicans had insisted that—out of fairness to the President—we call witnesses, and we had to call ten, not just the five John Doar's staff considered necessary. But after we had listened to the first five—Alexander Butterfield, Fred LaRue, Paul O'Brien, William Bittman, and John Mitchell—I was at a loss to explain what they were adding to either side's view of the inquiry.

When he had introduced Butterfield, back on July 2, John Doar had said that he would shed light on Haldeman's special relationship with the President, and Jenner had described him as an important witness who could show the line of authority within the Nixon White House. Well, in a sense, he did cover both those areas, but I thought it took a long time to get across the fact that Richard Nixon was not an innocent, nonparticipating bystander in his White House.

I admit that I was impressed by Butterfield's lengthy description of Mr. Nixon's attention to detail ("I know him to be a detail man . . . thanks to his close attention to these kinds of details, the White House staff functioned better") which included his great attention to meals, entertainments, arrangements of state gifts, whether or not there should be a salad (none at "small dinners of eight or less"). This did not sound like a man who would have paid, as he consistently claimed, so little attention to Watergate.

Butterfield also provided an interesting outline of the day-to-day functioning of the White House. He explained the special lighted board that indicated exactly where the President was in the White House; when Nixon left the Oval Office, for example, one of the Secret Service men would phone the switchboard with the destination, and when his arrival was verified the operator would punch the right button and the boards would show where the President was. These were called, he said, locator boxes, and there were four of them: two were wall mounted (in the offices of Steve Bull and Dwight Chapin), and two (those of Butterfield and H. R. Haldeman) were on desks.

Butterfield also testified that in all of his White House years (almost four) he had never seen Haldeman make a decision of any substance that wasn't cleared with the President first. He was not, as Butterfield phrased it, "a decision-maker," rather he was "essentially an implementer."

162

Still, Butterfield did not add anything new as far as *hard* evidence was concerned. Nor did Paul O'Brien or Fred LaRue, who began testifying on the 3rd and finished on the 8th.

The caucus held by the Democrats on the night of July 2 was the first of several "briefing sessions," in which—it was profoundly hoped—we would see some sense made of all we had been hearing for the last three months.

Because various segments of the inquiry staff had been specializing in particular areas, Rodino decided to have them summarize the weight of the evidence thus far so that we could look at the strength or weakness of the case in regard to the major allegations against the President. We were to have a briefing each night, a half hour after the regular session of the committee, which would cover such topics as Watergate, ITT, milk money, Cambodia bombing, impoundments, and personal finances.

Originally, it was to be for only the Democrats, but when Rodino learned that some Republicans were interested in attending, he opened them up to anyone on the committee. Pete Rodino was not going to be accused of partisanship.

We began at eight-thirty on July 2, with only a handful of Democrats, but Dick Cates, one of the four senior associate special counsels, and Evan Davis, who headed the staff's Watergate task force, had not been speaking long when numerous other members began to file in. The point of the discussion was, simply, to examine the possible intentions and purposes of the President in the various actions that he had taken. They began with John Mitchell's statement, on June 20, 1972, that the break-in was not connected to the Committee to Re-Elect the President, which long ago was proven to be a lie. That began the cover-up.

Cates and Davis also explained that we were within our rights to draw negative inferences from the fact that necessary evidence had been destroyed or refused to the committee. Slowly, step by step, they built a pattern of activities that made sense only if a cover-up were involved. And it all pointed to the President. This was the Watergate phase of the inquiry, and it was impressive to hear, after all this time, how the various acts and omissions fit together. The staff was building a strong case.

Another point that Cates and Davis brought out was that

163

when Nixon named Ehrlichman to investigate the Watergate affair, he must have known that John Ehrlichman was by no means an investigator. That too pointed toward cover-up. Then they moved to the question of "hush money." Listening to the facts as they were ticked off, so calmly and carefully, it was clear that the White House must have been worried about a domino effect: If Liddy and Hunt went to jail, then it could be Mitchell and Magruder next, followed by Gordon Strachan, and on down the line. But would it stop at the bottom rung, or would it start going up again, and up and up, all the way to the top?

When we broke off at ten-fifteen, I was more sure than ever that Richard Nixon didn't *dare* turn over all the material the committee had requested—because within that material was the missing evidence of his participation in the cover-up. I couldn't draw any other conclusion.

The remaining witnesses served only to buttress the opinion, held by many members, that we never should have called witnesses in the first place.

Not that there weren't moments of quiet drama. On July 10 I watched John Mitchell walk down the hall of the Rayburn Building after his appearance. Walking with his lawyers, he simply ignored the press. To me it was a terrible shame to see him, a former Attorney General of the United States, now under indictment and awaiting trial in the cover-up case, walking silently down halls where he had once been greeted with high praise and admiration.

But Mitchell had not lost all of his former bravado. On the evening he was to resume his testimony, I was sitting in the hearing room with a few other members when Mitchell walked in a bit early. He looked around, smiled that thin-lipped smile, and said, "I guess I'm not playing to a full house."

Mitchell's testimony was sharply limited by the requests of his counsel, who explained that he could not afford to subject himself to questions that would soon be matters for a jury or a judge to hear. And H. R. Haldeman never even made it to the witness table; his lawyers told us that he would have to take the Fifth, so Rodino said, in effect, why bother?

Petersen, Dean, Colson—the appearance of each one was ultimately anticlimactic. As Hungate cracked, "They didn't live up to their advance billing."

On the electronic trolleycar during the short ride to the House chamber, I sat next to Drinan, who said, "Mitchell is stone-walling it." Others felt much the same way, and there had been a brief argument between Democrats Walter Flowers and John Seiberling. Flowers asked John, "Why do you bother to object? It only gets the Republicans going, and thinking they have to object to counter you. This testimony isn't worth all the bother and the time it's taking." Another Democrat said, "You know, I like Harold Donohue. He knows when to turn his hearing aid off."

The staff memo laying out Mitchell's proposed testimony had indicated that he could shed light on the question of whether Nixon approved the payment of hush money, but it turned out that we were not going to hear anything, on important points, other than the fact that the witness "couldn't recall."

Realizing this, most Democrats either did not question him or did so quickly. Drinan came on very strong, however, and used up all his time before he'd exhausted his questions. He tried to continue, but Waldie and Flowers yelled out, "Your five minutes are up!"

Drinan put his hand over the mike and whispered, "I need more time." I looked over at Bob McClory, who had had the same problem often in the last few weeks, and he was smiling. (McClory had gone so far as to buy a watch with an alarm, and once when Rodino interrupted to say that his time was up, the watch began buzzing at that exact moment.)

I did not have many questions for Mitchell, but I got so involved in trying to get from him why he wouldn't tell the President what he knew about the break-in and cover-up when he knew it early on that I tripped all over my words, and my question made little sense. Del Latta, of all people, kindly let me have a part of his time, but the second phrasing wasn't much of an improvement. Mitchell smiled and told me that my question was a "non-sequitur," and that was the end of my turn. I had a lot to learn about the subtle art of examining a witness.

After Mitchell finished, and he had testified on both the 9th and the 10th, Latta said, "Mitchell didn't tell us anything, but when John Dean comes on he'll tell us more than he knows."

165

Dean was scheduled to begin his testimony on the morning of the 11th, but on the night of the 10th we had a Democratic caucus. It turned out to be an important one.

Rodino began by dividing the committee Democrats into "task forces," to marshal the arguments in specific areas that would most likely lead to proposed articles of impeachment. Rodino was trying to set the stage for the formal debate. It was clear to most of us, if only in just the last few days, that John Doar was going to "come out of the closet" by shedding his cloak of rigid impartiality and taking on an advocate's role, pressing for the impeachment of Richard Nixon.

Harold Donohue, too often the butt of jokes among the younger members, asked *the* pertinent question: "Is Jenner going to go along with Doar?"

Rodino said, almost loudly, "Yes." There were looks of relief and satisfaction all around the room.

Walter Flowers said, "I think there are areas where articles of impeachment don't lie, and I think we need staff on 'the other side,' because we need bipartisan support."

I agreed with Walter. We had never been a lynch mob, and we didn't want to appear to be one at the last moment. Then Jim Mann spoke up, quietly, and said, "I think what we need is to have informal discussions with some of the Republican members."

In the next fifteen minutes it was agreed that Mann, Flowers, and Ray Thornton would approach four key Republicans: Railsback, Fish, Cohen, and Butler. It would be a critical step in trying to form a bridge across party lines, and before we broke up for the night someone had already dubbed them "the swing seven."

I left the meeting that night with a strange feeling. For the first time in over three months we seemed to be on the doorstep of the formal debate. We had heard all the evidence, most of the witnesses, and some of St. Clair's defense. Now, it all seemed to hinge on the Republicans. Would they vote as a bloc, to protect the leader of their party? Or would they vote their individual consciences? And what about the Democrats? Were we a solid bloc, and if so, was it because of politics or conscience? We would be finding out soon, and it left me exhilarated and scared.

*   *   *

Amid a blaze of flashbulbs and followed by a gang of reporters, John Dean arrived in Room 2141 on the morning of July 11. Dean, as always, was carefully dressed, this time in a brown suit, blue shirt, and green tie, the familiar collar pin completing the neat picture. I could never understand why John Dean had become almost a hero to some of my progressive friends. Certainly he had attempted, almost by himself, to expose the cover-up, but his chief motive had always appeared to me to be that of saving his own hide.

Dean and his lawyer smiled and shook hands with several people, and someone remarked that John Dean had once been a counsel to the minority of this very committee. This prompted several members to whisper that he should never have left. Dean began his testimony in a firm but quiet voice, and as the story began to unfold in answer to Doar's questioning, I felt a grudging admiration for Dean. There was no whining or self-serving note of apology. When he had to go over some of his own misdeeds, he did so in a direct and forthright manner, almost as if he were talking about someone else.

Now I could see, firsthand, why he had made such an impact on television before the Senate Watergate Committee. His testimony was a remarkable display of memory. And because of this, the many damaging statements and inferences made Richard Nixon look even worse.

Late in the afternoon Dean's lawyer asked if we could take a break. Rodino quickly agreed, and as he walked past my end of the dais, Dean said, in a stage whisper, "Sorry. Nature calls." I smiled. We had been interrupted many times for vote calls and quorum calls, but this was the first time we had been interrupted for a nature call. (After that, Rodino said he would make it a practice to break more frequently. Jenner had told him that it was customary, during a trial, not to require anyone to testify for more than an hour and a quarter at one shot.)

Later in the day Dean had an interesting exchange with Wiley Mayne, my Republican colleague from Iowa, who asked, "Mr. Dean, at the risk of being indelicate, did I correctly understand you on at least two occasions during your testimony to say that you were pregnant?"

167

"I used that phrase."

Mayne, as if in disbelief, spelled it out, "P-r-e-g-n-a-n-t?"

And Dean replied, "I was pregnant with the cover-up, as I think I started testifying, and where the phrase first came from, I said I was a reluctant lady at first and soon I was pregnant. That is what I was referring to by the time I destroyed the Hermes notebooks."

A few minutes later, that same theme was picked up and expanded on by Caldwell Butler, another Republican: "My next question has reference to this unique biological phenomenon to which Mr. Mayne has referred. I take it from your use of this word that having found yourself a fallen man, your personal standards became somewhat demanding?"

"I think that is true, yes."

"My real question is this: At what point in time in your best medical opinion can you say that conception took place?"

Dean smiled, but it wasn't a particularly happy smile. "I would have trouble speaking in that vernacular. In retrospect, let's say that if I had stayed in Manila, I might not have been raped." (Dean had returned from a Far East trip on June 18, 1972, the day after the Watergate break-in.)

Caldwell nodded his head slowly. "Well, that is a pretty good response. Would you judge that, because as soon as you got back from Manila or shortly thereafter, you became involved in what amounted to a cover-up?"

"Yes, I did."

"Is it your feeling," Butler asked, "that this was the first instance in which, using the vocabulary which you have selected, would you say that conception took place at about that time, or were there some events prior to that that you personally wanted to cover up about yourself?"

Dean answered immediately, "No, sir, I would say that is when it happened, when I came back. I would say after I talked to Magruder and Strachan and Liddy, I was in."

I pushed back from the table, folded my arms, and thought for a moment as Dean went on with his answers. John Dean was not telling us anything that he hadn't put on the record before, but it was strange, after all the days and weeks and months of listening to the evidence, to suddenly hear one of the principal players speak so baldly about his role in the cover-up. I turned and looked down at the Republicans. They were a somber bunch.

That evening, at the briefing, Bernie Nussbaum and Smith McKeithen handled the personal finances and tax issues, and they did an impressive job of laying everything out. Paul Sarbanes mentioned to me how highly he thought of Nussbaum (who was taking a strong advocacy position) and expressed hope that he would be able to brief us on some of the other areas. I was glad to hear that, not just because Bernie was a friend, but because I knew that Paul, like Jack Brooks and a few other committee members, was concerned about working up his own set of draft articles of impeachment.

I noticed that Wiggins of California had sent a staff person in his place. Later Don Edwards showed up to say that he had attended the briefing on ITT. "And guess who was there? Dennis and McClory. And everything went very well. I think we just might be beginning to change some Republican minds."

He could have been right. I'd heard Tom Railsback described on the late news last night as a possible pro-impeachment vote; and when Rangel and Latta appeared on the *Today* show this morning, the host was visibly disappointed that they seemed to be in agreement. (Apparently he'd hoped for a strong partisan clash to excite his viewers over their morning coffee.)

When I saw Rangel later in the day, I kidded him about getting along so well, on television, with Del Latta. Charley said, "Yeah, I better be careful or the people back home are going to think I've gone bad."

Henry Petersen, the head of the Criminal Division of the Department of Justice, testified on the morning of July 12, and among other things told of his attempt to warn the President about the possibly illegal conduct of Haldeman and Ehrlichman. I found it interesting when he said, referring to Nixon's response to that warning, ". . . he didn't think that they were involved, that he thought they were fine people, and that they certainly considered themselves to be innocent of any wrongdoing. But he said that people usually do consider themselves innocent."

Then Petersen went on to describe his own reaction: "I guess I

169

must confess that I was a little exasperated perhaps considering the man's station, perhaps even a little bit rude in consideration of the calm with which he accepted what I thought was shattering information. I made it quite clear that I thought that they ought to leave and that, however clearly I expressed myself of that I can't be certain, but certainly that this was, in effect, at least in my judgment, the last chance for the Administration to demonstrate its integrity by removing those who might be involved in illegal activity."

At the briefing that night Paul Sarbanes came up and kidded me about how tired I looked. Then he said he had left his office at four in the morning, one day recently, "And I looked up and saw that the lights were still on in Wiggins's office—so I turned around and went back to mine." It reminded me of the oft-told story about how Bobby Kennedy, when he was after Jimmy Hoffa, would go past the Teamsters' Building late at night and if the lights were still on, he would go back and work some more too.

I tried to sleep late on Saturday, the 13th, but the weeks of early rising had become habitual, and I woke fairly early. I wished I had the time to get some exercise. Just several days ago, when I pulled into my parking space in the Rayburn garage, I felt pangs of envy when I saw Bob Kastenmeier getting out of his car in tennis shorts—but this morning there was something I had to do.

I ate a quick breakfast of fruit and juice, and drove down to the old Congressional Hotel to the offices of the inquiry staff to talk to a few of the people about taxes and other related matters. I figured Saturday would be a good day. I knew they'd be working. With things getting down to the wire, it seemed that everyone connected with the committee was *always* working.

John Doar was on the phone as I walked in. He looked terrible. I knew he'd had a cold but I'd thought he'd shaken it. Evidently he had not. There were several small envelopes, containing various pills, on the top of his desk, and a large glass of water. It looked like a television commercial for a cold remedy.

We began a candid discussion of the chances of getting the members to approve an impeachment article based on Nixon's

170

taxes, and Doar remarked that Ray Thornton "did not buy the tax article. He thinks there are other ways of getting to impeachment besides the tax question." I would have to talk with Ray, because his quiet but effective counsel would be most helpful if I could convince him that we had the evidence to impeach on taxes.

I told Doar that I wanted to work specifically on the tax article, and he looked at me as if to say I needn't have reminded him of that.

"Look, Ed, if it were your taxes or mine, with these same facts, we'd be indicted, but this inquiry is a peaks and valleys thing, and we can't always be on a peak. I think the last week has been very good for us. In particular, I think the release of the material helped a lot. Now the people can get some idea of how thorough we have been."

On July 11, the committee had released the edited (to protect certain individuals who would have been hurt by a total release of everything we had heard) version of eight books of evidence. Even though Walter Cronkite said, only a few hours after the thousands of pages of material had been made public, that it did not contain conclusive proof of the impeachment allegations, it was a good step, and one that Rodino had weighed carefully.

In one of the first briefing sessions there had been a discussion as to "politics," with one member saying that he thought the question of impeachment would turn on the political axis, and Rodino had heatedly disagreed. He had said, "Whether or not we vote to impeach will turn on the truth—and we better all realize that the people are way ahead of us on this thing. Which is why it's so damned important that we get those books out now!"

Doar and I talked, generally, about how the committee might handle the IRS and tax material. It was a continuing question as to whether certain material, once it had been presented, should be released immediately or should await the final report of the committee. But the full House would need the evidence before it could properly consider the final vote, so there was a good argument for early release. But we had to be careful that we weren't accused of playing politics.

Before I left, Bernie Nussbaum came in to Doar's office to bor-

171

row one of his cold tablets. He too was sneezing and blowing his nose. He was on his way back to his office to reinterview Chuck Colson, who was slated to testify on Monday.

On my way out the door I turned back and said, "Now you two guys get some rest. We're going to have a tough week next week, and we'll never get through it without you."

They grinned, tiredly. On the way home I stopped and bought some aspirin, some twenty-four-hour cold capsules, and some throat lozenges. Be prepared.

One thing you had to say about Chuck Colson was that he definitely had chutzpah. When he appeared before the committee, at 10:25 on Monday morning, July 15, he was wearing a dark blue pinstripe suit, blue shirt, dark tie—and a Nixon tie-clasp!

After all the concern on the part of the staff, who felt that Colson was less than candid in their interviews with him, plus the worry of many members on both sides of the aisle, Colson's testimony was a letdown. I had had a meeting with Harold Hughes, in his office in the Senate, to discuss whether we could rely on what Colson said. Hughes told me that he felt Colson's much-maligned religious conversion was genuine, and that *if* Colson decided to level with us, we could believe what he said.

The scope of his testimony, as outlined by the staff, indicated that he could provide information on a variety of dirty tricks during the campaign and also the work of Hunt and McCord. But under Doar's slow and careful questioning (and it was apparent that Doar had not yet shed his role of strict neutrality) the witness didn't seem to be telling much, if anything, that we didn't already know.

The complaints came quickly during the break, as did the humor. Caldwell Butler said to Drinan, "If he really did have a religious conversion, you ought to be able to give us expert testimony on that." Drinan shook his head. "I'd have to check his contributions first." Jack Brooks, as usual, was disappointed with the slow pace and the lack of new information: "What more does he have to tell us?" he asked Doar, and added, "Let's get it over with and send him back to the pokey!"

I don't know if it was intentional, but Colson got quite a laugh himself, while testifying about a meeting attended by Ehrlichman

172

and David Shapiro, Colson's law partner who was helping Colson prepare advice to the President on breaking open the Watergate case. Apparently Shapiro has a wry sense of humor, which was not particularly appreciated at the time by John Ehrlichman. Colson told the committee, "Mr. Ehrlichman took extensive notes throughout the meeting, which notes he produced at the Senate Select Committee hearings [the Ervin Watergate hearings] and which were printed much to Mr. Shapiro's distress, in the record of the hearing of the Ervin committee, because the final concluding line was that Mr. Shapiro volunteered to defend John Mitchell because he thought he had a brilliant defense of insanity and he thought whoever had ordered the Watergate had been insane."

After the laughter died down, Colson added, "This caused a brief distress between Mr. Shapiro and his colleagues at this time." I'm sure it did.

A few minutes later, Colson showed why he had always been considered one of Nixon's strongest supporters. "I also remember being furious when I first learned . . . that John Dean had gone to the prosecutors seeking immunity, because I thought that his first duty as the President's counsel was to try to help the President get out in front of Watergate and not go to the prosecutors and seek to, in effect, save his own neck and put the President in a difficult position. I felt that anyone as counsel to the President had his first duty to the President. It infuriated me."

During the lunch break the Democrats held a caucus in which Rodino and Doar laid out the areas that the members would be responsible for, named the members at least tentatively, and told us in general the day-by-day plans right up to the opening of the formal debate, which they thought might be on the 23rd.

A bit later, Sam Garrison, the Republicans' assistant counsel on the committee, came up to John Doar and asked him if his brief (which we all knew he was already preparing) would be "an advocate's brief."

Or, asked Garrison, who, it was said, was himself busy preparing an anti-impeachment brief for the minority, "Will it just be a neutral brief?"

The question seemed to miff Doar, and he snapped back, "It'll be a *facts* brief."

Later someone told Doar, "Hey, John, we ought to get Garrison to come up and talk to you every fifteen minutes. Then we can keep you mad."

When Colson finished his testimony, he stopped on his way out of the hearing room to shake my hand. He said, "Harold Hughes told me he's going to come and visit me."

I thought about Colson after he'd left. He really was an enigma. He appeared eager to testify, and in fact both he and his lawyer praised the committee at the end of the testimony, and he complimented Barbara Jordan for asking "tough questions." Yet I could understand why the staff had been concerned about him. It was hard to decide if he was telling the truth, or if he was simply doing what he'd accused Dean of doing—trying to save his own neck. I thought Colson had been a big question mark who really hadn't added a whole lot.

Hughes told me that Chuck Colson was "a babe in Christ," but after listening to him testify, I couldn't shake the doubts I had about the validity of that religious conversion. Colson told us that he still thought Richard Nixon was a great man and that he still believed in him. Well, I knew that Christians are taught to be compassionate, but Colson didn't believe the President had ever done anything wrong.

Herbert Kalmbach, once Nixon's personal lawyer and supposedly knowledgeable about various financial, tax, and campaign fund deals, took the stand after Colson. I had never seen Kalmbach, but after looking at him and listening to him for a few minutes, I began to feel sorry for him. Here was a man, fifty-two years old, conservatively dressed, thin, who had been a successful and highly respected Republican lawyer, husband, and family man. Now he was marked with the stain of Watergate, and it set me to thinking how many people's careers had been hurt because they'd been associated with Richard Nixon. And yet Nixon appeared to be, in Barbara Jordan's phrase, "the most secure man in the country." Sure, we were in a sense after him, but his stonewalling tactics had been successful for a long time—and there was no clear sign that we were gaining on him. (At dinner that same night, Paul Sarbanes and I were talking about the slim chances of finding what the press referred to as "the smoking gun," an irrefutable piece of evidence showing Nixon's complicity in the cover-up. Paul said, "You know, I've been having this dream, and in it, all the Democrats are running out of a room, shouting, 'We found it! We found it!' ")

Kalmbach testified that the most important thing to him had been his reputation, and it made me wish that Nixon and some of those around him had felt the same way. There is a world of difference between "reputation" and "image."

Kalmbach continued his testimony the next day and recounted the tales of money being collected in cash, and his being told to "get cash whenever possible." The whole campaign collection business was increasingly questionable and clandestine.

Kalmbach told us how he was contacted by then Congressman Louis Wyman of New Hampshire and told to get in touch with a Dr. Ruth Farkas, a wealthy woman who was interested in an ambassadorial post—and who had money to contribute to the re-election fund. In fact, the figure of $250,000 was specifically mentioned.

Kalmbach testified that he had met her for lunch and they had a very pleasant time except for one thing: Kalmbach was talking about her being named ambassador to Costa Rica, while Dr. Farkas had someplace else in mind. "So," the witness said, "when I started talking to her about being helpful to the President's 1972 campaign, she said words to the following effect: She said you know, well, I am interested in Europe, I think, and isn't $250,000 an awful lot of money for Costa Rica? I at that point thought I would just have a general conversation with her, because it was evident to me that she wasn't all that interested in Costa Rica and was more interested in Europe. I told her that I would support her candidacy for an ambassadorial appointment, act as a reference. She was very pleasant. We had a pleasant lunch. I said goodbye to her and I have not seen her or talked to her, as I remember, from and after that date."

"Was she ever appointed an ambassador?" Jenner asked.

"Yes, sir, she was."

"To what country?"

"Luxembourg."

The whole thing was so crass. It was buying and selling ambassadorships, plain and simple, and the White House denials couldn't change the ugly fact.

*   *   *

175

I went back to the office during one of the breaks in Kalmbach's testimony to catch up on the mail, but I was soon sorry I
had bothered. One of the staff members had left a pile of hate
mail on my desk, with a note saying I shouldn't bother reading
"this sick trash," but I felt I had to glance through it.

The first letter was dated July 3, and simply addressed "Mezvinsky." In a very neat hand, it said:

> Anyone with a name like this isn't fit to be in the U.S. Congress!
>
> For God's sake, fool, keep off television—the people know you are
> not a gentleman. You are small—dishonest!
>   A LIAR
> You are nothing but a cheating, lying foreigner like Rodino, and
> we Americans can't stand the sight of seeing you on our TV!
>
> $11,000 in one bribe alone you took. You belong in jail "Vinsky."
> You belong in an Out House—you stink!

It was signed "American People." It was too bad the letter was
anonymous, as I would have liked to respond by thanking the
person for linking me with Pete Rodino.

There was another unsigned letter, dated July 9, that simply
said:

> JEWS
> CHRIST KILLERS
>
> JEWS 1974
> NIXON KILLERS

One correspondent addressed me as "Dear Political Pimp,"
and warmed up from there, saying that I was a "G. damn whor,
don't have enough evidence to convict Nixon of a parking ticket." The letter writer, a man from Clearwater, Florida, closed by
telling me to "drop dead," but at least he signed his name.
Another Floridian, this one from Seminole, wrote, "My wife is
worried about getting our lawn mowed in the future and wants
me to write to you as she believes you will have some time to

spare." How can you dislike a man who writes letters for his wife?

The rest were of the truly ugly sort, the kind that make you feel sorry for people whose minds are so twisted that they pour out hate as a natural expression. I pushed the pile away.

There was another letter, of a quite different sort, and though I had read it many times in the last several months, I had purposely avoided doing anything about it. It had to do with the divorce proceedings. Under Iowa law, before a divorce can become final, there is a mechanism for conciliation. However, if the couple is convinced that there is no advantage to be gained in seeking the help of a marriage counselor, or "conciliator," the conciliation requirement can be waived. Sitting in front of me on my desk was a form, awaiting my signature, for that very purpose.

I'd had the form for weeks, but I could not—or would not—bring myself to sign it. For a long time I had fought all attempts to change the legal status from that of a separation, but on June 17—the second anniversary of the Watergate break-in!—Micky's new lawyer had sent me this form. If I signed it, divorce would be certain.

I almost hated that piece of paper. The language was so cold and final. One clause in particular grated; it read, ". . . your petitioner [Micky] states that there has been a breakdown of the marrige relationship to the extent that the legitimate object of matrimony has been destroyed and there remains no reasonable likelihood that the marriage can be preserved."

As a lawyer, I was familiar with that legal language, but it seemed particularly cutting and callous now. This was *my* marriage, *our* marriage being described in those terms. Perhaps I was being unrealistic, but I still thought of myself as a father and husband. On the one hand, I admitted that it looked improbable that Micky and I could ever again live together harmoniously. But on the other hand, I still wanted to try. Maybe I just wanted to try for *my* sake. I didn't know.

I put the paper back in the desk drawer and left the office.

"Let me tell you a story that really reflects the Republicans' dilemma."

177

I was walking back to the House with Hamilton Fish, a third-term Republican from New York and a fellow Judiciary Committee member whom I respected. It was July 18, and St. Clair had just concluded his defense of the President.

"I have a fourteen-year-old son," Ham said, "and we were discussing impeachment. My son said, 'Dad, you've got to vote for impeachment.' So I told him what the adverse political results of such a vote might well be, and he looked at me and said, 'Vote against it.' Then I went on to explain the important constitutional issues that were involved, and the importance of upholding the system, and can you guess what he said to that?"

"No, what?"

"He said, 'I think you better abstain'!"

That morning the final portion of St. Clair's long-awaited defense of Richard Nixon had taken about two hours. Anyone who had expected a show—say, a combination of Clarence Darrow and Billy Graham—would have been disappointed. St. Clair was low-key and methodical, speaking quietly and slowly. His opening remarks were somber:

> I think I would be less than candid if I didn't indicate to you the enormity of the responsibility that I feel in regard to this matter, representing as I do the President of the United States in a proceeding that, fortunately, is reasonably unique in our history. Frankly, the enormity of this responsibility sometimes seems to be, to me at least, somewhat overwhelming. I doubt very much if I can adequately, in the time that I contemplate using, or in fact in any time, fully acquit my responsibility in such a tremendously important proceeding. I hope you will bear with me. My only consolation is that I think that the enormity of this responsibility is even greater on your shoulders. After all, when I am through, I can get up and I can walk out that door. But you are going to have to sit here and you are going to have to make some very important decisions. And you are going to have to be counted with respect to those decisions and they are not easy. And they are not solely legal decisions. They are as much political as they are legal.
>
> So when I say I feel an overwhelming responsibility, I can only say, well, at least I can walk out that door and I think that you have even a greater responsibility and as we have been here in the last 9 or 10 weeks, I have seen nothing to indicate to me that you are not well aware of precisely what I am talking about.

178

* * *

Was it a good tactic to raise the red flag of "politics" so early in the presentation? I wasn't sure. It seemed to me that certain Republicans, especially those who were being classified in the press as "undecideds," might resent that remark as much as certain Democrats.

When he finished, it seemed to me that all he had really accomplished was to point out the obvious fact that a great deal of our evidence was circumstantial, that we had not found—although he didn't come right out and use the term—the smoking gun. Back in the cloakroom, waiting for a vote on the floor, several Democrats on the committee said they weren't impressed with St. Clair's performance or the strength of his defense. One said he thought St. Clair had made a weak presentation. I didn't agree; I thought he had done a good job with a weak case.

It was hard to guess how various members had reacted. Sarbanes told me that Walter Flowers had been impressed with St. Clair's presentation. That worried me a little, as the Southern Democrats, like Flowers, were vital to the key impeachment votes.

St. Clair had done one thing that I thought hurt his case, though I had to admit I couldn't say if it was his choice or that of his client.

Several months back, the committee had asked the White House for copies of John Ehrlichman's handwritten notes of certain conversations between the President, Ehrlichman, and other Nixon aides. As it turned out, those notes were of great interest to the Special Prosecutor's office, and they already had them. In attempting to respond to our request, someone at the White House had called the Special Prosecutor's office and asked for their copy. They were given a copy, but through a misunderstanding, we were sent a Xerox copy of the same notes by the Special Prosecutor's office. Apparently, no one on St. Clair's staff knew we already had the notes.

As John Doar told the committee, just before St. Clair began, ". . . there are about twice as many blank pages in the material that was sent by Mr. St. Clair to the committee as there were in the material that was over in the Special Prosecutor's office. . . . Now, our preliminary examinations of these two sets of materials indicate that there was blanked out of the material

179

furnished to the Judiciary Committee a considerable amount of material with respect to President Nixon's discussions with John Ehrlichman on the subject of the Ellsberg prosecution. There were also a number of other things eliminated."

I was surprised, a bit later, when Republican Del Latta voiced a strong objection to the fact that we had received less material than had the Special Prosecutor's office. I began to wonder if Latta might conceivably vote for impeachment. This issue of the lack of cooperation on the part of the White House was bothering a lot of members, regardless of party.

When he got to the question of Nixon's income taxes, St. Clair said that the President had had "a more searching audit than any person ever had." He went on to say that the President, because of his office, could not be guilty of fraud, but that the people who prepared the returns might be. There it was again. All the mistakes, whether we were talking about Watergate or taxes, were made *for* Nixon, but were not actually his fault.

After St. Clair finished, the reactions came quickly. Bill Dixon of the committee staff said, "I didn't realize how strong a case we had until I heard St. Clair."

Barbara Jordan was particularly annoyed at St. Clair's attempt to give us edited, rather than full, versions of notes and transcripts and said, "His actions indicate not just contempt for the committee, but contempt for the whole Congress!"

I told Barbara that I thought his performance today epitomized his whole approach to the question of impeachment. At the end of his presentation, St. Clair had repeated his statement that he was free to "walk out that door." And that is just what he did. I watched him go, watched the door close behind him, and I was struck by both the drama and the truth of what he had said. He could—and did—leave, but we had to stay behind and "do the responsible thing."

John Doar sat quietly, drumming his fingers on the table. At his side was his favorite, oldest briefcase. He was flanked by Bert Jenner plus a convoy of younger lawyers. He was ready to go.

Looking at him, seeing that comfortable, rumpled presence waiting so casually, made *me* nervous. For months, I had waited to see when and if the fire would flash out, to see if the man would take a hard position. One way or the other.

A few minutes were given to procedural matters, but Doar was barely started when it became clear that he had not just taken a stand, he had taken a strong stand.

". . . As an individual, I have not the slightest bias against President Nixon. I would hope that I would not do him the smallest, slightest injury. But I am not indifferent to the matter of presidential abuse of power, by whatever President, nor the identification and proof of that abuse of power, if I believe that it has existed.

"And if, in fact, President Nixon or any President has had a central part in the planning and executing of this terrible deed of subverting the Constitution, then I shall do my part as best I can to bring him to answer before the Congress of the United States for this enormous crime in the conduct of his office."

Room 2141 had become very quiet. This was not the John Doar we were used to.

". . . Now, as I listened to Mr. St. Clair yesterday, and I have listened to him before, I must be candid with you that I have had this one observation. It has occurred to me time and time again that Mr. St. Clair has things upside down. He's had things upside down throughout these entire proceedings."

Del Latta objected that Doar shouldn't be criticizing St. Clair in the latter's absence, but he was soon quieted down, and Doar went on. He had the attention of everyone.

". . . yesterday when I listened to St. Clair's argument and followed its symmetry and logic, I found myself writing in the margin of my notes, as incident after incident flashed back through my mind as to some of the things that Mr. St. Clair dealt with and didn't deal with, I thought to myself, if what Mr. St. Clair says is true, then, why, why, why did that happen? Why did this other incident happen? Some of the instances, and I am just going to touch on a few, seem to me inexplicable in terms of the picture or the portrait. . . ."

For the better part of an hour, John Doar built the case against the President. It was largely circumstantial, as he readily admitted, but not entirely.

"Now, during that same conversation [March 21, 1973] and in a number of other conversations, the President refers several times to the containment, the containment. Containment"—and Doar raised his voice noticeably—"was the plan, containment was the decision. Containment was the decision that was made early on, shortly after the break-in.

"On the 21st of March, he talks about having John Mitchell come down the next day. It's urgent he come down. Why does he want him to come down? He wants him to come down so that they can have a new strategy, not to develop for the first time a strategy, but to have a new strategy. All of that is direct evidence that the President directed and made the decision to cover up back shortly after the break-in.

"Now you move back to the September 15 [1972] conversation, and I won't go into that, but I say to you, anyone reading that as a whole, and taking into consideration what the President knew at that time, can only conclude that that too is direct evidence that the President made the decision to have a plan of containment or cover-up shortly after the break-in.

"You remember that when John Dean comes into the room, he says: 'Well, you have had quite a time, John, you have finally got Watergate on the way.' And he says, John Dean says, 'Quite a three months.'

"In the President's transcript, the quote 'quite a three months' which happens to go right back almost to the 17th of June, it's not there. And then you read the June 30 excerpt of the transcript and you see the discussion between Haldeman and Mitchell and the President. And if that isn't direct evidence of a presidential decision to cover up, then I am badly mistaken."

The room was so still that I forced back a cough. It would have been too loud. I looked out at the committee's and inquiry staff's lawyers who were sitting behind Doar and Jenner. Everyone looked grim. It was history we were listening to and we were all a part of it.

If the forcefulness of Doar's summation was a surprise to some people, they had to be jolted by what happened next. Bert Jenner, the minority counsel, agreed with Doar. And he did so in no uncertain terms.

He was more specific than John had been on the issue of what kind of evidence we needed in order to impeach. Unlike St. Clair, who called for evidence of a crime, Jenner spoke of evidentiary tests of relevancy and what is known, in the Federal Rules of Evidence, as "Habit and Routine Practice," and he told the committee we could apply these standards.

182

Shortly before he finished, he said something that had needed to be said for as long as we had been hearing the evidence:

"May I make one personal reference? I have been here now since January 7. I have been through all of these evidentiary materials, I have read those edited transcripts, I have listened to the tapes. And ladies and gentlemen, I have never heard the President of the United States or any of his aides ever say . . . by any manner of words written or oral—'This is my country.' 'This is the Constitution of the United States.' 'It is my duty to preserve, protect and defend the Constitution, to see that the laws are faithfully executed.' 'The people of the Nation will be affected one way or the other by what I do or fail to do with respect to that which I have been or should have been alerted.'

"I haven't heard or seen any of that. There isn't a word. There isn't a phrase, there isn't an inference to be drawn from which that may be found in the record."

For some reason, I turned and looked up at Peter Rodino. The chairman had tears in his eyes.

Twelve: *Resolution to Impeach*

The sun was unmercifully hot, and the humidity was typical of
Washington in late July. But I refused to move into the shade,
and instead just let it pour on my face and body. It didn't make
much sense, but some of the tiredness seemed to be oozing out
of my pores. I could hear the children splashing and yelling in
the water a few yards away.

I'd come out to the Highlands pool in McLean to be with the
girls, to take over for Micky, but today instead of leaving, she
stayed and sat with me. It was pleasant, Micky was in a great
mood, and I could relax.

"You look beat, Eddie."

"I know. Everybody's beat. Someone said Walter Flowers has
an ulcer. And all last week Railsback and Cohen were sipping
Coke, even during the hearings, to settle their stomachs."

Micky laughed, lightly, "If you were a Republican, you'd probably be drinking Coke too."

"Yeah, or maybe chicken soup."

"So where do things stand?"

"Let's see, what day is it? Wait, I know. Sunday the 21st. Well,
on Thursday, St. Clair finished his defense and Doar and Jenner

184

made their statements, and they both said, in effect, that Nixon should be impeached. God, was it dramatic. Oh, and then Jenner was replaced by the Republicans . . ."

"I read about that this morning."

". . . who thought he was supposed to uphold Nixon, so they replaced him with Sam Garrison. Now Jenner will assist Doar on the impeachment inquiry staff."

"Do you really think any of the Republicans are going to vote for impeachment? I mean, you've all heard the same evidence and everything, right?"

"Yeah." I wiped the sweat off my face. I could feel the pinkness beginning. "I really don't know, right now. McClory made a statement, I think it came out in the *Star*, on the 18th, and he said he was going to vote his conscience. But he's kind of funny. He comes on at times like a real Nixon loyalist in the committee, and then he goes out and tells the press that maybe he'll vote for impeachment after all.

"And there have been some bipartisan meetings, all last week. I think there's a chance that we'll get Tom Railsback, or maybe Ham Fish, and maybe Bill Cohen and Caldwell Butler. Bernie Nussbaum thinks that some of the Republicans are definitely coming around."

"What about that one from Maryland, Hogan?"

"That would surprise me very much. But, I'll tell you, he was coming on strong in some of his questioning last week. You know, he's a former FBI man, and the evidence about Nixon using the Bureau and other agencies for extralegal stuff, well, that wouldn't sit too well with a guy like Larry."

Exuberant Evie came running up, splashed water all over her mother, and then announced in a loud voice that she had almost gone to the bathroom in the pool. Micky got up and led her away, but she turned back with, "Aren't you glad I stuck around? How would you have handled this one? She's getting a little big for the men's room."

I watched them go. I was overwhelmed with regret. Micky was such a terrific person. Why couldn't we keep it all together, make another try? That "waiver of conciliation" form was still in my desk drawer, still unsigned. Maybe, when the inquiry is over . . .

Or was I kidding myself again? After a while, you have to admit that some things in life are simply inevitable.

". . . if this case were to go to the Senate, and managers of the House were to begin presenting evidence, they would be able periodically in the presentation of that evidence to reach into a quiver and pull out an arrow of adverse inference for evidence, and I am suggesting, ladies and gentlemen of the committee, that you might reach in the quiver and pull out a bunch of toothpicks and it doesn't matter how many toothpicks you pull out, they won't kill a bear.

"Now, turning to the facts of the Watergate situation. . . ."

It was the morning of July 22, and Sam Garrison was making the case for the President, the case most Republicans had thought Bert Jenner would make—until he stunned them by agreeing with Doar that the evidence supported impeachment. I listened carefully to Garrison, to give his arguments the benefit of the doubt, but it was hard going. I wasn't impressed with his presentation. I wondered if Nixon wouldn't have been better served with someone like Wiggins to argue on his behalf.

Apparently Barbara Jordan shared my lack of enthusiasm for Garrison's presentation. As we were answering a quorum call, she said, "I'd hate to miss a quorum call because I had to sit and listen to that."

On the floor of the House we were debating a resolution for press coverage of the hearings. Would we or would we not open the hearings to television and radio coverage? We would, by a vote of 346–40, but that did not come about without some bitter argument, both on the floor and off.

I voted to bring the TV cameras in. We had met too long in secret, and it was time for the people to see the results of all those executive sessions, secret caucuses, and closed briefings.

A few hours later, in a Democratic caucus, Rodino said that he had been asked by several Republicans on the committee what we had worked out in regard to draft articles of impeachment. The main question was this: Would we bring up all the articles and then vote on them all at the end; or would we bring them up and vote on each one, one at a time?

186

Rodino said that question was being hashed out, but that he would have an answer at our main caucus that evening.

I really felt for Rodino. When he took over the Judiciary Committee from the "deposed" Emanuel (Manny) Celler, he could have had no idea what he was in for. No one could have. And the pressure on him was not just from his fellow members.

After the meeting Rodino was talking with me, Jerry Waldie, and a few others, and he said that a man from the National Citizens Committee for Fairness to the President, the Rabbi Korff group (which had been demonstrating around the Hill for the past few days), had come up to him and grabbed him by the arm and started talking to him in Italian. Apparently this upset Rodino. It must have seemed to him that the man thought the chairman would listen to him more seriously because of their common background. Rodino said, "And I also told him that I didn't like being grabbed." Waldie said, "That's really stupid. This whole thing is getting to be like a circus."

Coincidentally, when we got to the trolleycar platform for the ride back to the office buildings, we were met by several representatives of the Fairness Committee. One of them, a woman, was holding an American flag, and she said, "Be fair to the President. He likes you. And you can like him." God, I thought, if she only knew. Just three days before, Ron Ziegler held a press conference at San Clemente (where the President was resting after his foreign trips) to accuse us of conducting a "kangaroo court" and charge that we had made "a total shambles out of what should have been a fair proceeding."

That didn't give me the feeling that anybody in the White House liked us. And certainly not the President.

Late in the afternoon Garrison finished his defense, and McClory told him that he had made a "major contribution," and David Dennis said that he appreciated having this "position."

Walter Flowers could not resist ribbing them. He asked, in an aside, "What position?"

Bert Jenner was preparing to follow Garrison's presentation, when Charley Sandman of New Jersey intervened. "I would suggest, Mr. Chairman, we resolve this here. I mean, this man [Jenner] was supposed to be the attorney for the minority. He has

187

been anything except the attorney for the minority. He has already come out . . ."

At this point he was interrupted by several members who called out, "Regular order."

Railsback waded in, stating that Jenner had been "working on the case from the very beginning . . . it is ridiculous to bring this up right now, and I want to hear Mr. Jenner, and there are others as well."

To his great credit, Sam Garrison spoke up: "If I might, with all due respect to Mr. Sandman, say that I have very high personal regard for Mr. Jenner, and I for one would like to hear what he has to say."

With that, Sandman's resistance faded, and Bert Jenner began to speak. Within moments it was clear to everyone that Jenner was speaking with even more than his normal degree of seriousness.

. . . And as I said when both you, Mr. Chairman, and Mr. Hutchinson questioned me in January of this year, when you probed as to whether I had any biases one way or the other, I responded that I had none, that I would bring to the committee my litigation experience and sense of professional responsibility to bear in any effort to bring the whole truth to this committee, to the House, and to the country. And that is what I have been doing.

I am also a human being. I have love for my country, and I have love for my Constitution, and love for my profession and my family. My Constitution and country come first, and my profession next. And I regret to say that in my career my family has to come third. Especially is all this so when the office of the Presidency of the United States is in any respect in jeopardy. And that is the manner and fashion in which I want to say to all of you that once the evidence was put together I did come as I said last Thursday, I believe it was, whatever day it was, I came to the professional judgment that I stated on that occasion.

I could have no other judgment in my heart, and I am not talking about the weight of the evidence now, I am talking about Bert Jenner. When I reached that conclusion then true to what I think I have been as a lawyer for over 43 years, I voiced it. It was not easy. Should I be put in the same situation again in the future, I would do it again. The truth is whole. It is not many-sided. It is not political.

When he finished, more than fifteen minutes later, I thought there might be applause. He had taken Garrison to task—kindly but firmly, and after praising him for his obvious "fairness"—on Garrison's charge of "two trials," and inferences, and other evidentiary points. And he used examples to back it up, examples such as the fact that the transcripts prepared by the committee clearly differed with those supplied to us, and the country, by the President. And the differences were harmful to the President. It was quite a performance.

Jerry Waldie said, on the record, "I have found Mr. Jenner's contribution to be enormously worthwhile, and I have found his presentation just now to be extremely moving and I have been most pleased to have been part of an inquiry in which he has had a significant role."

Just before we adjourned, one of the senior Republican members made a request that surprised several of the people on my side of the aisle.

Wiggins said that he had heard that some Democrats and the staff had been preparing draft articles of impeachment, and that he would appreciate seeing them as far in advance as possible of the formal debate. This surprised us because we assumed that the Republicans had been working on their own articles.

Somebody pointed out to me that Flowers, Mann, Thornton, Railsback, Cohen, Fish, and Butler were planning a meeting. Hungate had started to call the group "the big seven." Perhaps Bernie was right that the Republicans were beginning to come around. It wouldn't be long before we all found out.

When I crawled into bed late that night, I was bone-tired. We'd had a Democratic caucus that began at eight and ran for more than two hours, covering a host of important points. At the heart of everything, however, had been the realization that political animals of very different stripes were going to have to work together.

Walter Flowers was concerned about whether or not a general abuse of power article would also include the Cambodia issue. He didn't want this, because of the feeling of the conservatives in

189

his Alabama district, and he was afraid that including Cambodia would necessitate his voting against an article that he might otherwise support. Liz Holtzman had the opposite problem. If Cambodia was left out, she would be in trouble with her constituents.

Finally, John Conyers spoke up. "What I'd like to know, Walter, is what is your irreducible minimum?" I had become impressed with Conyers. For a guy who likes to speak out early, to lead on hard issues, he had been almost conspicuously quiet. I thought he had been statesmanlike.

We talked about the Republicans—Railsback, Fish, Butler, and Cohen—who were expressing interest in getting together with the Democrats to see if there were any areas of common ground.

Finally, toward the end of the meeting, Walter Flowers said, "Come on. Let's get on with it. If I'm going to face the music I want to face *all* the music."

What was needed at that moment was a light touch, which Charley Rangel provided by saying, "Walter, don't worry. *I'll* join you." There was laughter from everyone, for they knew the effect on some of Walter's constituents if he was linked with a black from New York City.

Without finally resolving it, we had discussed whether we should have an actual final draft of impeachment articles drawn up before Wednesday—when we hoped to begin the televised portion—or should we simply have a general debate. How odd, I thought, that we should have come as far as we had without having agreed on the format and procedures. Well, there weren't any members of Congress experienced in the area of impeaching a President.

Rodino made it clear that he did not think that he should be the one to offer the article, or articles (if it came to that), of impeachment, but that he would serve as chairman—and anchorman—and that Harold Donohue, the second-ranking Democrat, would introduce the article. So the stage was set, for Harold Donohue, after twenty-seven years in Congress, to be the man who would introduce a resolution that might conceivably lead to the impeachment of President Richard M. Nixon. What a way to end almost three decades in the People's House.

When we broke up, Jim Mann said, very seriously, "Now not a word of this to anybody. Not even your top aides!"

Before I fell asleep, I thought about the way things were accelerating. I knew the committee would be debating at least one article of impeachment. But I wasn't sure whether we would pass one.

I knew that I could vote with conviction for an abuse of power article, and a Watergate article, and for one dealing with the President's refusal to cooperate with the inquiry. As for taxes, I was not only sure I could vote for it, I was beginning to consider the possibility of sponsoring it.

Just that morning, walking out of the Rayburn garage, I had run into John Dent of Pennsylvania, and he said, "I won't ask you how things are going in the committee, but if I were on it, the one thing I'd push would be the money. That's the impeachable thing."

As far as I was concerned, that was what a lot of people around the country thought too.

I fell asleep with images of tax forms, backdated deeds, and the spacious, well-improved grounds and buildings of the President's "mansions" dancing in my head.

We had a caucus set for two o'clock on the afternoon of July 23, but it started late. There were many reasons why it was delayed, one of them being that a member of the Judiciary Committee had called a two P.M. press conference to announce his decision on whether or not he would vote for impeachment. It was not a Democrat, though, it was Republican Larry Hogan of Maryland.

That morning, Paul Sarbanes, who knew of the press conference, told me he was sure Hogan would announce his opposition to impeachment. Larry was running for governor in Maryland, and I wondered if that was why he had decided to come out early for non-impeachment.

A group of us were standing around in the hearing room, waiting for the caucus to begin, when Rangel walked in carrying a portable radio. I could hear the announcer's voice grow louder as Rangel approached: ". . . to repeat . . . Republican Lawrence Hogan of Maryland's Fifth Congressional District, and a

191

member of the House Judiciary Committee now holding hearings on impeachment, announced this afternoon that he will vote *for* the impeachment of President Richard Nixon. . . ."

There were gasps all around. A few members claimed to have known about it ahead of time, but I'm not sure anyone believed them. We were a wide-eyed group. Finally, Rangel broke the silence by kidding Flowers, "Walter! Hogan wasn't even one of the Republicans you've been conferring with!"

The caucus got under way, and we began again the discussion of how to bring up the articles. Rodino was in favor of having the votes "ad seriatim," or voting on each particular article, but Seiberling countered by suggesting that we push one major article and "vote it up or down," meaning go all the way to a final vote, "and then the members will have crossed the Rubicon."

"But the Republicans," Rodino cautioned, "have a tougher row to hoe."

Flowers said, "Yeah, and remember, you don't have a majority without *us*." He was referring to the conservative Southern Democrats. He was dead right, on the numbers, but no one had an accurate head count at that point. Walter went on to explain that he had no intention of being an obstructionist force.

After the meeting I walked with Rodino for a while, and he told me that he'd had a short talk with Larry Hogan prior to his announcement and he'd told Rodino that he was upset over the way Nixon had been characterizing the work of the committee. I wondered how many other minority members felt that way.

Rodino also mentioned some of the strange comments he was getting in reaction to the potential scheduling of the vote. A Republican had told him he hoped there wouldn't be a vote on the night of Tuesday next, because Jerry Ford was visiting his district and he had to be there. And then Silvio Conte of Massachusetts had told the chairman that the same night would be bad for him because he coached the baseball team of the House Republicans and they had a game scheduled for that night which would include some of our committee members.

Later that afternoon I went to Jerry Zeifman's office, along with Rodino and Sarbanes, and there was a big birthday cake sitting on a desk outside Jerry's office. One of the staff members had a birthday, and I was given a piece of the cake. As I was eating it, I strolled into Jerry's office, but I stopped short when I saw the look on his face.

"What's the matter?"

He looked up at me for a moment, and then he handed me a piece of paper that he had just finished signing. It was a notice to all members of the Judiciary Committee that "final debate on impeachment will begin at 7:30 P.M. on Wednesday, July 24, 1974."

"Never, in my wildest dreams, did I think I'd be signing a notice like that one day."

That afternoon, at the committee's business meeting, we began arguing again over how to approach the votes—either one by one on each article, or all votes at the end. Walter Flowers was mad, and he was hardly the only one. While the argument raged, one of the young staff lawyers passed my spot, leaned over, and said, "Boy, if this kind of arguing goes on tomorrow night when you're on television, you guys'll be dead." His point was well taken. The last thing we wanted the nation to see was a committee that, after six months of incredible work, still couldn't even agree on the procedures. It wasn't a pleasant thought.

The next morning I got up and ate immediately. I wanted the milk and french toast and juice to hit bottom before the butterflies woke up and started flying around. With the first televised debate scheduled for that night, I knew it was going to be some day.

The politics of impeachment got up early too. In the morning I talked with Paul Sarbanes, and he told me he was worried that because of the ruling that each member could speak for fifteen minutes during the public debate, the last to speak in the evening would be Wiggins. Paul didn't want that, because he thought Wiggins would do too good a job of muddying the waters. Later, I saw Rodino and he warned me to think twice about bringing up the tax article before the full committee, since its defeat could hurt the chances of the "stronger" articles.

Shortly before noon I was in a caucus of all the House Democrats when suddenly there was an excited buzzing, and the business at hand was immediately forgotten. The Supreme Court had voted—eight to nothing—that Richard Nixon had to turn over the tapes subpoenaed by Jaworski! It took a moment for the news to travel around the House chamber and then the applause began, growing louder and louder. It was the outcome I'd hoped for, despite some serious doubts.

This was turning into quite a historic day.

"Before I begin, I hope you will allow me a personal reference. Throughout all of the painstaking proceedings of this committee, I as the chairman have been guided by a simple principle, the principle that the law must deal fairly with every man. For me, this is the oldest principle of democracy. . . ."

It had finally begun, the formal debate, and Peter Rodino was delivering his opening remarks. The television cameras were less noticeable than the lights, and the room was bustling until the chairman began to speak. Then it became quiet. Rodino sat above me and to my left, on the higher level of the two-tiered dais. I wanted to turn and watch him as he spoke, but I didn't. Instead, I sat with my hands folded in front of me and listened to the quiet power of this man who had aspired to be a poet and now found himself at history's stage.

"Almost two centuries ago the Founding Fathers of the United States reaffirmed and refined this principle ["that the king, like each of his subjects, was under God and the law"] so that here all men are under the law, and it is only the people who are sovereign. So speaks our Constitution, and it is under our Constitution, the supreme law of our land, that we proceed through the sole power of impeachment.

"We have reached the moment when we are ready to debate resolutions whether or not the committee on the Judiciary should recommend that the House of Representatives adopt articles calling for the impeachment of Richard M. Nixon.

"Make no mistake about it. This is a turning point, whatever we decide. Our judgment is not concerned with an individual but with a system of constitutional government."

That was the official beginning. My hands had begun to perspire and I rubbed them dry—under the table and away from the eyes of the cameras.

Ten minutes later, by prearrangement, Harold Donohue was recognized by Rodino, and he said, "Thank you, Mr. Chairman. Pursuant to the procedural resolution which this committee adopted yesterday, I move that the committee report to the

House a resolution together with articles of impeachment, impeaching Richard M. Nixon, President of the United States. Now, a copy of this resolution is at the clerk's desk and I understand a copy is also before each member."

How strange it sounded—"I understand a copy is also before each member." I'd heard that phrase scores, maybe hundreds of times, and I had only been in the Congress for little more than a year. And yet I was hearing those simple words, in my first term, in reference to a resolution calling for the House to impeach the President.

We were now at the beginning of the phase during which each of the committee's thirty-eight members could speak for fifteen minutes. These speeches were officially labeled "opening remarks." There was no requirement that a member give his or her position in regard to impeachment. The nation was watching on television, or at least it had the opportunity, and many viewers were eagerly awaiting assurances (even hints) that one was "for" or "against" impeachment.

One of the many ironies of the situation was that the members of the committee did not know a whole lot more about the eventual outcome than did the members of the television audience.

Harold Donohue did not take his full fifteen minutes. But he *did* say that he was ready to vote. He'd heard all he needed to hear. Then Bob McClory spoke, slowly and seriously and with great care in his choice of words. He said that he could not go along with John Doar on the Watergate charge; he felt, as did Sam Garrison, to whom he referred, that the evidence was not strong enough to show direct presidential involvement. But then he turned to the areas of abuse of office and the President's failure to respond to our subpoenas, and it was soon clear that if he hadn't yet made up his mind to support articles in those two areas, he was close.

In regard to the former, he mentioned the long string of presidential aides who had been convicted of crimes that involved Watergate in its broadest aspects, and said, "After receiving evidence for weeks and weeks, evidence which has been frequently peripheral, as it relates to direct involvement of the President in Watergate and other crimes, I ask myself, is this any way to run a White House, or a country?"

In regard to the refusal to respond to the subpoenas, he said,

". . . . the President's failure to comply threatens the integrity of the impeachment process itself. His action is a direct challenge to the Congress in the exercise of its solemn constitutional duty."

There were murmurs from the crowd when McClory finished, and the television cameras were panning back and forth, probably trying to pick up reactions from the facial expressions of the other members. I don't know if my face showed it, but I was surprised at McClory's firmness. Surprised and pleased.

There were other surprises. Jack Brooks did *not* reveal how he would vote, and Henry Smith of New York said, "Except for the area of the secret bombing in Cambodia at the President's order between March 18, 1969 and May 1, 1970, where I have not yet made up my mind, I should have to vote against impeachment of the President on the state of the evidence which we have seen." The second part of his statement was expected, but I was intrigued by his reference to the Cambodia bombing.

The next surprise was that no sooner had Bob Kastenmeier gotten the last words of his statement (in which he called for Nixon's impeachment in very strong terms) out of his mouth than Rodino gaveled down hard and called a recess. I looked around in surprise, and heard someone whisper. "It's a bomb threat. Let's shake our tails."

As we swept out, the Capitol Police and the specially trained German shepherds came bounding in. Fifteen minutes later we were back in our places. The threat had been a hoax.

Sandman followed with a performance that must have startled the viewing audience. He ranted and raved, and he even got laughs (when he said "I ran for governor in my state last year and Richard Nixon did not help me one blessed bit, so I have no reason to feel kindly toward him") and he concluded that he had yet to see evidence that the President should be impeached. He left the door open a crack, when he ended, by saying: "All right. There are 37 of you. Give me that information. Give it to 202 million Americans, because up to this moment you have not."

The door may have been open, but I didn't get the impression that his mind was. I figured Sandman would hold out to the bitter end, along with Dennis and a few others.

Don Edwards came next. The California Democrat set the rec-

196

ord straight on a couple of inaccurate statements by Sandman, and in a very somber explanation of his position said that he would vote for impeachment. And then he added, "A number of my colleagues on the committee, a majority, I think, and I, are prepared to present in the next few days what we think is overwhelming evidence to support this conclusion. On my part I am willing to face my constituents, my family, myself, and history with this sober conclusion."

Before the hearings had begun, several people had said that they were afraid the evening's viewing would turn out to be dull, possibly even boring. But as I scanned the room and looked at the other members, I did not see anyone who wasn't listening intently. And now, at ten minutes after ten, we were about to hear from Tom Railsback, one of the key Republicans. Tom's attitude was crucial to the final outcome of the impeachment inquiry.

At first Railsback seemed to be meandering; unlike the others, he was speaking without notes. His voice, sounding a little higher than usual, reflected the tension, but after a while he settled down. And I don't think that anyone in the room doubted that he was speaking right from the heart.

He said that he found impeachment an awesome responsibility, in particular because Nixon had campaigned twice for him in Illinois and Railsback regarded him "as a friend." He added other details to explain why he found the task so difficult, and then there was a noticeable shift in his tone as he began to discuss what he called his "serious areas of concern."

Dismissing ITT, the milk scandal, and Cambodia, he said, "But, I do have some problems I want to share with my colleagues and I do want to share with my constituents my concerns. They relate to what I would call abuse of power. I cannot think of an area where a conservative, or a moderate, or a liberal should be more concerned about the state of our government."

And then he went into the relationship between Dean and the President, and Haldeman and Ehrlichman and the President, and the whole business of how the White House "investigated" Watergate. He was getting close to the end of his time, but he was really worked up. He waved his arms, to make one point, and I could tell that he was aching to get even more things off his chest.

197

The more people he wove into his narrative, the more you could sense that he found nothing to exonerate the President. I looked toward Rodino to see if I could catch his expression. Apparently, Railsback's time had already run out, but Pete still held the gavel poised. He was hesitant to cut him off before he finished his thought. Finally, though, he had no choice and gaveled him down.

But Bill Hungate, a Democrat and the next speaker, said quickly, "Mr. Chairman, I yield two minutes to my distinguished colleague and neighbor from Illinois, Mr. Railsback."

Tom nodded gratefully and picked up where he had been forced to leave off. (I learned later that the relinquishment of Hungate's time had been prearranged by Jimmy Mann. Mann had approached Hungate before the hearing began and told him Railsback would need more than fifteen minutes. Hungate was the only member who could yield to Railsback and I was told he good-naturedly agreed to Mann's request, saying, "I'll yield two of my fifteen minutes because thirteen is really my lucky number. That is, I'll yield if I like what Railsback's saying.")

With his extra time, Tom mentioned that Nixon had refused to give us a very important tape—one in which the President talked with Haldeman for five hours right after Haldeman had spent two whole days listening to the Watergate tapes.

"I just can't help but wonder, you know, when you put all of this together in that kind of perspective, I am concerned and I am seriously concerned. I hope that the President—I wish the President could do something to absolve himself. I wish he would come forward with the information that we have subpoenaed. I just am very, very concerned."

Hungate followed with a ringing denunciation of the President's actions and when he finished we were ready to file out. I looked over at Tom Railsback. His face looked gray, and drawn.

At eight-thirty the next morning, Thursday, July 25, I walked into Jerry Zeifman's office for a Democratic caucus. It seemed that I was *living* in the Capitol buildings, I spent so little time in my apartment. If we didn't get finished soon in committee and get impeachment to the full House, I would consider moving a bed and a hot plate into my office.

There was a good deal of approving talk about the way the first night's opening statements had gone but Rodino was not satisfied. He cautioned us to be more specific, to begin our remarks by laying out just why we were taking one stand or the other. Someone pointed out, one of the junior members, that no one had any advance notice of what the others were going to say, and that you could find yourself with a paper full of wonderful remarks—that another member had just made, sometimes using the exact words you'd planned to use. I was keenly aware of that problem because I would be the last one to give an opening statement!

We talked for a while about the tax article, and it was soon clear that it was nowhere near being finished in draft form. Unlike the Watergate article, and the one on failure to comply, the tax question had not received the attention I thought it deserved, either from the staff or the members themselves. I realized that we did not have the same kind or amount of evidence in regard to the tax and personal emoluments issue, but I still felt we could be doing more, even if we were running dangerously close to the wire.

Then the discussion turned to subpoenas, and Bill Hungate grumbled, in what was definitely not a kidding tone, "I'm not so sure, if we can't even enforce our subpoenas, that I want to work around here."

At 10:10 A.M. we were back in the hearing room, ready for the remaining twenty-seven members of the Judiciary Committee to give their opening remarks. Twelve and a half hours later—at 10:48 P.M.—we had finished. It was one of the longest of many long days.

Every Democrat—including Rodino, who made his first public statement of intention—indicated he or she would vote for impeachment. Of the twelve Republicans, seven said they could not vote for impeachment, but in varying degrees the other five said they might. The five were Hamilton Fish, Larry Hogan, Caldwell Butler, Bill Cohen, and Harold Froehlich.

Along the way, there had been many statements that brought quiet to the room, many moments that caused everyone to reflect and to realize anew the terrible seriousness of what we were about.

199

Ham Fish mentioned his distress ". . . at the use of the enormous power of the United States Government to invade and impinge upon the private rights of individuals."

Jerry Waldie, in a strong presentation, raised a critical point: "To this day there is not one single instance where this President has come before any authority with evidence or with his understanding of the evidence to ask for clarification."

Walter Flowers put one central issue right on the line when he said, "What if we fail to impeach? Do we ingrain forever in the very fabric of our Constitution a standard of conduct in our highest office that in the least is deplorable and at worst is impeachable?"

And Larry Hogan, in an extremely forceful statement, had me almost in tears. I didn't care about the rumors that Hogan's position was "politically motivated." He sounded absolutely sincere to me, especially when he said, in a firm voice, "I cannot, in good conscience, turn away from evidence of evil that is so clear and so compelling."

I thought Jim Mann was good, as were Paul Sarbanes and Barbara Jordan. Especially Barbara Jordan.

I remembered how Jack Brooks had kidded Barbara about being able to turn on her Southern accent when she was back in the district, but I forgot about that entirely within moments. She spoke with more dignity of purpose than anyone else.

"Earlier today we heard the beginning of the Preamble to the Constitution of the United States, 'We the people.' It is a very eloquent beginning. But when that document was completed on the 17th of September in 1787 I was not included in that 'We the people.' I felt somehow for many years that George Washington and Alexander Hamilton just left me out by mistake. But through the process of amendment, interpretation, and court decision I have finally been included in 'We the people.'

"Today, I am an inquisitor. I believe hyperbole would not be fictional and would not overstate the solemnness that I feel right now. My faith in the Constitution is whole, it is complete, and it is total. I am not going to sit here and be an idle spectator to the diminution, the subversion, the destruction of the Constitution."

At nine minutes after ten P.M. I had looked at my watch.

Wayne Owens of Utah was nearing the end of his statement. I looked at what remained of the typed copy of my remarks. It was covered with changes, slashes, linear additions and deletions. In the best of moments my writing is not easy to read, like that of most left-handers; now it looked like nervous hieroglyphics, more like picture drawings than words.

I was just about to scratch out another word, when I felt someone tap me on the shoulder and pass me a folded sheet of paper. It was written on Judiciary Committee stationery, and it read:

> DEAR CONGRESSMAN MEZVINSKY,
> Thank you for relinquishing your time.
> THE CHAIRMAN.

Startled, I tried not to turn around too quickly. When I did, I saw Bob Kastenmeier and Don Edwards grinning at me. It was their idea of a joke.

"The time of the gentleman has expired. I recognize the gentleman from Iowa, Mr. Mezvinsky, for purposes of general debate only for a period not to exceed 15 minutes."

"Thank you, Mr. Chairman." I pushed my hands down on the table in front of me, to quiet them, and cleared my throat for the third time in ten seconds. From just behind me, I heard Barbara Jordan whisper, "Go get 'em, Ed."

"I know that I am one of the last speakers but I shall not have the last word because we all know that the last word belongs to the Constitution. My colleagues and I who have anguished over this task know this all too well. You can tell it from the words they have spoken, whatever side of the aisle they were on.

"I just hope that I am able to make a contribution to a further understanding of our grave responsibility.

"Now, the American presidency is a rare trust. It is truly a culmination of a national trust and confidence. And what we are called on to do by our Constitution is to scrutinize the treatment of this sacred trust by Richard Nixon. By putting the impeachment process into motion, we have accepted the challenge laid down two hundred years ago by the Founding Fathers, the challenge to preserve the government that they created. I think it is important for us to remember that the authors of that Constitution provided that process not as something to be feared by the Nation, but rather as an essential provision to reassure and protect the people from the abuse of the great powers of the presidency.

"The Founding Fathers really insisted that the President be held to the highest standard of accountability and we know that the impeachment process is really the ultimate guarantee of that accountability.

"The Congress is called on to enforce that guarantee. And for this reason it is not only Richard Nixon that is on trial: So are we, every member of this committee, every member of this Congress.

". . . I take a look at my own background, a background where my parents were immigrants who were genuinely inspired by America as they compared it to their homelands of czarist Russia and turn-of-the-century Poland. I grew up in Iowa with a great admiration for our Presidents, whether they be Republican or Democrat, and I now find it personally unsettling to be faced with the harsh evidence that Richard Nixon has abused the presidency. But the committee must face the evidence and that is what it is. It is evidence. To do otherwise would be a grave dereliction of our duty."

By this time, late in the evening of the 25th, the three main articles were in nearly finished form, based on the cooperation of many parties, but the tax article was not, and in fact the whole question of Nixon's taxes had seldom been mentioned in the opening statements. So I turned my attention, and I hoped that of others, to that question.

"I want to focus on an area that is not now covered in the articles: That is the evidence on the President's taxes because I believe this evidence falls into a pattern of abuse which the committee must consider and I think the tax question is especially important because it is readily understandable. All of us pay taxes. All of us deal with the Internal Revenue Service.

"Now, let us review the facts about the presidential taxes. Here is the story."

Based on the report of the congressional Joint Committee on Internal Revenue Taxation, I laid out the following facts:

202

YEAR	INCOME	TAX OWED	TAX PAID
1969	$460,000	$220,000	$72,000
1970	360,000	90,000	793
1971	250,000	94,000	878
1972	250,000	90,000	4,000

"Now that means in four years Richard Nixon underpaid his federal taxes by nearly $420,000."

I went on to explain the backdating of the deed that supposedly gave him the tax shelter necessary to legitimize these huge deductions, the deed for the papers that were appraised at more than half a million dollars. And I traced the history of how all of this was finally rectified, with the result that the President had paid his back taxes for the last three years (all the law required) and that despite his promise to pay the extra $148,000 for 1969, he had not yet done so.

I mentioned the opinion, given the committee, by Fred Folsom, who had been the head of Justice Department's Criminal Fraud Division. Folsom said that if the department had that much evidence on any other taxpayer, and if that taxpayer refused to answer any questions (which is what the President had done) he or she would have been indicted by a grand jury and ultimately sent to jail.

I was really getting worked up by this point, about two-thirds of the way through my allotted time. "But, Mr. Nixon tells us that he is not responsible for what is on his tax returns, even though he is the one who signed 'under the pain of perjury' on the bottom line. . . . Now, I think this committee has to face up to the question of whether Richard Nixon has willfully evaded his taxes.

"I believe this matter falls into a pattern of abuse of office because it is evident that the President entertained an expectation for and took advantage of favorable treatment by the IRS. I view this as a grave misuse and serious violation of public trust that demeans the Office of the Presidency."

My words were coming so fast that some were tripping over others. I knew my time was almost up.

"Mr. Chairman, as you so eloquently noted at the opening of this general debate, we are at the crossroads for America. Whatever this committee decides, it will have a major impact on the future of our country. What legacy shall we leave for the future?

"Will we condone Richard Nixon's presidential conduct and sanction his claims that he is the defender of that grand office or will we record our abhorrence at the way he has defiled the office?

"Will we ignore the actions which have already brought so many of our children to hold such a low regard for the highest office in our land, or will we make it clear to our fellow citizens that we cherish the Office of the Presidency and will take up the constitutional challenge to protect it?

"As we proceed with the debate on these articles, on the question of whether or not we are to bring Richard Nixon to account for the gross abuse of office"—I could hear the gentle tapping of Rodino's gavel—"I think we must all ask ourselves, if we do not, who will?"

Bang. Down it came. "The time of the gentleman has expired."

The next day I was talking to Jerry Zeifman, and he remarked that he thought the members, in their opening remarks, gave the accurate impression that we were speaking from our hearts. That pleased me.

Later, around noon, when I went onto the floor, the reaction of the non-committee members was positive and warm. Several said they thought the committee was doing a fine thing for the Congress as a whole, that we were renewing people's faith in the House.

In the offices behind the hearing room, it was another tedious, but important day spent in going over the articles, drafting and redrafting, trying to work into one document the various efforts of the staff and members of the committee, with Jim Mann coordinating the swing coalition of three Southern Democrats and four Republicans. At one point, Bob McClory brought in an article he had drafted, and after reading it through, both Jack Brooks and I said, "My God, it's stronger than the Democrats' version!"

It was turning into an emotional day. At noon some people had to be removed from the hearing room because they suddenly stood up in the audience and started screaming, "Why don't you impeach for war crimes?"

Then, a bit later, two of my fellow Democrats on the committee suggested that I sponsor the tax article—so that they would have something to vote against! I guess they were afraid, for political reasons, of appearing too anti-Nixon, and wanted to be able to show they had not voted for *all* the articles of impeachment. It gave me an uncomfortable feeling.

As had happened so often before, it was Bill Hungate who added some levity to a very slow period of debate, and helped to improve my mood. He said, "I tell you, if a guy brought an elephant through that door and one of us said, 'That is an elephant,' some of the doubters would say, 'You know, that is an inference. That could be a mouse with a glandular condition.'"

But there wasn't much more in the way of humor on Friday afternoon. Paul Sarbanes had proposed a substitute to the original first article, the one dealing with obstruction of justice in regard to the Watergate cover-up. Sarbanes's substitute tightened up the wording of the original, and was not radically different, but it brought on a long and heated debate. Those who spoke against Sarbanes's substitute were in reality attacking the obstruction of justice article itself. And they hung it all on one word, a word that was used so often throughout the afternoon and evening that the press began to joke about it. The word was "specificity."

Sarbanes had listed nine separate areas of offenses but had not included (just as the original had not) the specific times and places and events that backed up the allegations. The opponents seized on this, arguing that the President was not being put on notice of the charges against him, that the whole thing was unconstitutional.

Sandman, Dennis, Wiggins, and Latta were vocal opponents, and their concern was apparently shared, at least to some degree, by Caldwell Butler and even Jim Mann from our side of the aisle.

Rodino used Doar and Jenner to explain away as many of the objections as he could, but he was forced to open up debate when Sandman moved to strike the first subsection of the Sarbanes substitute (which charged Richard Nixon with "making false or misleading statements to lawfully designated investigative officers and employees of the United States").

As the debate raged, and the nation watched, we saw a lot of people talking about the final issue—the potential impeachment and removal of an American President—through the mechanism of a simple motion to strike some language.

Finally, in a statement every bit as moving as her opening remarks of the night before, Barbara Jordan said, "It is apparently difficult for the committee to translate its views of the Constitution into the realities of the impeachment provisions. . . . Some of the arguments offered earlier today . . . are phantom arguments, bottomless arguments. . . . If we have not afforded the President due process . . . then there is no due process to be found anywhere . . . this committee suffered, if you will, the counsel of the President to sit in these proceedings every day. . . . The President's counsel was allowed to cross-examine the witnesses. . . . This is due process tripled, due process quadrupled."

When my turn came I was close to being openly angry: "We are supposed to be considering an article on impeachment concerning whether Richard Nixon has prevented, obstructed, and impeded the administration of justice. Somehow it seems that some of my colleagues have been more concerned about possibly starting a crusade to make the word 'specificity' as common in our conversations as the word 'Watergate' has become."

Maraziti tried to get me to yield, but I went right on. "I think it is demeaning, really, to the President to think that he cannot understand the meaning of what is in this Sarbanes substitute. I think it has been spelled out quite well and I think we understand the [Sandman] tactic as really being diversionary. I just want to say to my colleagues, the evidence that the gentleman from California [Waldie] and others have pointed out is overwhelming. And I also want to say that the evidence will not go away."

Shortly after I finished, Sandman formally moved his amendment. There was more debate, however, and it was clear that tempers were becoming frayed. Rangel pointed out that Sandman had similar objecting amendments to make to the remaining eight points in the Sarbanes substitute article, and that if we handled each one the way we were handling this one it would take "27 hours of this committee's time to deal merely with Mr. Sandman's parliamentary requests." That sobered a few people up.

I was distressed that we would have to vote in this fashion, after all the time we had spent behind closed doors trying to avoid just this kind of partisan fight, but there was no way out of it.

It was already past eleven P.M. when we got down to the actual vote on Sandman's amendment. Rodino tried to make it quick by calling for a voice vote, when he said, "The noes appear to have it."

But Charley Sandman was not to be put off so easily. He demanded a recorded roll-call vote. I wasn't sure he knew what he was doing. It was risky, because he was giving the members an opportunity for a dry-run vote on impeachment—especially risky at this late hour with everyone hot, tired, and less than calm.

The room quieted noticeably as the clerk called each member's name. By the time I voted "no," Sandman had already lost, as all nineteen Democratic members ahead of me had also voted to defeat the amendment. He got most of the senior Republicans and all the hard-core votes, but he didn't get Henry Smith, Railsback, Fish, Hogan, Butler, or Cohen. The vote was 27 against, 11 for.

Not that the vote would necessarily go the same way on Article I, but it wasn't a good omen for Nixon partisans—or the President.

At 11:35 P.M. the chairman said, in a markedly tired voice, "And the motion is not agreed to. And the committee will recess until twelve noon tomorrow."

The committee met at 12:45 on Saturday, July 27, following a morning of intense work on the redrafting of the articles, which the staff had worked on all through the night.

As I was walking into the hearing room, I was stopped by Eric Engberg of Westinghouse Broadcasting, who said, "In view of what happened on the Sandman amendment last night, and

207

considering your spot as the twentieth Democrat to vote, when it comes to the vote on Article I, yours could be the deciding vote on impeachment."

I hadn't thought of that before! Yet it was undeniably true, and it gave me an eerie feeling. Perhaps I hadn't thought of it because, up until now, I had my doubts that we could ever get Flowers, Mann, and Thornton to vote for any article of impeachment. But now, after all the good and careful work of Rodino, and John Doar and Bert Jenner, the staff, and the swing coalition itself, their votes on at least one article were considered all but certain.

What a queer way history unfolds. Two years ago I was a young lawyer in Iowa, passing out campaign lollipops in what many thought was a doomed effort to unseat a Republican Congressman with long years of experience in the House. And now I stood on the threshold of history, at "the crossroads for America," readying myself to cast what might turn out to be the deciding vote in the first step of the constitutional process of impeaching an American President.

I thought of my father, and I wondered what his reaction would be, remembering the kind of special insight he must have had, way back at the beginning, when he said, "Who needs that aggravation?" Well, what had begun as a "third-rate burglary" had become an aggravation for the President and then eventually a crisis for the nation—and at last the committee was coming to grips with it.

As I walked through the doorway, I was both proud and scared. But I wouldn't have traded places with anybody.

Throughout the afternoon it became apparent that most members wanted to avoid the wrangling (over "specificity") of the day before, but if there was any chance of bringing Article I to a vote that evening, we had to counter the objections of the President's hard-core supporters. To that end, in the morning caucus, Rodino had announced that the staff would be providing the members with memos giving the specific matters of evidence that supported the clauses in the article.

Almost immediately everyone started to call them the "scripts," and although there was joking, and some of the players either forgot their lines or heard someone else speaking their parts, it helped to organize the debate and keep it from getting out of hand.

Shortly after we began, Sandman earned the respect of the committee by withdrawing the rest of his proposed amendments challenging the "lack of specificity" in the remaining clauses of the Sarbanes substitute article. He also earned fulsome praise from various members, which must have pleased his constituents. He admitted that to do otherwise would simply take up too much time for what was, in view of the previous vote, a lost cause. Latta agreed with him, saying candidly, "We don't have the votes."

About halfway through the afternoon, a day on which the heat outside was slowly defeating the capacity of the air-conditioning system, we were getting close to a vote on a clarifying amendment offered by George Danielson. I thought the vote, which involved adding the words "and congressional committees" to the list of official investigations that the President had allegedly interfered with, would be a simple voice vote. So I slipped out of the room.

I knew I was cutting the time rather close, but I couldn't help it. I was answering what John Dean had described as a "call of nature," a call that had gone unheeded to the point of discomfort.

I was right in thinking it would be a voice vote, but I had neglected the possibility of someone calling for a roll-call vote, which Railsback did. When the clerk called "Mr. Mezvinsky," there was no answer. In fact, there was no Mr. Mezvinsky, which (I was later informed) the camera recorded for all to see when it focused on my empty place. I was still in the bathroom.

I got back in time to signal the chairman, who nodded, and let me register my "aye" vote, joining the twenty-three other members who supported the Danielson amendment. As I slid into my chair, I prayed that the cameras were busy elsewhere, because anyone with a color set could have seen the extent of my embarrassment.

Throughout the afternoon we continued to make changes in the wording of the article, and though I didn't know how it looked to the viewing audience, I was positive that we were functioning well, and according to the wise plan laid down so long ago by Chairman Rodino. The phrase that came to mind, even though it might have been shopworn, was "democracy in action." To see this group that represented such widely diverse areas and attitudes working toward a consensus was thrilling to me.

By six-fifteen I realized I was tired. But it wasn't just a physical tiredness. It was emotional as well, for it was now clear that within the next hour we were actually going to be ready to vote. The question before us would not be Article I itself. Rather, it would be for approval of the Sarbanes substitute, but everyone knew it amounted to the same thing. Those who favored substituting Sarbanes's draft for the original would vote for its passage. And those who opposed it would then vote against the actual article.

It was white-knuckle time.

Just before the chairman "put the question"—called for the vote on the Sarbanes substitute—two important committee members revealed where they stood.

Walter Flowers, the conservative Democrat from Alabama, said, in a voice filled with emotion, "There are many people in my district who will disagree with my vote here. Some will say that it hurts them deeply for me to vote for impeachment . . ." There it was! ". . . I can only assure them that I probably have enough pain for them and for me. I have close personal friends who support President Nixon. To several of those close friends who somehow I hope will hear and see these proceedings, I say that the only way I could vote for impeachment would be the realization to me anyway that they, my friends, would do the same thing if they were in my place on this unhappy day and confronted with all of the same facts that I have. And I have to believe that they would, or I would not take the position that I do."

The room was still as Walter continued, and then there was another voice, asking that Flowers yield. It was that of Ham Fish of New York, a man I knew had been wrestling, from the beginning, not with political concerns as much as with the deep questions of conscience.

"I thank the gentleman for yielding, and Mr. Chairman, for this opportunity to address not only the members on this side of the aisle who have labored these last seven months, but also my friends and supporters in New York who are also by and large supporters of the President. Mr. Chairman, I intend to vote in favor of this, the first article of impeachment. This comes after long deliberation, but it comes because an analysis of the evidence in this proceeding has led me to this inescapable conclusion.

"I am sure you realize that my vote is not cast lightly. My decision has not been reached hastily. It is reached at all with deep reluctance only after I have been persuaded that the evidence for such a vote is clear, evidence warranting the recommendation by this committee of this article of impeachment to the House of Representatives.

"I thank the gentleman."

"The question . . ." Rodino was ready for the vote *now,* but he was interrupted by McClory.

"Will the gentleman withhold?"

". . . The question is"—Rodino did not withhold— "the question is before us and, there being no objection, I am going to put the question, and the question occurs on the substitute offered by the gentleman from Maryland, as amended.

"All those in favor of the substitute of the gentleman from Maryland as amended, please signify by saying aye.

"The clerk will call the roll."

The names of the twenty Democrats would be called first (since we were the majority of the committee), then the seventeen Republicans, and the chairman would cast his vote last. I reflected for a second on the strangeness of the fact that while my hands were damp, my mouth was getting very dry.

"Mr. Donohue."

"Aye."

"Mr. Brooks."

"Aye."

"Mr. Kastenmeier."

"Aye."

"Mr. Edwards."

"Aye."

"Mr. Hungate."

"Aye."

"Mr. Conyers."

"Aye."

Still there was no sound in the room other than the flat voice of the clerk and the quick answer of the member. On down the list he went, all "ayes": Eilberg, Waldie, Flowers, Mann, Sarbanes, Seiberling, Danielson, Drinan, Rangel, Jordan (a firm-voiced "aye"), Thornton, and Holtzman.

And then he got to me, and it was as it had been predicted: I was the twentieth vote, and all nineteen ahead of me had voted to impeach.

"Mr. Mezvinsky."

"Aye."

And so we had voted for what would certainly turn out to be the first article of impeachment. But the important votes were still to come. Neither the House nor the rest of the country would be satisfied with a straight party-line vote.

The first Republicans, with various degrees of loudness, voted "no." Hutchinson, McClory, Smith, and Sandman.

Then it began to change.

"Mr. Railsback."

"Aye."

Flashbulbs went off throughout the room and you could hear the steady clicking of cameras.

"Mr. Wiggins."

"No."

"Mr. Dennis."

"No."

"Mr. Fish."

"Aye."

"Mr. Mayne."

"No." (That disappointed me. I thought my Iowa colleague had come around on this article.)

"Mr. Hogan."

"Aye."

"Mr. Butler."

"Aye."

"Mr. Cohen."

"Aye."

"Mr. Lott."

"No."

"Mr. Froehlich."

212

"Aye."

The last three Republicans, Moorhead, Maraziti, and Latta, voted "no." Chairman Rodino said, quietly, "Aye."

It was finished. Immediately, we moved to the article itself, "Article I of the Donohue resolution as amended by the Sarbanes substitute as amended."

The vote was exactly the same. And at five minutes after seven P.M. on Saturday, July 27, 1974, the House Judiciary Committee approved one article of impeachment against President Richard M. Nixon.

At once the quiet was broken, though there were no outbursts. The moment was too solemn. People began milling around, reporters ran for the door, and some of the members went down from the dais to meet family.

I got up quickly and headed for Rodino's small back office behind the hearing room. I didn't want to cry in front of everybody. I might as well have, though, for when I got to the office, there weren't too many dry eyes. Both Walter Flowers and Barbara Jordan were emotionally choked up. No one said much.

A short time later, driving home, I purposely avoided the route that would have taken me past the White House. As I drove, I realized that I was more tired than I had been in years, and more sad.

THIRTEEN: *Final Curtains*

When Peter Rodino walked into the Democratic caucus in Jerry Zeifman's office Sunday morning, there was a loud burst of applause. He smiled, but it wasn't a big smile. A moment later he said, "You know, during the vote last night"—and everyone knew which one he was talking about—"the voices were so quiet that it was like a funeral." As usual, it was Rodino who brought us back to the terrible seriousness of what we were about.

There was a long discussion as to who should introduce the second article of impeachment, the abuse of power article. Some wanted to see a Republican introduce it, and the names of both Larry Hogan and Bob McClory were raised. I feared that Hogan would no longer have the ear of a sufficient number of Republicans because of his "premature" announcement that he would vote for impeachment. I liked the idea of McClory for several reasons, one of which was that he favored a lesser standard of proof than had been drawn up by the inquiry staff.

In the end, though, a Democrat, Bill Hungate, was chosen to play the role that Sarbanes had played on Article I. Sarbanes later warned Hungate, "Be careful, when you're sponsoring something, you're all right for the first five minutes, but when your fellow Democrats run out of steam—or show they haven't done their homework on the 'specifics,' then they yield back to you the balance of their time—you better be ready to carry the ball."

I thought, as a freshman member, I was learning some things about the rough and ready of congressional debate that otherwise might have taken me years. Being on the Judiciary Committee was educational in all sorts of ways.

For once we broke up early, so I hurried out to the pool in McLean. Again, Micky was still there when I arrived, and she stayed for a while.

I swam with the children for a few minutes to cool off, and then joined Micky, who was reading *The Washington Post*. That morning's edition carried an editorial calling the tax issue worth treating as a separate article of impeachment. I was pleased to see that it echoed some of the thoughts I'd expressed to Meg Greenfield of the *Post* when I'd spoken to her last week, especially the idea of taxes being the "cutting edge."

Micky talked about the vote of the night before, and told me she was proud, not just of me, but of the committee and the Congress. She said it made her feel good as a citizen.

Driving home, all of the old "couldn't we try again" feelings returned in a rush, but this time they didn't haunt me as long as they usually did. Micky now seemed to be living a more peaceful, more settled, and normal life—if a single parent taking care of four young children can be thought of as "normal."

It was clearer to me than it had ever been that the official end of our marriage was not far away. How odd, though, that it seemed to be running on a parallel course to that of Richard Nixon's presidency.

On the floor of the House the next afternoon, during a break in the committee's hearing, the politics of impeachment surfaced once again. A member from Kentucky asked Rodino if the Judiciary Committee was going to meet the next night. He was concerned because Kentucky Republicans had scheduled a kick-off function for the reelection campaign of Senator Marlow Cook, and the Republicans had arranged for two hours of television time. He knew that if the hearings were on also, they wouldn't get much of an audience.

And then, Silvio Conte renewed his plea on behalf of the con-

215

gressional baseball game, which had also been planned for months. This time he was more specific; he said that the Republicans needed the services of Bill Cohen (who was a fine pitcher) and Tom Railsback—and that the Democrats were counting on the prowess of Paul Sarbanes! Rodino said sorry, but the Judiciary Committee would indeed meet on Tuesday night. "Gee, Pete," Silvio kidded, "couldn't you just postpone the hearings until after the ball game?"

Several times during the afternoon, when the time seemed ripe, I approached a few of the members to see if I could get their support on the tax article that I was now convinced I would introduce. Ham Fish and Larry Hogan said they were seriously considering it, and promised they would think about it some more, but Tom Railsback was firm in his disagreement.

In the early evening the general question of the IRS came up during the televised debate, and I got the member holding the floor to yield. I wanted to get across the point that it was not only the use of IRS to harass Administration "enemies," but also its use to help the President's friends.

". . . [W]hy is the friends list as significant as the enemies? Because impeding the due administration of the Internal Revenue Act by issuing a directive from the White House to turn off an IRS audit is a violation of the law. It is another kind of cover-up. It means another kind of protection. And we have evidence to show that is exactly what happened. . . ." To show that Nixon was directly involved, I quoted the President. "What does the President say directly: 'Do we need any IRS stuff?' That is the answer to direct involvement."

Not long after I spoke, Jim Mann of South Carolina began to explain why he was in favor of the abuse of power article. He had every ear and eye, and the room was still as could be while he spoke. He went into the "rule of law" argument, and laid out what he felt was the President's—any President's—duty under that rule and the oath of office.

He said that he had wondered, during the last few days, when other members complained about the lack of evidence, if they had really sat along with him for all the weeks and months we had been hearing the evidence, evidence he was certain did exist; ". . . because it is on that evidence that each of us is making

216

our decision, and as we seek a way to escape that decision, we cannot escape that still, small voice. And so, as Thomas Paine wrote, 'Those who expect to reap the blessing of freedom must, like men, undergo the fatigue of supporting it.'

"And in this situation, as we look at how the office of the Presidency has been served by an individual, I share the remarks of George Danielson that it is not the presidency that is in jeopardy from us. We would strive to strengthen and protect the presidency. But if there be no accountability, another President will feel free to do as he chooses. But, the next time there may be no watchman in the night."

It was a moving and, in my opinion, an eloquent speech. It set the tone for the remainder of the evening. One of quiet seriousness.

At 10:45 p.m we took a short break. I went to Rodino's little office in the back. Barbara Jordan and Walter Flowers were there, and they both admitted to being exhausted. I knew what they meant.

A few minutes after eleven, McClory told the committee, and the nation, that although he did not, could not, support Article I, he was going to vote for the second article of impeachment. He said that his decision to support the abuse of power article stemmed from his belief that in this case there was a constitutional—as opposed to a criminal—standard that had been broken. He was very moving, as he said, "While I bear no malice and no hostility to the President, it seems to me that I have an obligation myself as a member of this committee when I see the constitutional obligation in default to support an article of impeachment."

And so, once again closing in on the hour of midnight, the nation watched as the committee approved another article of impeachment.

This time the vote was 28 "aye" and 10 "no." Robert McClory of Illinois was the only member of the committee to change his or her vote as cast on Article I. McClory, a Republican who had to have some concern as to what he might be doing to his own political future, voted for impeachment.

We caucused in Jerry Zeifman's office at 9:15 on the morning of July 30. There were three main issues to discuss: Article III

217

(based on the President's failure to comply with our subpoenas), the Cambodia bombing article, and the tax article—which I had come to think of as "my" article.

The consensus was that we were doing fine, that we had a good chance on Article III, but there would be problems with the other two.

Jim Mann said, and I was afraid he was speaking for more Democrats than just himself, "You know, you get a person charged with three murders, but it's enough to convict him of just one."

Rodino was particularly sensitive to what he viewed as the Democrats' "pushing too hard," trying to pass all five articles. He felt that if we did that, the Republicans would retaliate and the "fragile alliance" would break down. I was not pleased to hear him say that, for I was more convinced every day that the tax article was one—perhaps even *the* one—that most citizens could understand and identify with.

I had to admit that the chairman had an arguable point, even if I didn't happen to agree with him. I knew Railsback was dead set against the tax article, that he had talked to Rodino and made his opposition clear. Without Railsback, it was questionable how many more of the "swing" Republicans, and perhaps even a few Democrats, thought that after passing two articles of impeachment, and having a good chance at passing a third, to go after Nixon on Cambodia and taxes would look like overkill. Liz Holtzman did not agree with that point of view and she argued, in the caucus, for pushing both taxes and Cambodia.

Rodino shook his head. "No, it would be like raising a red flag in front of the Republicans."

I was beginning to suspect that taxes was such an emotional issue that the leadership had worried from the beginning that we would never be able to get it across, and perhaps that was why we never had the same intensity of effort on taxes (and Cambodia) that we'd had on the other articles. At the moment I had no answers. Maybe we simply didn't have the time.

Discussion on these same points continued throughout the day, both in caucus and during the breaks. I had Jack Brooks on my side in regard to taxes; he not only had worked up drafts of the various articles, but he had been conducting his own investigation into the emoluments problem, such as the improvements at Key Biscayne and San Clemente, and the $5,000 earrings for Pat Nixon paid for out of leftover campaign funds.

I was buoyed up by Jack's continuing support, especially after I heard that pressure was being put on John Conyers to drop his Cambodia article, which he, rather than Drinan, was going to introduce sometime today. Still, I didn't worry about Conyers. He was used to pressure.

We broke for a recess at 12:40, and at 2:40, when I was on my way back, I ran into Charley Sandman. He said, "You know, Ed, this debate has enhanced the House."

I was impressed by his comment. I liked Sandman, and disagreed with those who had been telling me for the last few days that he was some kind of blind loyalist who would go to his grave for Nixon. Sandman's and my political philosophies were a long way apart, but I believed that he held his conservatism sincerely. On television, he had come across as the "heavy," according to many people, but to me he was supporting his conscience, not Richard Nixon's image.

As we neared the hearing room, Don Edwards joined us. He said to Sandman, "I think it's been very good to have you and Wiggins on the other side." That struck me as perceptive. Wiggins came on like the cautious constitutional lawyer, and Sandman like the bulldog. As a result, they made an interesting "odd couple."

We walked toward the room, and Sandman said to me, "It's better not to have too many articles, because then the ones we pass are diluted." I didn't agree with him, and I hoped his wasn't the prevalent view.

We voted on Article III just after four P.M., and though it was approved 21 to 17, there was a good deal of erosion. Not only did we lose two Democrats (Mann and Flowers), we also lost most of the coalition Republicans (Fish, Railsback, Cohen, and Butler) plus Froehlich. But we held Hogan and gained Bob McClory, who introduced the article. The committee had reaffirmed the importance of the subpoena power for all present and future congressional investigations. Mr. Nixon's notion that he alone, as President, could decide what the Congress was entitled to see and hear, in the face of a subpoena calling for specific

219

material, did not prevail in the Committee on the Judiciary. In many ways, we were sending the White House the same message that the Supreme Court had just sent in regard to the tapes subpoenaed by Leon Jaworski.

There was an almost palpable sense of relief and of letdown in the air after the vote. Three proposed articles, three votes to impeach, and now we would see if the committee would approve two more.

At 4:15 we went into yet another caucus, this one to determine how—and if—to handle the two remaining articles. John Conyers held firm, which relieved me, because I knew that if he had been talked out of bringing his Cambodia article the pressure would come down on me to do the same in regard to taxes. It was decided that the Conyers resolution would be brought up first.

Later, there was a roll-call vote on the floor and we all hurried over to the House. I saw Wilbur Mills, and he waved me to one side and began to caution me about bringing up taxes in the committee. He said he was worried that if we lost it might be construed as a vote of confidence for Richard Nixon in regard to his tax problems, and that would make it more difficult to prove fraud in the future. I felt he was probably worried that it might also reflect badly on his own Joint Committee on Internal Revenue Taxation report. There might be some implied criticism of his Joint Committee for not wrapping up the package on Nixon's tax matters, but I didn't mention it to him.

As Mills walked away, I marveled at how much had transpired in such a short time. It was not even two years ago that I had come, hat in hand, a newly elected Congressman, to seek the advice of Wilbur Mills, the one man who probably knew more about tax law and the tax code than anyone else in Congress. And here he was coming to me with some unsolicited advice. Watergate and impeachment had certainly wrought some changes.

When we got back to Room 2141 we began the debate on the Cambodia article. It was soon clear that we had a fundamental problem, a conflict of interest, in a sense. Unlike the tax and personal emoluments issue, the secret bombings of Cambodia related to a much larger issue, the Vietnam war itself, in which the House and the Senate were also involved. Congress had had nothing to do with Nixon's tax decisions or with his spending at his homes away from the White House. But the House and the Senate had had a lot to do with the fact that the war had not ended sooner than it had.

John Seiberling put it very well:

> I feel particularly deeply about this. I am not known as a hawk in the Congress to put it mildly. I voted against continuing the bombing of Cambodia last summer for even one more hour. Kent State University is in my district. Four Kent State students died four years ago because of the fact that the President of the United States again abused his power and invaded Cambodia without consulting the Congress. And if there is anything that we can do, that we haven't done, to stop that from happening again, we should do it. But we should not use our impeachment power to impeach this President for acts of the sort other Presidents have taken with impunity . . . and for which the Congress bears a very deep measure of responsibility.

By a vote of 26 against, and 12 for, the measure failed to pass. No Republican voted for it, only 12 Democrats—Brooks, Kastenmeier, Edwards, Hungate, Conyers, Waldie, Drinan, Rangel, Jordan, Holtzman, Owens, and I. And, with that, we recessed from 6:25 to 8:00 P.M.

And now, at a few minutes after eight, it was finally my turn.

As I began to speak, I knew that the chances were not strong in favor of the article, and I knew that several of the Republicans were upset because they thought (wrongly) that the Democrats had purposely scheduled the tax debate for prime time knowing it would embarrass the President, even if it didn't pass.

I was so nervous that I interrupted the clerk's reading of the article, thinking he had finished, and had to be set straight by the chairman. And I did something else, early in the debate, that might have looked to some people like the product of nervousness but actually wasn't. I let Wiggins amend the bill to include the word "fraudulently."

221

That one-word insertion made the standard of evidence much more rigid, and opened up several new objections by the minority. But I felt it was only fair. Cut down to the essentials of the tax issue, if we weren't talking about fraud, then we weren't talking about an impeachable offense.

I should have realized how tired, and angry, and embarrassed the President's stalwarts were, but I was too concerned with getting the tax issue before the people.

The debate that followed was, unfortunately, the most bitter and rancorous of the entire hearings. I guess some Republicans felt beaten, and thought we were piling it on. Certainly some of them had said as much privately, but I didn't expect the partisanship to erupt so strongly.

I finished my statement by saying, "Well, let me say that I think this falls in that category [impeachable offenses] because we have a President who, due to his position, could assume that his tax returns were not subject to the same scrutiny as those of other taxpayers. Rather than taking care to ensure that his tax returns complied with the laws, he took advantage of the presidency to avoid paying his proper tax.

". . . And when the President of these United States refuses to be bound by the revenue laws and if he escapes the judgment here as he evaded his taxes, then it is not just the treasury that is poorer. The very integrity of our system of self-government is diminished."

As the nation watched, the debate grew angry, then bitter, then calm, and then angry again.

About an hour and a quarter into the debate I turned the floor over to Liz Holtzman (who had been a member of the "tax and personal finances task force") and she began to hit home on the President's emoluments, the use of public and campaign money he had received that was turned to his own benefit.

As soon as she had finished, Charley Sandman came on like a bulldog, a rabid one. Perhaps he thought he could get away with what he said—he suggested libel was being committed—because Holtzman was female.

As soon as she could be recognized Holtzman called for the floor. "Mr. Chairman. I would like to be heard on a point of personal privilege with respect to that."

Rodino nodded and said, "The gentlelady is recognized as a matter of personal privilege."

"I would like to state that I resent the remarks of Mr. Sandman"—this was unusual; she was dropping the polite cover of "gentleman from New Jersey"—"because I have presented this as fairly as I could in terms of my reading of the Senate reports and materials before me. I certainly agree that we must be fair and honest and honorable, and I have tried my best to do that, and I think by casting aspersions on my integrity, Mr. Sandman is trying to undermine the integrity of the committee, and I personally resent it, and I wish he had considered his remarks."

It was a stinging rebuke. Sandman tried to respond, but Rodino recognized someone else.

At about 10:40, we voted.

My tax article lost. The vote was 26 to 12. That same count had defeated the Cambodia resolution, but this time there were some surprising shifts.

I lost Hungate, Waldie, Drinan, and Owens, all Democrats who had voted *for* the Cambodia issue; but picked up Eilberg, Seiberling, Danielson, and Rodino, all Democrats who had voted *against* the Conyers resolution.

I couldn't figure out why we had lost Hungate. That was a surprise. As for Waldie and Drinan, I guess they simply didn't think taxes was "big enough" to be an impeachable offense. Owens? He either didn't feel the case was strong enough, or he needed to vote against *something* and maybe he agreed with Railsback's view that the article was a symptom of "impeachmentitis." Owens's district happened to have favored Richard Nixon heavily in the last election.

Rodino's support pleased me deeply.

Leaving the hearing room, I was disappointed. I had expected to do better. Jack Brooks stopped me and gave me a few words of commendation, which I appreciated. When I got back to the office, the staff looked glum. They had manned the phones, and the tally wasn't very encouraging on that front. Most of the callers had accused me of trying to kick the President while he was down.

I wish they'd had some idea of the hours of work that had gone into the tax article, the efforts of people like Bernie Nussbaum and Smith McKeithen. They had worked such unconscionably long hours trying to put the case together without a major support team.

On the way out of the Rayburn Building, I had run into Nussbaum. Tired as his face looked, it was good to see it.

"Well," he smiled at me, "we tried."

That we had.

"Well, Ed, tell me, what's going to happen?" Doris asked the moment I walked into the office. It was the fifth time I had been asked that question in the ten minutes since I parked my car in the Rayburn Building garage.

"I don't really know. Maybe a Checkers speech. Maybe he'll come back out fighting. Or maybe, like one of the policemen told me, he'll disappear in the night and show up in a South American country seeking sanctuary."

"Do you think he'll resign?"

"I really can't see that happening, yet. It just doesn't seem like Richard Nixon."

She nodded her head. "I know what you mean."

All the speculation about what the President would, or would not do had come to a head last night, August 4, with the news that Nixon had summoned various of his top aides to Camp David for "talks." The news accounts, especially on the radio, had all the flavor of dispatches from the battlefield, reports of troop movements.

This morning's *Washington Post* suggested the meetings had to do with how the President should respond to the Supreme Court order that the tapes be turned over to Judge Sirica. An article by Woodward and Bernstein quoted an unnamed source as saying that the tapes would be devastating to the President's case. That wouldn't surprise me.

But no one really knew.

At the moment, I was more concerned with my congressional duties, many of which had been neglected during the long months of the impeachment inquiry. In fact, the last few days had been spent in trying to get back to the normal routine, while still grappling with the unfinished work of the committee.

There was the report to write, which would be a joint effort that had to include all the supplemental, minority, concurring, and dissenting views. I had a lot of work to do on the tax question. All of this had to be finished before the full House could take up the articles of impeachment.

Still, there was a sense of relief as the pressure had begun to lessen and the committee members were coming back to earth. The air of the impeachment inquiry had been rarified, especially for the junior members, so totally unused to being the focus of national attention. We'd all grown in the experience. I knew that, but it was good to come down from the mountain.

Just how different our experience had been from that of the members of other committees was brought home to me, vividly, a few days after the final vote, by a conversation I had with a staff member on the House Agriculture Committee.

"While your committee was struggling with impeachment, we were also debating the future of a great American."

"Really? Who's that?"

"Smokey the Bear."

He wasn't kidding. They had passed a resolution providing that when Smokey died, his body would be returned to his native New Mexico for burial. Poor Smokey. He'd been the biggest tourist attraction in the history of the National Zoo, until the pandas from China had upstaged him in the twilight of his life. Ironically, he had Richard Nixon to thank for that.

And Nixon was in a fight that could well send *him* back to his native state. Unlike the beloved symbolic animal, the President would fight it.

One other thing was certain: Impeachment would pass in the House. Everything I saw and heard indicated that the mood of the full House would ultimately match that of the committee members who had passed three articles of impeachment. That much was inevitable.

Later in the afternoon, the Democratic members of the Judiciary Committee held a caucus in one of the many small rooms that fill the nooks and crannies in the Capitol building. Someone said it had been a favorite room of the late Speaker, Sam Rayburn, a place to sit with other powerful members over "bourbon and branch."

225

While we waited for the meeting to begin, I talked with some of the members, and was annoyed to learn that certain people had voted against the tax article simply because political wisdom dictated that they vote against something. Paul Sarbanes at least had the good grace to say he felt he probably should have voted for it, but he was the only one.

Rodino announced that House debate on the articles of impeachment would begin on August 19, and would take about two weeks. The tentative schedule called for meeting each day at ten A.M. and going until six P.M., Monday through Saturday. And though it had not yet been approved, no one doubted that the debate would be televised. Although the debate in the House would probably change few minds, an orderly and powerful debate was necessary, both for the Senate and for the public. A careful, fair presentation would reiterate the strength of the evidence and would keep the political momentum for impeachment growing.

There were a number of details to be worked out—such as whether or not the actual tapes should be played (minus the "bleeps," which would undoubtedly shock the nation), if the electronic voting system should be put aside for voice votes, and whose name (or names) should be listed as sponsor of the impeachment resolution—and we worked slowly and carefully and long.

But later in the day, everything turned upside down. The White House issued a statement in regard to the impending public release of three crucial tapes, tapes that had never been turned over to anyone before. Richard Nixon, in this statement, admitted that his long-held claim of not learning about the cover-up until March 1973 was "incomplete and in some respects erroneous."

Though the words were carefully chosen to mask all but the slightest error of judgment or wrongdoing on the part of the President, the smoke screen did not alter the basic fact:

This was Richard Nixon's confession!

Accompanying the statement were transcripts of three June 23, 1972, conversations that scraped away the euphemistic veneer to bare the truth: Mr. Nixon had been lying all along.

226

The transcripts, recounting conversations between the President and H. R. Haldeman, then his chief of staff, showed Nixon personally ordering that the CIA be enlisted to obstruct the FBI investigation of the Watergate break-in.

The statement accompanying the transcripts offered a good example of back-against-the-wall candor. The tapes had already been turned over to Judge Sirica, and there was no doubt that, sooner or later, they would become public, or at least be available for the Senate trial.

In his statement Mr. Nixon admitted that the June conversations showed that the decision to use the CIA was not based on a desire to avoid exposure of sensitive national security matters but rather to avoid exposure of his campaign organization to felony charges.

". . . I was aware of the advantages this course of action would have with respect to limiting possible public exposure of involvement by persons connected with the reelection committee," the President's statement said.

Beyond admitting that he'd directed the Watergate cover-up, Mr. Nixon also acknowledged that he'd been pursuing a course designed to cover up the cover-up. In early May he had reviewed the June 23 tapes and "recognized that these presented potential problems."

But he kept it to himself for three months.

"This was a serious act of omission for which I take full responsibility and which I deeply regret," the President said.

While resigning himself to the fact that impeachment by the House is "virtually a foregone conclusion," Mr. Nixon's statement concluded: "I am firmly convinced that the record, in its entirety, does not justify the extreme step of impeachment and removal of a President. I trust that as the constitutional process goes forward, this perspective will prevail."

I was on the floor when Nixon's statement was released and, as that morning's *Post* had predicted, "all hell broke loose."

The three transcripts were immediately proclaimed by many to be "the smoking gun." And Bella Abzug declared, "Now, even the fig leaf is gone."

Wayne Hays paraphrased Nixon's statement: "Mea culpa,

227

mea culpa, I'm guilty as hell, but I'm sorry." Later, Majority Leader Tip O'Neill said, "Confession is good for the soul, but it doesn't save the body in this instance."

A clerk who works in a small library off the House floor walked up to me and shook my hand. "You shouldn't have any trouble getting reelected, you were right," he said.

Rodino had a copy of the President's statement and read several paragraphs to Hungate, Mann, and me as we gathered off to the side of the chamber. The chairman showed special interest in Mr. Nixon's comments about withholding the damaging evidence. Beyond refusing previously to surrender it to the Judiciary Committee, which had subpoenaed it, Nixon said he "did not inform my staff or my counsel of it, or those arguing my case."

That seemed a clear concession to St. Clair, giving him an alibi to show that he hadn't been lying to the committee about the President's role, but was only a misled victim himself.

But if St. Clair had been duped, he seemed a willing patsy to me. Back in May I had warned that he was putting himself in a "precarious position by telling us that the transcripts [released earlier] tell it all about Watergate." At that time I suggested that the President's lawyer exercise care to avoid "the delicate position of possibly being involved in covering up the cover-up of a cover-up." Unsurprisingly, he didn't take my advice and demand to hear the tapes.

"It's all over," I heard Bill Steiger of Wisconsin telling someone. Steiger was a Republican and, while that sentiment was echoing throughout the Democratic side of the chamber, it was the reaction of Republicans that would be most significant, and most devastating.

The cloakroom was crowded, but I managed to squirm my way to an area where I could see the television set. I had heard that Charlie Wiggins had reacted to the new transcripts with a demand that Nixon resign, and if he didn't that Wiggins would vote to impeach him.

There he was on the screen—Wiggins, choking back tears, his stricken face making him as painful to watch as it must have been for him to have gone before the television cameras.

The Californian had been the President's most effective defender on the Judiciary Committee. While the White House engaged in its counterproductive frenzy of attacks on the committee, Wiggins had staked his reputation, his integrity, on his patient and eloquent discussion of the evidence, arguing that it was not sufficient to justify impeachment.

He had surely won a large following around the nation and now they saw their champion humiliated by the man he defended.

"After considerable reflection, I have reached the painful conclusion that the President of the United States should resign," Wiggins said, basing that conclusion not on anger but on "information which establishes beyond a reasonable doubt" that Nixon had interfered with the FBI investigation of the Watergate break-in.

If the President failed to heed his advice, Wiggins announced that he was "prepared to conclude that the magnificent career of public service of Richard Nixon must be terminated involuntarily and I shall support those portions of Article I . . . which are sustained by the evidence."

Wiley Mayne also announced that he now would vote for impeachment and the other eight members of the committee who had steadfastly opposed the articles of impeachment announced that they were reassessing their positions.

The television news was a parade of statements abut the transcripts that echoed conversations on the floor—expressions of shock, feelings of betrayal, assurances that the vote for impeachment in the House would be overwhelming and that conviction by the Senate was all but assured.

As I left the cloakroom, Jake Pickle of Texas came up to me, put a hand on my shoulder, and said, "Thanks. The Judiciary Committee has helped give the House a better name."

In the statement accompanying the June 23 transcripts, Mr. Nixon said he recognized "that this additional material I am now furnishing may further damage my case. . . . "

By August 6, the extent of that damage may have won for that comment the understatement of the year award. The media was talking about the "tidal wave" against Nixon and the "impeachment fever racing through the House."

229

Before the day was over, all the members of the Judiciary Committee who had voted against impeachment had released statements that they had now shifted their position on Article I and the verdict on the obstruction of justice charge was now 38-0.

John Rhodes, the minority leader, labeled the fresh transcripts "cataclysmic" and announced he'd vote for impeachment.

While his predecessor as House Republican leader didn't go as far, Jerry Ford finally decided to bow out of the impeachment debate. Ford had announced the evening before that he would stop criss-crossing the nation, proclaiming the President's innocence and lashing out at his critics. The Vice President, who had been talking about our committee proceedings as a "travesty," said he still stuck by his earlier statements but would quit repeating himself. Ford's silence was one of the kindest things Nixon was hearing.

John Tower, chairman of the Senate Republican Policy Committee, told reporters after the group met to discuss the President, "The majority sentiment among Republican Senators is that he should retire from office."

News of each new defection spread quickly—adding momentum to the snowballing conclusion that it was no longer a question of if, but of when and how Richard Nixon would be ousted from office.

As Wiggins had done, most who were convinced by the June 23 transcripts that Nixon was guilty of an impeachable offense called for resignation. The phones in our office were ringing all day with the staff fielding the latest rumors on when the President would give in to pressure and quit.

Late in the afternoon of August 7, word spread through the chamber that Senator Barry Goldwater and Senate and House minority leaders Hugh Scott and John Rhodes had been called to the White House to meet with the President. This could be it!

Since early in the year, when asked my opinion about whether Nixon would resign, I had held that he would voluntarily step down only if leaders of his own party called on him with an ultimatum: You can leave gracefully or you can leave in disgrace, impeached, and convicted.

Maybe that "scenario" was now being played out at the Executive Mansion.

"I'm frustrated," Don Riegle, the Michigan Congressman who had defected from the Republican Party to become a Democrat in early 1973, told me. "I may not get a chance to vote." But I knew I had many colleagues who would shed no tears at being deprived of the opportunity to cast a vote on impeachment.

The tension was extremely high while the Republican leaders were closeted with the President. The television cameras were set up on the White House lawn to let the nation in on the results of the meeting immediately.

"There were no decisions made," Goldwater announced. "We made no suggestions. We were merely there to offer what we see as the condition on both floors."

Scott added that it had not been a cheerful prognosis. "We have told him that the situation is very gloomy on Capitol Hill." The President's mental state was the subject of many of the rumors engulfing Washington, and a reporter asked about Mr. Nixon's mood.

"Serene," Scott said. What a word to use!

Although reporting that no decision, either way, had been reached, the trio implied that one was near, and Scott assured that whatever Mr. Nixon decided on resignation "will be in the national interest."

When I left the chamber after watching the news, a reporter hailed me in the hallway. He asked about resignation. Did I think it was the right course, did I expect it?

I replied, "Just give the President time, there's no need to rush him."

Doris and I were in the office just after noon on August 8, sorting through material that had been sorely neglected in past weeks. I got a call from a friend who said she'd just driven by the White House. A crowd of several hundred people had gathered on the sidewalk in front of the mansion, she told me, and was spilling into Lafayette Square across the street. "It's like a deathwatch," she said. "They're waiting for the guillotine to fall."

We were waiting too. The portable television set in our office

231

was on, tuned to CBS, which featured a soap opera called "The Young and the Restless."

Doris suddenly shot from her chair to turn up the sound. There was that moment of fear that strikes when a television program is abruptly interrupted for a "special news bulletin." But the tension quickly dissolved into weary relief and jumbled nerves as Walter Cronkite delivered the simple news: President Nixon would address the nation at nine P.M.

In announcing the speech, Nixon's press secretary, Ron Ziegler, had not mentioned what the subject of the address would be. But he didn't have to. Any suspense that had survived the day disappeared when Vice President Ford cancelled several scheduled appearances and met with Nixon at the White House.

Shortly after the announcement, I got a call from Dick Levitt, a friend from Des Moines who is a successful businessman. He amazed me by saying, "Don't be too sure that the American people don't want Nixon to go to jail."

I assured Dick that I was not behind and would not support any of the various immunity proposals being talked about. And our conversation was a vivid reminder that even if Nixon resigned, that would not mean an immediate end to the question of his future.

It was possible, of course, for impeachment proceedings to continue even after the President resigned. Senate majority leader Mike Mansfield had suggested that the Senate trial be held whether or not Nixon remained in the White House.

But that was doubtful. Tip O'Neill, Mansfield's counterpart in the House, had rejected the notion as "overkill."

I'd talked with Rodino the day before, and he told me, "There will be no impeachment if Nixon resigns. Enough is enough."

Ironically, the bill being debated on the floor on the afternoon of August 8 was a piece of legislation that had grown directly out of the Watergate morass. It was a campaign reform measure designed to curb the kind of big-money abuses in election financing that led to the scandal.

It was a sensitive issue, for many of the proposed regulations would apply to our own campaigns. Tempers flared often during the debate. The shouting and snarling that punctuated some of the debate made me wonder what would happen when and if impeachment came to the floor.

One of the most heated exchanges concerned a Republican-sponsored amendment that would have deleted a provision for public financing of presidential nominating conventions.

John Brademas was steaming when he walked to the well to speak out against the amendment. He began by reminding us that many people expected the President to resign before the day was over. "And why?" Brademas asked. "Because we have witnessed over the last several months, month after month, revelations of the most spectacular lawlessness and corruption in the two hundred years of the history of this country." The Indiana Democrat's voice reached the level of a shout and was aimed at the Republican side of the chamber: "It seems to me that upon your party . . . there should now be some sense of public responsibility to . . . help clean up federal elections in this country." He warned the Republicans that if they voted to eliminate public financing of conventions, voters would reject them at the polls "even as the American people are rejecting the present President of the United States." The boos and hisses from the Republican aisle nearly drowned out Brademas's "I urge the defeat of the amendment."

David Dennis rose a few minutes later in support of the amendment. He began by complaining that the level of the debate had been lowered "to the ordinary partisan level which one might normally expect from the other side of the aisle."

At that Flowers engaged in animated mock applause. Quite appropriate, I thought, considering Dennis's performance on the committee. But Dennis didn't seem to notice, or didn't care. He was wound up.

Saying he wanted to "retreat to a slightly more statesmanlike stance," Dennis went on to blame Watergate on the Democrats. His logic: Special-interest money runs the country because government is so large and powerful that everyone has to beg its permission to live. And, "Every single person in this country who has two nickels . . . naturally tries to pay the bureaucrats and the politicians off," Dennis explained. "Who created this situation?" he asked, and then supplied the answer: "The party on the other side of the aisle, for the last thirty years, did that. Now, the President of our party who, unfortunately, perhaps learned your lessons too well," he shouted toward the Democratic side, "is about to pay for your sins. . . ."

Now angry boos came from our side and Wayne Hays rose to reply. "I noticed he used the word 'retreat' and I would say that he has had some good experience in retreating lately. I am only sorry he did not get to retreat on TV like he made his defense on TV." Things were getting ugly. Fortunately, someone called for the vote.

The amendment was defeated by about a hundred votes and after he cast his vote, Flowers walked over to where I was sitting with Waldie and Holtzman. "You know," he said jokingly, "I think I'll sit with you hard-liners. The others don't seem to want me anymore."

A little later, I talked with Speaker Albert, who told me one question he'd been asked repeatedly by reporters during the day was how Nixon's resignation would affect the November elections. "We have to face it: it will affect them," he told me, "and I've been saying, 'Look, I'm not going to be coy about this, it's going to hurt Democrats' chances.'" The Speaker told me that he had figured that with Nixon in office, 325 Democrats would have been elected in November (a gain of 75 seats) but with the albatross gone, Albert had scaled down his prediction to 275.

He also said he planned to "talk straight with Ford when he becomes President and warn him not to try to crucify the Democrats." Albert said he'd remind Jerry that one of the first things ahead was confirmation of a Vice President.

"Speaking of that," Albert said with a slight smile as he pointed at Rangel, Sarbanes, and me, "you guys aren't on the Judiciary Committee. You're on the impeachment and confirmation committee!"

About 6:15 P.M., Doorkeeper Fishbait Miller boomed out, "A message from the President." A hush fell over the chamber. Maybe this was it, an advance notification of his resignation.

But what it was was the "18th Annual Report of the President on the Trade Agreements Program."

Waiting for President Nixon to come on television and make it official at nine o'clock, I sat at my desk reading incoming impeachment mail. It was overwhelmingly favorable and one of the most recurring phrases was "Thank you for doing what had to be done." But, now and again, I'd come across a note filled with animosity.

One writer, from Davenport, noted that in my televised speech I had referred to being the son of immigrant parents and added, "This merely proves that the immigration laws need tightening up." Another letter proposed that I be deported as "an undesirable alien." Another told me, "You're the kind of Jew that made Hitler necessary."

Alexander Hamilton had warned that impeachment would "agitate the passions of the whole community and divide it into parties more or less friendly or inimical to the accused." I knew the divisiveness would not evaporate if Nixon resigned, but I hoped that it would be tempered. Much would depend on what Nixon said tonight.

The television screen focused on the scene outside the White House where a large crowd was milling about. I was hoping that Mr. Nixon would take the high road, be humble, contrite, attempt to douse the passions rather than inflame them.

"Good evening. This is the thirty-seventh time I have spoken to you from this office, where so many decisions have been made that shaped the history of the nation. . . ."

He looked composed, his voice was steady.

Kevin McCormally, who was with me to help draft a statement on my reaction, lit his pipe, sent a huge cloud of smoke sailing toward the ceiling, and settled into his chair.

"Throughout the long and difficult period of Watergate," the President said, he had considered it his duty "to make every possible effort to complete the term of office to which you elected me."

He was staring directly into the camera, his left eyelid appeared to be quivering. His expression was serious.

"In the past few days, however, it has become evident to me that I no longer have a strong enough political base in Congress to justify continuing that effort."

With that, my last flicker of doubt died. He was leaving.

"I would have preferred to carry through to the finish, whatever the personal agony it would have involved and my family unanimously urged me to do so," Nixon said. But he would sacrifice his desire and forfeit his office, he said, because "the interest of the nation must always come before any personal considerations.

"To leave office before my term is completed is abhorrent to every instinct in my body. But as President, I must put the interest of America first. . . . To continue to fight through the months ahead for my personal vindication would almost totally absorb the time and attention of both the President and the Congress. . . .

"Therefore, I shall resign the Presidency effective at noon tomorrow."

Expressing "deep sadness that I will not be here in this office working on your behalf to achieve those hopes" that were high when he entered his second term, the outgoing President assured the nation that with Gerald Ford "the leadership of America will be in good hands."

Looking ahead, Nixon said, "The first essential is to begin healing the wounds of this nation: to put the bitterness and the divisions behind us and to rediscover those shared ideals that lie at the heart of our strength and unity as a great and as a free people.

"By taking this action, I hope that I will hasten the start of that process of healing which is so desperately needed in America."

When it was over Kevin and I prepared a short statement:

"By acknowledging that the constitutional process, the rule of law, had been followed, the President stepped down gracefully. There is no joy for anyone in his resignation and it is important that we accept this appeal that there be no recrimination.

"We must now turn to the future, with Gerald Ford as President, and with our confidence strengthened by the vitality of our Constitution and the stability of our system of government."

Kevin began calling it to the newspapers and wire services, and I started down the list of radio stations that had requested my reaction.

Just as I finished punching out the number of the first station, I noticed that Gerald Ford was on television. I hung up and listened.

He was standing outside his home in Alexandria, Virginia,

saying that the resignation was "one of the very saddest incidents I have ever witnessed." A year ago, he was a member of the House. Tomorrow, he would be President.

Leaving the Longworth Building, after giving nine repetitious radio interviews, I thought I saw John Doar driving toward the Congressional Hotel.

I wondered if he was heading home or going to work at the hotel. For an instant I considered hailing him and presumptuously demanding that he take the rest of the night off. But he was already past.

When I got to my car, I headed instinctively toward the White House. I wanted to see it on this night. Driving down Pennsylvania Avenue, surrounded by the eerie orange hue given off by the anticrime streetlights, I remembered something I hadn't thought much about since my days in law school, and the President's speech had brought it to mind. The overall impression given by Mr. Nixon's remarks had been that he was oblivious to what was happening to him, and why.

M'Naghten Rule. That was it. The classic test of criminal insanity—the right-wrong test of criminal responsibility. It holds that if a person does not know that his actions are wrong, he is not culpable. (Of course, the law then requires that such a person be put away.)

Could it apply to Nixon? I asked myself. Could his conception of the presidency, and his inability to distinguish himself from his office make him believe that he was sovereign, above the law? Could it be that he truly did not know what he had done was wrong and did not understand why he was being called to account?

A traffic cop was directing a stream of cars away from Pennsylvania Avenue in front of the White House; the street was blocked by a large crowd.

I swung around a few blocks and was able to drive by the rear of the mansion. It was beautiful, elegant, and shining in the spotlights. What a historic place . . . and time!

The traffic was crawling along. A lot of people had the same idea as I, to see the White House. No troops around it, no riots . . . quiet, stately, serene.

On the radio, a newsman was talking about whom Ford might

choose to be his Vice President. Mel Laird's name was mentioned as a likely possibility. I remembered that among all the speculation about whom Nixon would choose to replace Agnew, it was reported that his top choice was John Connally. But Nixon had reportedly been dissuaded from nominating the former Texas governor primarily to avoid a bruising battle in Congress over confirmation.

Imagine the problems, I thought, if Connally had been chosen and confirmed! The week before, John Connally had been indicted on charges of receiving a $10,000 bribe and engaging in perjury and conspiracy to cover it up.

Other "what if" questions came to mind as I drove by the Executive Office Building and toward my apartment.

What if George McGovern had been believed when, standing on the University of Iowa campus on the eve of the 1972 election, he had so accurately described Nixon's Administration as the most corrupt in our history?

What if, during that campaign, it had come out that Agnew was a crook rather than that Tom Eagleton had suffered depression and had undergone electroshock treatment?

I turned *what might have been* to my own marriage. Through the last weeks, absorbed by impeachment, I had tried to put the strong possibility of divorce out of my mind. But, now, I'd have to face it and deal with the pressure from Micky's attorney to sign the waiver of reconciliation so that our life together could be formally, legally severed.

What if, I wondered, I'd been as jealous of my time with Micky and the girls, as concerned about Micky's feelings before the separation as I had tried to be during these long months of attempting to patch up the marriage? Could it have been different?

The intersection of Wisconsin and Massachusetts avenues is one of the busiest during Washington's rush hour madness—and an unfortunate place to have a flat tire. But that was my luck on the morning of August 9. Fortunately, I'd gotten a late start; it was almost nine-thirty and the traffic wasn't too bad. I nudged the limping Chevy over the curb and onto the grass.

It was nearly time for Mr. Nixon's farewell to his staff and I decided to sit in the car and listen.

He was introduced, probably for the last time, as the President of the United States, and as he spoke to his staff it was evident, though I could not see him, that the composure demonstrated the night before was gone. His voice cracked, he sniffed often, and although I couldn't see him, I imagined a broken man, tears streaming down his face.

Mr. Nixon said he was not a wealthy man, spoke of having to come up with the money to pay his taxes, quoted Teddy Roosevelt, talked of his parents, thanked his staff, and expressed his pride in them. Occasionally, there was laughter, and, a few times, applause.

Near the end of his rambling final address, the President offered this advice: "Always give your best. Never get discouraged. Never be petty. Always remember, others may hate you, but those who hate you don't win unless you hate them. And then you destroy yourself."

Hearing his emotional farewell, I pitied him, and tears filled my eyes. As much as I disliked Richard Nixon for what he'd done to the country, for tearing us apart, affecting every institution of government and leaving a scar that will last for years, I was listening to him and responding to his tears with my own. As relieved as I was to see him go, as certain that he had brought this tragedy upon himself, I was moved by the spectacle of a man being brought to such a wretched end.

Nixon concluded his remarks. The radio announcer said the President walked with his family to the south lawn of the White House. A red carpet had been rolled out to a helicopter that was waiting to take him to Air Force One.

According to the radio account, the play-by-play, before boarding the helicopter, Mr. Nixon turned to the people gathered by the White House, threw his hands into the familiar V salute, and smiled, as he had done so many times in triumph.

I shut off the radio and hailed a cab, figuring that I could send a summer intern from the office to rescue my car later. As the cab sped down Massachusetts Avenue, I kept my eyes fixed in the direction of the White House, staring at the overcast sky and hoping to catch a glimpse of a helicopter, moving southeast, carrying history.

Back in my office, the staff joined me around the 12-inch portable television set to watch the inauguration of the new President. Before the ceremony began, someone said, "Gee, Ed, you'd think Ford would have invited you down since you helped make this all possible."

It was moments after noon when Chief Justice Warren Burger appeared on the screen. (I'd heard earlier that Burger had been summoned back from a vacation that he'd begun shortly after the ruling against Nixon in the tapes case.)

Ford took the oath of office in the very room where, about two hours earlier, President Richard Nixon had spoken to his staff. The transfer of power was smooth, yet another tribute to the system designed two hundred years ago.

President Ford—*President* Ford!—labeled his brief inaugural address "just a little straight talk among friends" and asked that since the nation had not elected him by ballot that the people "confirm me as your President with your prayers."

He talked of openness and candor, emphasized his belief that "truth is the glue that holds government together," and firmly declared, "My fellow Americans, our long national nightmare is over.

"Our Constitution works: our great Republic is a Government of laws and not of men. Here the people rule. . . ."

Near the end, the new President asked the nation's prayers for his fallen predecessor. "May our former President, who brought peace to millions, find it for himself," he said in a voice cracking with emotion.

A report following the speech said that the end of Richard Nixon's presidency had come while he was airborne somewhere over the Midwest, just beyond the Mississippi River. I wondered if he had been over Iowa when his presidency ended.

FOURTEEN: *Afterthoughts*

"Nixon's not very good, is he?"

"What?" I was concentrating on my driving, and I didn't expect a five-year-old, my Evie, to come up with such a question. We were driving back from the beach, the Eastern Shore on the Atlantic, several hours by car from Washington. It had been the perfect way to spend the weekend after Nixon's resignation.

"Ah, no, he isn't."

"That's what I thought. He lies, you know. Nixon promised low prices, but prices go up." She waved a package of gum in front of my face. "Just look, this used to be a nickel and now it costs a dime."

Sagely, the three other girls agreed.

Then Margot, the biggest sister, cut in, and I could tell she was serious by the tone of her voice. "I don't want Dad ever to be President, 'cause Dad's honest."

Again, the others agreed, firmly and quickly. I couldn't think of anything to say.

The wisdom of an eleven-year-old suggested the legacy and the tragedy of Richard Nixon—a distrust and negativism so deeply rooted that it dismissed the possibility of honesty in the

241

Oval Office, as though morality had to be checked at the door of the White House.

I prayed, for my daughters' sake, that I could contribute to efforts that would ensure that the House did not squander its newfound reputation but instead would build on it to make "the people's house" more deserving of the people's confidence and pride.

On Monday, Richard Nixon was in exile at San Clemente and I was in Washington, still engulfed by impeachment. I was still working on the committee's final report. While Jack Brooks was writing a separate addition to the report on the emolument section of our article, I was concentrating on the tax-evasion portion.

With the assistance of Bernie Nussbaum and Smith McKeithen of the inquiry staff, and Kevin McCormally, I was trying to strike a middle ground between what Bernie called "waving the bloody shirt" of emotionalism and a dry, legalistic presentation of the evidence.

I also wanted to dispel the idea that the tax article was somehow superfluous, or a symptom of "impeachmentitis," since it came after three other articles of impeachment had been approved.

Though we all admitted to one another that it was "hard to get worked up" about the report since Nixon was gone, we still wanted it to be *just right*. Beyond setting out the case, I (with Doar's encouragement) also wanted to use the defeat of the tax article to say something about the impact of the tapes on the impeachment process.

"There'll never be another impeachment," John Conyers had told me, explaining that his conclusion was not based on a belief that it might never again be necessary to call a President to account, but on a belief that there would never again be tapes.

"Just look at you, Mezvinsky . . . cleancut, Midwestern," he said. "You sponsor a tax article that the public understood and it wouldn't pass."

Nussbaum attributed the defeat of the article to both the lack of tapes containing evidence of tax fraud and the fact that the tax case had not gone as far before impeachment as had the other charges—it hadn't been delved into by the Senate Watergate Committee and none of Mr. Nixon's aides had yet been indicted in connection with the President's tax returns. It was a sorry state of affairs, as Bernie outlined it. Yet, I agreed with him.

I would be the last to question the overwhelming value of the tapes, but I was concerned that they might have become a technological prop, the reliance on which could adversely affect future investigations.

The point we wanted to make in the additional views, after laying out the evidence, was that the evidence met the most stringent standards of proof. And I raised the question of whether the availability of the tape recordings led some members to expect that type of evidence. The draft of the views we were working on included carefully chosen language, such as:

"Most cases, however, whether criminal or civil, do not turn on the availability of tape recordings. They are decided on an evaluation of all the proven facts and circumstances and the logical inferences to be drawn from those facts and circumstances."

That evening, August 12, the new President addressed a joint session of Congress. Understandably, Mr. Ford didn't mention impeachment, but he was about the only one who didn't.

Before the President arrived in the House chamber, I was talking with Father Drinan. He grumbled, "You know, I introduced the first impeachment resolution—way back in July of '73—and now, look, Wiggins is getting all the credit."

I replied by telling him that earlier in the day I'd been on an elevator with Wiggins and Pete McCloskey. "Pete was calling him a hero," I said, and Drinan shook his head slowly.

A few minutes later Drinan told several of us, "Last weekend in Massachusetts, I saw a bumper sticker that said IMPEACH FORD BEFORE IT'S TOO LATE. Just goes to show you that Massachusetts is ahead of the times."

After Ford's speech, I ran into Angelo Roncallo of New York, who was in a noticeably good mood, still exuding the jubilant relief that Republicans had exhibited when Ford entered the chamber and spoke as the President. Roncallo nodded hello, and then said, "Thanks, you sure got us out of a hotbox!"

243

* * *

On August 20, the Judiciary Committee's final report came to the floor: more than five hundred pages presenting the recommendations of, and the evidence supporting, the three approved articles as well as twenty-four additional views by members. The ten Republicans who had stuck by Nixon until the end, when the June 23 tape drove them away, said near the opening of their lengthy *minority views* that "our gratitude for his [Mr. Nixon's] having by his resignation spared the Nation additional agony should not obscure for history our judgment that Richard Nixon, as President, committed certain acts for which he should have been impeached and removed from office."

With that unanimous conclusion, the report was sent to the floor, accompanied by a carefully worded resolution that sought that the House acknowledge the work of the committee, but not be required to approve or reject our findings. The resolution would make the report an official House document and provided a means to get it on the record without actually adopting articles of impeachment and setting a Senate trial in motion.

It also, of course, would mean that no member of the House, other than the thirty-eight of us on the committee, would ever have to cast a vote in judgment of Richard Nixon.

According to the resolution, the House "takes notice that" the committee was directed to investigate impeachment, the committee recommended three articles of impeachment, the President resigned; and that the House accepts the report and commends the committee for its "conscientious and capable efforts in carrying out" its responsibility.

That approach, of course, miffed some members who wanted an impeachment vote on their record, but it also placated those who did not want to have to take a stand.

The resolution was put to a vote and passed 412 to 3, with two Democrats (Otto Passman of Louisiana and Sonny Montgomery of Mississippi) and a single Republican (Earl Landgrebe of Indiana) refusing to accept the report.

Officially, it was over.

But, within a few minutes, the doorkeeper announced a message from the President.

It was the formal presentation of something President Ford

244

had announced earlier in the day: his nomination of former New York Governor Nelson Rockefeller for Vice President. The nomination was referred to the Committee on the Judiciary, where at least we had some practice in that area, some fresh precedents to apply.

Before diving into the Rockefeller nomination, however, there would be a three-week recess.

The vice presidential nomination would cut deeply into the time I would have nearer the election, and I had to get out to Iowa to do some campaigning.

Generally speaking, I was in good shape politically. Impeachment had been a plus, especially as far as recognition went. But, as my campaign manager, Don Gibson, kept reminding me, it was crucial for me to be out in the district and talking about other issues—especially bread-and-butter economic issues—and reminding constituents that the record of my first term included far more than those votes on impeachment.

Trying to make up for lost time and anticipating that Congress would be in session up to the eve of the election, my schedule was necessarily intense.

I tried to hit the issues I knew were on people's minds, inflation, the threatening recession, congressional reform and governmental accountability, and energy, but no campaign event passed without discussion of impeachment.

Most of the reaction was good—I particularly remember a jovial, back-slapping gathering at the Moose Lodge in Burlington—but there was also lingering resentment.

Once, in early September, I was in Keosauqua for a parade and barbecue celebrating Sheep Empire Days. Riding in the parade through this small town, I noticed two women sitting in a car off to the side of the street. They were shaking their fists and appeared to be yelling at me, though I could not hear them. I didn't think much of it at the time because I thought they were kidding.

But later, at the fairgrounds, a woman burst through the group of people I was talking with and furiously began berating me. She had been one of the two in the car.

"You Communist!" she screamed. "Look what you did to our President. You Commie, I don't want anything to do with you.

245

I'd never vote for you." She was furious, and began poking me in the chest. "I'll never talk to you," she screamed, "look what you've done to our President!"

I was stunned, speechless. Somebody convinced the woman to stop and she went away, her body heaving with anger.

I said something about having to get to my next appointment and turned to walk to the car. Tom Baldridge, my campaign driver, motioned for me to hurry.

What a long way we'd come, I thought, from two years earlier when I was trying to get people to remember my name, but was not really being identified with any issue other than the war and the need for change in Washington.

My personal ambitions had gotten me to Washington, to the job I had wanted so badly and for so long. I knew I would always be proud of the role I played in history. But sacrifices had been made. My family suffered. The divorce was a certainty. I had come to see what Micky had known for so long—our union was not to be saved. Only the paperwork needed to be completed to formally sever the legal bonds. To Micky's everlasting credit, she and I and our daughters were on excellent terms, which was a major accomplishment considering the quiet agony of divorce we had endured.

My first two years in Congress was surely a term to remember.

As I slid into the front seat of the car in the dusty lot in Keosauqua, I remembered the words a friend had written to express his feelings just before the first impeachment vote. He had written, "How incredible it is that you would have to face such an historic responsibility in your first term. Perhaps that is an omen: that this had to be done now because there is so much else to do."

Baldridge put the car in gear and we moved on, toward another election and the challenges of the future.

AUTHOR'S NOTE

I began thinking about this book shortly after the Saturday Night Massacre in October, 1973, when Richard Nixon and Watergate began pulling me toward some unknown destination. As first conceived, *A Term to Remember* was to be an account of my journey, heavily laden with the evidence that would decide my vote on the question of impeaching the President of the United States.

The proud manner in which Chairman Rodino led the Judiciary Committee and brought the public into our deliberations, however, freed me to put down a more personal story. This was not easy for me. I did not want to open the private side of my life. Yet, from the earliest stages I knew I could not tell my story honestly without doing so. The family man could not be disembodied from the public man.

Through the months since I began writing, my life has changed significantly. I am no longer in Congress, I am living under a new, elected President, and I am now happily married to a very special person: Marjorie Margolies. (Ironically, it was the war in Indochina, which I went to Congress to end, that brought Marj and me together and brought me the beginning of a new life. During the final writhing days of the Saigon government in the Spring of 1975, Marj, a TV reporter with WNBC (NBC News), interviewed me about the airborne evacuation of infants from South Vietnam. Six months later, we were married.) My family has grown from my four daughters—Margot, Vera, Elsa, and Eve—to include Lee Heh from Korea, and Holly from Vietnam, the children Marj adopted as a single parent.

I will not forget the 93rd Congress of 1973 and 1974. From the experiences of those years, I am discovering that hope and trust are returning to our institutions of government. And, I have realized that my love for my family has become the motivating force for my life.

EDWARD MEZVINSKY
May, 1977

INDEX

249

Cambodia, bombing of, 39–42,
44, 80, 196
Cates, Dick, 163
Caulfield, Jack, 134
Celler, Emanuel, 93, 94, 120, 187
Central Intelligence Agency
(CIA), 87, 227
Chapin, Dwight, 162
Chicago Tribune (newspaper), 137,
138
Chung, Connie, *photo insert*
Clark, Dick, 11–12, 23, 159
Cohen, Sheldon, 112
Cohen, William S., 98, 184, 185,
photo insert; during impeach-
ment hearings, 147, 160, 166,
189, 190, 199, 207, 212, 216,
219
Colson, Charles, 150, 172–74, *pho-
to insert*; Committee for the Re-
election of the President, 134,
163
Connally, John, 238
Constitution, U. S., 25th Amend-
ment to, 59, 60
Conte, Silvio, 192, 215–16
Conyers, John, Jr., 69, 95, 105,
242, *photo insert*; on Ford
confirmation hearings, 59–60;
during impeachment hearings,
142, 152, 190, 211, 219–21
Cook, Marlow, 215
Court of Appeals for the District
of Columbia, U.S., 58, 63, 122
Cox, Archibald, 156; firing of,
64–67, 69, 71; requests for
tapes by, 50, 63–64
Cronkite, Walter, 171, 232
Culver, John, 159

Danielson, George E., 95–96, *photo insert*; during impeachment
hearings, 209, 212, 217, 223

Davenport Times-Democrat (newspaper), 67–68
Davis, Evan, 163
Dean, John, 43, 88, 134, 135, 182,
197; on Colson, 173, 174; "ene-
mies list" and, 89; as Judiciary
Committee witness, 164–69;
resignation of, 45; Senate tes-
timony of, 49, 61, 72–73, 87; on
White House tapes, 138
Delta Queen (steamship), 45
Democratic Convention (1960),
27
Democratic Steering and Policy
Committee, 45
Dennis, David, 97, 101, 122, 223,
photo insert; during impeachment hearings, 147, 156, 169,
187, 196, 205, 212; on subpoenas, 128–29
Dent, John, 191
Department of Defense Appropriations Act of 1973, 39–42
Des Moines Register (newspaper),
121
Diem, Ngo Dinh, 90
Dixon, Bill, 180
Doar, John, 80, 87, 124, 125, 237,
photo insert; as advocate of impeachment, 166, 179–82, 195,
205, 208; hiring of, 79, 92; during impeachment hearings,
135–36, 138–39, 141–42,
145–47, 151, 155–58; investigative methods of, 111; on Nixon's taxes, 112–13, 170–71;
questioning of witnesses by,
172; St. Clair and, 103–5; staff
selection by, 99–100; in transfer
of materials from grand jury,
122–23
Donahue, Harold D., 94, 106, *photo insert*; during impeachment

hearings, 137–39, 166, 190, 194–95, 211; on subpoenas, 128
Drew, Elizabeth, 132
Drinan, Robert F., 61–62, 96, 243, *photo insert*; during impeachment hearings, 149, 172, 212, 219, 221, 223; in questioning of witnesses, 165; on subpoenas, 104–5, 129

Eagleton, Thomas, 238
Edwards, Don, 94, 96, *photo insert*; during impeachment hearings, 147, 169, 196–97, 201, 211, 219, 221
Ehrlichman, John, 103, 169, 182; indictment of, 86; Nixon and, 164, 179–80, 197; resignation of, 43, 45; Senate testimony of, 49, 173
Eilberg, Joshua, 95, *photo insert*; impeachment votes of, 212, 223
Eisenhower, Dwight D., 140
Ellsberg, Daniel, 43, 45
Engberg, Eric, 207–8
Ervin, Sam, 48, 50
Ervin Committee, *see* Senate Select Committee on Presidential Campaign Activities
Evans, Rowland, 100–1
Examination of President Nixon's Tax Returns for 1969 through 1972, 114–16

Face the Nation (TV show), 113
Farkas, Ruth, 175
Farm Bureau, 83
Federal Bureau of Investigation (FBI), 87, 227
Fish, Hamilton, Jr., 97, 185, *photo insert*; during impeachment hearings, 147, 166, 178, 189,

190, 199–200, 207, 210–12, 216, 219; on subpoenas, 129
Flowers, Walter, 93, 95, 102, 120–21, 165, 184, 233–34, *photo insert*; during impeachment hearings, 147, 166, 179, 189–90, 192–93, 200, 208, 210, 212, 213, 217, 219
Flynt, John, 40
Folsom, Fred, 203
Ford, Gerald, 42, 192, 232; hearings and confirmation as Vice President, 59–62, 74–77; impeachment proceedings and, 70, 83, 230; as President, 234, 236–37, 240, 244–45
Frame, W. C., 109
Freedman, Doris, 67–68, 231–32
Froehlich, Harold V., 98; during impeachment hearings, 199, 212

Garrison, Samuel, III, 101–3, 173–74, 185–89, 195, *photo insert*
Gibbons, Sam, 32
Gibson, Don, 245
Goldwater, Barry, 230–31
Gray, L. Patrick, 43
Greenfield, Meg, 215
Gulf of Tonkin Resolution, 40

Haldeman, H. R., 21–22, 103, 134, 169, 182; indictment of, 86; Judiciary Committee and, 164; Nixon and, 162, 197–98, 227; resignation of, 43, 45; Senate testimony of, 49, 87; on White House tapes, 138
Haldeman, Mrs. H. R., 136
Hamilton, Alexander, 235
Harlow, Bryce, 106–7
Hays, Wayne, 124–26, 133, 154, 155, 227–28, 234